T0305583

All Fall Down

For Gerald Epstein, Robert Pollin, and Tom Schlesinger
with thanks

All Fall Down

Debt, Deregulation and Financial Crises

Jane D'Arista

Research Associate, Political Economy Research Institute, University of Massachusetts, Amherst, USA

Cheltenham, UK • Northampton, MA, USA

Published by
Edward Elgar Publishing Limited
The Lypiatts
15 Lansdown Road
Cheltenham
Glos GL50 2JA
UK

Edward Elgar Publishing, Inc.
William Pratt House
9 Dewey Court
Northampton
Massachusetts 01060
USA

A catalogue record for this book
is available from the British Library

Library of Congress Control Number: 2018943993

This book is available electronically in the **Elgar**online
Economics subject collection
DOI 10.4337/9781788119498

ISBN 978 1 78811 948 1 (cased)
ISBN 978 1 78811 949 8 (eBook)

Typeset by Columns Design XML Ltd, Reading
Printed and bound by CPI Group (UK) Ltd, Croydon, CR0 4YY

Contents

Tables

Foreword

For decades now, Jane D'Arista has been among the tiny handful of people in the United States and globally who truly understand how financial markets and institutions both function and malfunction. A lot of complex razzle-dazzle does certainly take place in contemporary financial systems. And among the Wall Street operators, academic finance professors, and government policymakers and regulators, there is no shortage of people claiming expertise on every possible topic in the realm of finance. Most of them are compensated handsomely for proffering their views. D'Arista stands apart from all such people, for the simple reason that she has always deployed her formidable talents on behalf of the general good. She has never sought the approval of either mainstream economists or Wall Street titans. This has enabled her to examine reality undistracted, with a powerful combination of depth, breadth, and clarity.

All Fall Down builds from D'Arista's long list of distinguished previous contributions. These earlier works include her classic 1994 two-volume monograph *The Evolution of US Finance*, and a wide range of research papers and policy studies she has published subsequently.

Many of these previous publications came out of her 20 years of work, from 1966 to 1986, as a staff member with, respectively, the US House of Representatives Banking Committee, the Congressional Budget Office, and the Energy and Commerce Committee. She continued to publish steadily as Director of Programs for the Financial Markets Center and while teaching Ph.D. courses at the University of Massachusetts Amherst, the New School for Social Research, and the University of Utah from 1999 to 2006. Most recently, in the aftermath of the financial crisis, many of D'Arista's writings grew from her involvement with SAFER—A Committee of Economists for Stable, Accountable, Fair and Efficient Financial Reform, a project that she co-directed with Gerald Epstein.

With *All Fall Down*, D'Arista is able to synthesize and significantly extend this earlier work to deliver original perspectives on two fundamental questions: first, what caused the 2007–2009 global financial crisis; and second, what needs to be done to prevent another such calamity?

The army of finance experts have, of course, provided a plethora of answers to these two questions. But these people were mostly oblivious to the worsening fragility that had been spreading throughout the financial system for decades. Given their track record, it is reasonable to ask why their views should carry credibility now.

In stark contrast, D'Arista's earlier work identified deep problems with the US and global financial regulatory system that were growing over time. In *All Fall Down*, she traces how these developments encouraged excessive financial speculation, which led to the formation of a global financial market bubble. This in turn brought us to the 2007–2009 crisis.

The significance of this overall point—that D'Arista had long recognized the deepening fragility of the US financial system while virtually all mainstream observers were asleep at the switch—cannot be overstated. The reason is simple. The 2007–2009 financial crisis was the most severe since the 1929 Wall Street crash and Great Depression 70 years earlier. Eight million US workers lost their jobs between 2007 and 2009, 9 million US families lost their homes between 2006 and 2014, and $17 trillion in US household wealth—i.e. 24 percent of all household wealth—was wiped out between 2006 and 2008. The patterns were comparable in Western Europe. Moreover, the crisis would have been far more severe still had not the US and Western European governments engaged in massive countercyclical stimulus programs and bailout operations to prop up the collapsing financial system. This was socialism for big banks on the grandest possible scale.

More still, this crisis was by no means an historical aberration. The classic 1978 book *Manias, Panics and Crashes* by Charles Kindleberger makes clear that, throughout the history of capitalism, unregulated financial markets have persistently produced instability and crises. The 1929 Wall Street crash and subsequent Great Depression was only the most severe instance of an overwrought financial market leading to an overall economic calamity.

Amid the 1930s Depression, Franklin Delano Roosevelt's New Deal government put in place an extensive system of financial regulations in the United States. The single most important initiative was the Glass-Steagall Act of 1933, which divided up the banking industry into two distinct segments: "commercial" and "investment" banking. Commercial banks were limited to the relatively humdrum tasks of accepting deposits, managing checking accounts, and making business loans. Commercial banks would also be monitored by the newly formed Federal Deposit Insurance Corporation. This provided government-sponsored deposit insurance for the banks in exchange for the banks accepting close scrutiny of their activities. Investment banks, by contrast, were free to invest their clients' money on Wall Street and other high-risk activities, but had to steer clear of the commercial banks. Similar regulations were imposed on savings and loans and other depository institutions.

For the most part, the Glass-Steagall system did its job. For the first 30 years after the end of the First World War, US and global financial markets had become dramatically more stable than in any previous historical period. This was while GDP grew at a healthy rate and unemployment remained low in the US and other advanced capitalist economies. But even during the New Deal years themselves, financial market titans were already fighting vehemently to eliminate or at least defang the regulations. Starting in the 1970s and continuing through to the 2007 crisis, they almost always got their way. As a result, the increasingly unregulated financial markets were able to operate again according to their own self-destructive logic.

As D'Arista explains in *All Fall Down*, one of the critical developments that contributed to the weakening of the Glass-Steagall regulatory system was the emergence of the Eurodollar market, beginning in the late 1960s. Through the Eurodollar market, non-US banks, and even US banks operating offshore, could create dollar-denominated accounts for their customers. This enabled these offshore institutions to perform virtually all the functions of banks located within the US, but without having to abide by the Glass-Steagall regulations.

A related development was the emergence of what D'Arista (and her co-author Tom Schlesinger) initially called the "Parallel Banking System" in a prescient 1993 paper.[1] D'Arista and Schlesinger described the development of entities such as the General Motors Acceptance Corporation and General Electric Capital, GE Capital, which were able to operate like banks within the US without facing the US regulatory laws that applied to banks. These entities initially grew out of the operations of their parent non-financial corporations, such as GM and GE.

But this parallel banking system burgeoned over time into what is now more broadly termed the "shadow banking system." The shadow banking system includes mutual funds, holding companies, and finance companies among other non-bank intermediaries. As with the Eurodollar institutions, the shadow banks became capable of performing most of the lending and other functions of traditional banks, but without facing the same regulatory requirements. As one indicator of how the shadow banks grew in importance, as of the decade 1970–79, traditional banks and

1 Jane W. D'Arista and Tom Schlesinger (1993), "The Parallel Banking System," in Gary Dymski, Gerald Epstein, and Robert Pollin, eds, *Transforming the US Financial System: Equity and Efficiency for the 21st Century*, Armonk, NY: M. E. Sharpe, ch. 7.

other regulated depository institutions accounted for 47 percent of all lending in the US economy while the shadow banks accounted for 5 percent. For the years immediately prior to the 2007 crisis, the traditional banks' share of lending had fallen to 20 percent while the shadow banks' share had risen to 28 percent.[2]

Of course, all the experts extolling the virtues of unregulated financial markets were forced to retreat in the aftermath of the 2007–2009 crisis. This is the context in which the new financial regulatory system—the Dodd-Frank system—became law in the United States as of 2010. Dodd-Frank was a massive, 2300-page tome of legalese. Nevertheless, it provided only a broad framework for implementing a new regulatory system, leaving large numbers of critical details to be hashed out at the various regulatory agencies. This was because the big-time Wall Street players calculated that they could dominate the rule-writing process once their lawyers and lobbyists could caucus quietly with the day-to-day regulators after the public's attention had drifted elsewhere.

D'Arista's own assessment of Dodd-Frank in *All Fall Down* is typically unvarnished. She writes that the measure "seemed to go through the motions of a major reform effort, giving nominal recognition to problem areas without confronting the underlying structural issues that contributed to the collapse." But even with these weaknesses, as of this writing (March 2018), President Donald Trump and the Republican-controlled Congress have been maneuvering to repeal or at least roll back Dodd-Frank. D'Arista's perspective here is that "those who favor repeal give little weight to the belief that the role of regulation is to protect the public whose money is at risk. Their proposals seem to argue that the role in making policy is to support a profitable financial system."

By contrast, the concluding chapters of *All Fall Down* develop a clear regulatory structure that would be capable of "protecting the public whose money is at risk." One centerpiece of D'Arista's proposal is a new system of reserve requirements, i.e. requirements that financial institutions maintain a cash reserve to fortify themselves during periods of market downturns, when the value of income-generating assets experience sharp declines. Financial institutions would generally choose to minimize their cash reserve holdings so that they can use these funds to earn profits from making loans or investments. Under the old regulatory system, banks were required to hold cash reserves but non-bank intermediaries—i.e. shadow banks—were not. This created a serious

2 Robert Pollin and James Heintz, *Study of the US Financial System*, FESSUD, 2012, p. 126, http://fessud.eu/wp-content/uploads/2012/08/USA-Financial-Systems-Studies10.pdf.

regulatory disparity favorable to shadow banks, which in turn undermined the entire regulatory system.

As D'Arista explains, one of the strengths of her proposed system of uniform reserve requirements is that it will strengthen the ability of the Federal Reserve to counteract speculative bubbles. As speculative bubbles begin to form, the Federal Reserve would have the capacity to increase the cash requirements for financial institutions, which would, in turn, slow down the flow of credit channeled into speculation. Indeed, during the late 1990s speculative "dot.com" stock market bubble, then Federal Reserve chair Alan Greenspan himself acknowledged that this type of regulatory intervention would work effectively, observing at one point that "I guarantee that if you want to get rid of the bubble ... this will do it."[3] But Greenspan, like so many other regulators and policymakers before and since, was simply unwilling to confront Wall Street at that time or any other time. Hundreds of millions of ordinary people worldwide paid the price of such behavior with the 2007–2009 financial crisis reckoning.

Jane D'Arista makes abundantly clear in *All Fall Down* that we cannot allow Wall Street to continue setting the rules that govern our financial system. She makes equally clear how we can transform our financial regulatory system so that, first and foremost, it serves the interests of ordinary people, in the US and throughout the world. *All Fall Down*, in short, deserves to be read, reread, and pondered over by anyone who cares about creating a more just, equitable, and sustainable economy.

Robert Pollin

3 See William Grieder, "Il Maestro's Failed Magic," *Nation*, March 27, 2002, p. 6, https://www.thenation.com/article/il-maestros-failed-magic/.

Acknowledgments

The good fortune in my working life began when I was hired by US House Banking Committee chairman Wright Patman of Texas to write a history of the early years of the Federal Reserve System. Working for two exceptional public servants, Chairman Patman and his staff director, Paul Nelson, who became my mentor, was a remarkable learning experience. The next two committee chairmen I served under, representatives Henry Reuss of Wisconsin and Timothy Wirth of Colorado, asked me to write additional studies of the financial system in connection with work on hearings and legislation. Working with Tim, his staff director, David Aylward, and my research assistant, Mary Jo Parrino, on financial restructuring was another notable experience that laid the foundation for my writing and teaching in the years that followed.

My good fortune continued after I left Washington in the early 1990s; Hyman Minsky invited me to attend his summer programs at the Levy Institute. During the same period, I also became part of a growing network of progressive economists that joined in meetings sponsored by the Economic Policy Institute under Jeff Faux. It was there that I met Jerry Epstein, Bob Pollin, Gary Dymski, and Jim Crotty and renewed a friendship with Jamie Galbraith that began when we both worked for Henry Reuss, all of whom became a core group of colleagues and close friends whose work has greatly influenced my own. Other valued colleagues I met over the years include Robert Blecker, Lance Taylor, John Eatwell, Eileen Appelbaum, Ilene Grabel, Andrew Cornford, Perry Mehrling, Tom Pally, and Stephany Griffith-Jones, who later became a co-author and close friend, as did Jim Boyce and Korkut Erturk.

After leaving a teaching and administrative position at Boston University School of Law, I joined the Financial Markets Center, a think tank founded and directed by Tom Schlesinger, where I began writing a series of quarterly reports on the Federal Reserve's *Flow of Funds Accounts* and on international capital flows. Tom's drive and dedication were infectious and his support for the reports I wrote under his rigorous guidance was critical in shaping the direction of my subsequent work.

I owe the chance to resume teaching to Bob Pollin, who acted on a suggestion by Ellen Russell to include a seminar on financial institutions and markets for graduate students in the Economics Department at the University of Massachusetts Amherst. Several years later, Lance Taylor invited me to teach a seminar on international financial institutions at the New School; following the seminar, I taught a half semester at the University of Utah at the invitation of Korkut Erturk. I am grateful to have had these opportunities and grateful to the students in those seminars for the discoveries that emerged in the process of sharing issues and ideas with them.

I owe special debts to: Bob McCauley who, as an intern in the late 1970s, joined in my quest to follow developments in the Eurodollar market and is now my source for that information; Matias Vernengo, who shares many of my interests, including the ideas of central bankers in the 1930s; Robert Wade, who informed my understanding of the crises about which he writes so well; Mario Seccareccio, from whose work as editor of the *International Journal of Political Economy* so many have benefited; and Jan Joost Teunissen who, as director of FONDAD, organized a series of memorable meetings on multinational issues with an exceptional group of multinational participants.

I need to mention several others whose work and contributions to my personal and professional life I value: Patrick Bond, a family friend since his teens; Leanne Ussher, Gokcer Ozgur, and Codrina Rada.

Alan Sturmer and Erin McVicar at Edward Elgar have been immensely helpful in guiding this book to publication, as have been my friends Mary Guitar and Douglas Nielson, whose editorial skills and suggestions were an important source of support during the months of writing.

But this is a book that would not have been written without the encouragement of my daughter, Carla, and the ongoing support she and my son-in-law, George Frampton, gave me. Their willingness to read and comment on many drafts of the introduction and summary set the course and kept me going. I am indebted to them for many things and certainly for this.

Abbreviations

ABS	Asset-based securities
AMLF	Asset-Backed Commercial Paper Money Market Mutual Fund Liquidity Facility
BIS	Bank for International Settlements
CD	certificate of deposit
CDO	collateralized debt obligation
CDS	credit default swap
EME	emerging market economy
ERISA	Employee Retirement Income Security Act
FDIC	Federal Deposit Insurance Corporation
FRB	Federal Reserve Board
FRS	Federal Reserve System
GDP	gross domestic product
GSE	government-sponsored enterprise
ICA	international clearing agency
IMF	International Monetary Fund
IRA	individual retirement account
LOLR	lender of last resort
LTCM	Long-Term Capital Management
MBS	mortgage-backed securities
MMMF	money market mutual fund
NAFTA	North American Free Trade Agreement
OECD	Organisation for Economic Co-operation and Development
OFR	Office of Financial Research
OPEC	Organization of Petroleum Exporting Countries
OTC	over-the-counter
PDCF	Primary Dealer Credit Facility
QE	quantitative easing

SCF	*Survey of Consumer Finance*
SDR	special drawing rights
SIV	structured investment vehicle
TAF	Term Auction Facility
TSLF	Term Securities Lending Facility
UK	United Kingdom
US	United States
VaR	value at risk

1. Introduction and summary

INTRODUCTION

A broken economic system that can no longer be effectively patched is ending. It is an interconnected global system shaped by the use of key currencies for cross-border payments by citizens and governments of countries other than the countries in which those currencies are issued. Since the 1980s, the dominant key currency in the global system has been the United States (US) dollar but, from the beginning, the constraints inherent in US acceptance of that role for its currency have created strains on its economy and on the global system that, in time, became unsustainable.

The flaw in this system is the basis for the confidence on which it depends. The choice to use the dollar for payments or investments outside US financial markets rests on belief in the ongoing strength of the American economy and its continued growth. Holdings of dollars by the rest of the world are in fact claims on the American economy that require confidence in its ability to pay its debts. Of course, the ability to attract savings from the rest of the world while running trade deficits seems to create a substantial advantage for the key currency country. US economic growth would have been much weaker over the last three decades without the build-up of debt financed by sizable inflows of foreign savings that helped provide both the ample credit that supported the US consumer-based economy and the credit Americans used to buy the imports that generate those savings. It has allowed the US to live beyond its means. But the continued dependence on debt-fueled growth that underpins this global system is the Achilles heel which led to its near collapse in 2008 and which will lead to another collapse in the not too distant future.

In addition to the debt-fueled growth dynamic that drives the American economy in its role as a key currency country, the global system has been shaped by the requirement that all countries except the US adopt an export-led growth model for their economies. Those countries that cannot use their own currencies to pay for cross-border transactions must run trade surpluses to acquire the dollars or other strong currencies needed to engage in international trade and investment. While the creation of the euro allowed the European Union to trade among its members without that constraint, those countries, too, structure their economies to favor export-led growth and their markets are less open to the rest of the world than the US market. Consequently, the US has become the buyer of last resort for the world's economy; its ability to accept the ongoing trade deficits that sustain that role is a critical factor in allowing the current system to continue.

The debt-fueled, export-led growth models that shaped the global economy developed in tandem with dramatic changes in financial functions brought about by the creation of offshore markets, financial product innovation, and deregulation. The outcome was an erosion of control over the expansion of credit in national economies that led to extraordinary growth in debt relative to their economic output. The ratio of private sector debt to gross domestic product (GDP) for many countries, including the US, rose to levels that constrained the ability of their households, businesses, and financial sectors to generate the income needed to service and repay what they owed.

The rise in debt to historical levels constituted the primary threat to the global economy. Moreover, it was one of the clearest warning signals of the collapse that caused the financial crisis of 2007–2008. The crisis was not, as many asserted at the time, unforeseen (Galbraith, 2009), except by those who declined to read those signals. For those who did foresee the scale of the coming disaster, developments during the crisis confirmed the underlying fault lines that had emerged as changed institutions, products, and practices shifted the structure of the global system over the preceding decades.

These changes resulted in the transformation of national bank-based systems into a market-based global system dominated by large, multinational institutions based in major developed countries. The context for this transformation was neglect or abandonment of existing regulatory frameworks without attention to the implications of those changes for systemic soundness. Among the major indications of systemic vulnerability were the unprecedented growth of financial sectors relative to the economies in which they were located; the interconnectedness of financial institutions; and the extraordinary increases in international capital flows that exacerbated the pro-cyclicality of finance in both boom and downturn.

The outcome of the crisis has been deeply punishing for real sectors in many of the world's economies. It has led to numerous serious efforts by public agencies and independent analysts to ascertain its causes. But the effort to address those causes in ways that will prevent a recurrence is still a work in progress. The Dodd-Frank Act of 2010, for example, seemed to go through the motions of a major reform effort, giving nominal recognition to problem areas without confronting the underlying structural issues that contributed to the collapse. The regulatory framework the act proposes continues to assume that the US financial system remains essentially bank-based. It fails to confront the many new issues that must be addressed to ensure the soundness, effectiveness, and transparency of the market-based system now in place. As a result, US financial law and regulation remain in the shadows of the bank-based system designed in the 1930s that began to morph into a market-based system as early as the 1960s.

The primary activity in the market-based system that has emerged over the last half century is investing and trading, not traditional bank activities like deposit taking and lending. The development of parallel offshore markets was a major factor in the shift toward trading, but other developments in US financial markets also contributed to this change. When Lehman Brothers collapsed in the fall of 2008, intermediation between non-financial savers and borrowers had become a less important function for the financial system than speculating in and insuring financial assets issued and held by the financial sector itself.

Many believe stronger limits on leverage and trading are needed to ensure that a future crisis is not already in the making. The outcome of the 2016 election in the US, however, produced a political climate that placed repeal of the 2010 Dodd-Frank Act on the Congressional agenda. Those who favor repeal give little weight to the belief that the role of regulation is to protect the public whose money is at risk. Their proposals seem to argue that their role is to support a profitable financial system. Some advocate a return to self-regulation and the self-dealing by and within the financial system that resulted in the excessive speculation that triggered the crisis of 2007–2008, which will lead, once again, to an environment in which such anti-regulatory ideology will excuse policymakers from making pragmatic assessments of the risks and problems that regulations are—or should be—designed to fix.

This book attempts to provide an assessment of how the monetary and financial frameworks for the US and global economies unraveled over the last 50 years. It offers proposals to reform the broken system now in place and calls for continued attention to the need for reform despite—or because of—the hostile political environment. The first section is a brief summary of the developments and proposals described in greater detail in subsequent chapters. The author hopes this summary will help the reader follow the progression of seemingly disparate issues that, like pieces of a puzzle, are indispensable parts of a narrative that describes how the vulnerabilities in the current system emerged and how they continue to threaten the US and global economies.

SUMMARY OF THE BOOK

Part I

The first major shift in market structure was initiated in the 1960s by the development of unregulated markets for financial transactions denominated in national currencies outside their countries of origin. Institutions operating in these parallel markets for dollars, pounds, marks, and other currencies fundamentally changed how and by whom they were funded and how and to whom those funds were channeled. In time, those changes were incorporated into the operations of financial institutions in national markets, transforming the structure of domestic markets and forcing regulatory accommodations to meet the new functional configurations that resulted.

As early as 1970, offers of financial guarantees began to increase with the strategy established by the US Federal Reserve to solve the commercial paper crisis that resulted from the default of the Penn Central Railroad, inaugurating a trend toward contingency lending in which banks promised (for a fee) that they would lend to companies that were unable to sell their commercial paper. The growth in these guarantees led to swollen off-balance sheet positions for contingent liabilities held by banks and fueled the growth in non-bank lending funded by commercial paper. By the 1980s, what had evolved was, in effect, an unregulated parallel banking system. With finance companies as issuers and money market mutual funds as buyers of commercial paper, these sectors operated in tandem as lenders and funders of credit without the regulatory costs imposed on depository institutions.

But while the parallel non-bank system reduced banks' share of total financial assets, the parallel system itself was, in time, dwarfed by the ways banks found to evade regulatory costs and the innovative products they developed for guaranteeing and hedging against losses on financial assets. In the build-up to the crisis, selling and buying over-the-counter (OTC) derivatives contracts became a major area of activity for the largest financial institutions and led to the engorged off-balance sheet positions that became known as shadow banking.

Another critical development that hastened the shift from a bank-based to a market-based system was passage of the Employee Retirement Income Security Act (ERISA) in 1974. Rules and regulations that required companies to back their promises of benefits with actual holdings of assets increased demand for securities and had the effect of encouraging a seismic shift in household savings from bank and thrift deposits to pension funds. The effect was to open a new and large channel for the flow of household savings to securities markets, and to increase their vulnerability to the volatility of market forces without protections such as those provided by deposit insurance.

The shift to a market-based system prompted little or no change in securities law and regulation. The emphasis on transparency initiated in the 1930s that had made US securities markets a model for the world was lost by the growth and increased dominance of opaque markets for buying and selling foreign exchange, mortgage-backed securities (MBS), OTC derivatives, and securities repurchase agreements (repos). With no information available on the volume and price of transactions, these markets posed increasing risks to the system as they became the dominant areas of credit creation and trading.

During those weeks of crisis in September 2008, it seemed almost ironic that reports on prices on the US stock market continued to be broadcast at the end of each day, even as they were being unraveled by developments in much larger markets—the market for MBS, for example, where, as early as 1984, trading was estimated to be larger than that in all the world's equity markets combined (Maxwell, 1984). In 2008, the scale of price collapses in the MBS and other OTC markets were disastrously unavailable to participants trying to make decisions on trade, as well as to regulators and the public at large.

Meanwhile, acceptance of these and other changes in financial structure seemed to support what the Bank for International Settlements (BIS) termed the rise in "free market ideology" that prompted a wave of deregulation in the domestic US market. At the beginning of the 1980s, Congress passed legislation ending limits on interest rates paid by banks and savings associations—critical provisions of the 1930s reforms—that led to widespread failures of thrifts and greater reliance on fee income for banks. Later in the 1980s, the Federal Reserve began to loosen reserve requirements in an effort to equalize costs for banks competing with other financial sectors and costs between banks' offshore and domestic markets, in order to bring more of their activities back into the home market and under surveillance by the central bank. But, as traditional banking operations lost their dominant role, banks also moved into new activities and, in 1999, succeeded in obtaining congressional approval for repeal of the 1933 Glass-Steagall Act that had separated commercial and investment banking.

At that point, the compartmentalized structure put in place in response to the Great Depression disappeared along with the particular missions and responsibilities of individual financial sectors. On paper, however, this regulatory structure and its institutions remained unchanged. Because of this disparity, regulatory responsibilities became muddled and effective systemic oversight was lost.

Part II

With the adoption of capital requirements and adherence to the belief that market forces should and would act as an appropriate regulator for the financial system, the unregulated offshore financial markets became the model for the US domestic system. Banks and other major financial institutions in the US took on functions developed offshore, where 80 percent of borrowing and lending occurs between financial institutions. They assumed the function of monetizing debt by using the opaque market for repurchase agreements to raise short-term funds from other financial institutions. This funding strategy enabled higher levels of leverage and trading for their own accounts as they used borrowed funds to buy assets that could be pledged for additional borrowing. Using this strategy, they effectively seized control over market liquidity—previously a central bank function—and created debt levels for financial and non-financial sectors that were unsustainable relative to economic activity. In addition, it was a strategy that tightened the web of interconnectedness that linked the fortunes of many to the performance of the largest institutions. As a result of the growth in interconnectedness in both domestic and offshore markets, the loss of confidence that developed as housing prices fell—one of the traditional asset-price triggers for financial crises—originated in the financial system and led to a run on the financial sector by the financial sector (D'Arista and Epstein, 2011).

The US Comptroller of the Currency—the primary regulator of national banks—ignored this growth in interconnectedness when, in the late 1990s, he failed to question whether the National Bank Act's restrictions on loans to individual borrowers in relation to capital should also apply to financial counterparties. The Federal Reserve, too, ignored its oversight responsibility in failing to assess developments underway in the run-up to the crisis. Before March 2008, the Fed had not moved to acquire information about the interconnectedness and exposure to risk among counterparties in the enormous credit risk transfer markets where collateralized debt obligations (CDOs) and credit default swaps (CDSs) were traded. The CDS market was estimated to have been a $62 trillion market—about four times larger than the US economy—at the time of Lehman Brothers' collapse.

The Fed also seemed unconcerned about the implications of the build-up of positions among dealers in the OTC market for derivatives. Since OTC derivatives are tailored to the needs of a single customer and thus cannot be traded, buying and selling contracts among dealers to hedge their positions pushed up the nominal value of outstanding contracts to many multiples of the value of underlying assets. The beginnings and ends of layers in these markets were obscured and most of the so-called assets involved had become impenetrable froth.

But the US Congress, too, shirked its oversight responsibility when it gave a boost to securitization in 1984 by exempting private issues of MBS from registration and disclosure, relying instead on the ratings of a few nationally recognized credit rating agencies. Since the issuers paid the agencies, one of the more glaring conflicts of interest in the MBS market was baked into the pie at that point.

Securitization was a boon to the banks: a way to evade capital requirements while earning profits on originating and servicing a rising volume of lending for mortgages. Moreover, it allowed a new class of unregulated institutions—mortgage brokers—to enter the system as originators without having to raise capital to hold the loans. But the absence of capital restrictions on banks' and other lenders' securitization exposures resulted in an undercapitalization of what had become the largest US credit market, one which fed the housing bubble and ensured that MBS were held and traded by almost all financial sectors, including pension and mutual funds.

The pervasiveness of MBS holdings meant that, when the bubble burst, homeowners experienced a double whammy: their net worth fell because of the drop in the value of their homes and then fell further as the value of MBS in their pension and mutual funds declined. In addition, the lack of disclosure about underlying mortgages in securitized pools dealt a third blow to households: it made negotiating loan workouts more difficult and exacerbated the rate of foreclosures.

As a result of securitization, small businesses, too, were dealt a heavy blow by the crisis. Banks had used business owners' residences as collateral to channel lending to these borrowers because the collateral could be securitized and the loans would no longer be held on their balance sheets. After the crisis, the position of small businesses as borrowers with underwater collateral and no access to credit became a significant and tragic drag on recovery.

Another critical development overlooked by regulatory authorities and Congress was the growing level of concentration in almost all financial sectors. The growth in concentration accelerated as institutions expanded both their international reach and their share of financial activity at home. When Continental Illinois, the large Chicago-based bank, threatened to cause ripple effects throughout the system in 1984, "too big to fail" became a common term of reference for the dilemma of interconnectedness. That a single institution with liabilities for deposits, commercial paper, and commercial paper guaranties could damage the well-being of a wide range of other financial institutions, however, was not a new concern. Similar concerns about Franklin National Bank's interbank deposits and foreign exchange contracts had led the Fed to intervene in 1975 when Franklin failed and, of course, the Fed did so again in 1984.

Concentration was evident in other sectors as well, especially among securities firms and institutional investors who, as managers of household savings invested in pension and mutual funds, held an unprecedented level of market power. Looking at an already high level of concentration in the 1980s, some argued for stronger anti-trust laws. But, given the widespread belief that markets free of government regulation are more efficient, that view was ignored in favor of the assumption that markets would curtail concentration.

In the end, however, government reinforced the market's decision to permit ever higher levels of concentration. Beginning with the thrift failures in the 1980s, "supervisory mergers" and "purchase and assumption" transactions became the preferred method of handling failing depository institutions. A Federal Reserve paper noted that, between 1980 and 2005, 17,500 mergers involving small, medium-size, and large institutions took place—about 700 a year (Mester, 2007). In 1984, 64 banks held half of all banking assets. By 2009, that number had been reduced to five. Along the way, in 1991, Congress passed the Federal Deposit Insurance Corporation Improvement Act, authorizing federal regulators to rescue large banks and cover their uninsured deposits if their failure would create a serious risk to the banking system.

As a result, the erosion of regulation and abandonment of prudent financial practices proceeded at an even more rapid pace. Among the most egregious of the unsound practices that had become embedded in the system was the widespread engagement of large banks and investment banks in proprietary trading—that is, trading for the institution's own account in addition to trading for customers' accounts. Proprietary trading increased these institutions' reliance on borrowing funds from other financial institutions to increase leverage to expand speculative positions involving carry trade transactions. "Carry trade" is a term for borrowing short term at low interest rates in order to invest in higher-yielding long-term assets. It was a strategy that diverted a sizable share of financial resources away from transactions with non-financial customers in order to augment the profits of large institutions. In addition, the interconnectedness and leverage associated with carry trades added an increasingly higher level of risk to the financial system.

A reasonably strong version of former Fed chairman Paul Volcker's proposals to curb these activities was included in the Dodd-Frank Act in 2010. By December 2014, however, the proprietary traders had succeeded in adding an amendment to the government spending bill that weakened the force of the Volcker provisions. And, as noted, Dodd-Frank remains vulnerable to further weakening, rather than the strengthening hoped for by so many who made reform proposals during and after consideration of the bill.

The good news about the Dodd-Frank Act is that it fully recognized the importance of government regulation. Even so, it failed to recognize the extent to which changes in the structure of the financial system have altered relationships among financial institutions, regulators, and the monetary authority; and between finance and the real economy.

To deal with those changes in ways that will restore the financial stability necessary for sustainable growth in economic activity, regulations must be clarified and sharpened, and must apply in the same way to all institutions engaged in a given activity. In addition, a new system of financial guaranties must be put in place to protect household savings. Based on the kind of information about holdings already reported by financial institutions for tax purposes, such a system would insure individuals rather than institutions, using social security numbers to identify the individuals' accounts. It would cover holdings wherever held, whether in banks, pensions, or other retirement or savings accounts, up to the existing amount of $250,000, and would charge a minimal insurance premium as the Federal Deposit Insurance Corporation does now.

Parts III and IV

Other efforts needed to strengthen US financial regulation and protect the public and the economy on which it relies must take into account how globalization has shaped both the financial system and the US economy over the past 50 years. The US balance of payments accounts were and are at the heart of globalization. Becoming a debtor nation in 1989 signaled the beginning of the ongoing loss of opportunities for the US economy to sell more goods abroad and at home. But, despite the vigor of the debate over trade, it almost always casts the trade deficit as a stand-alone phenomenon that can be blamed on the policies of other nations.

In fact, the US trade deficit stems from a broad set of causes—in particular, the dollar's central role in global payments and investments—and represents a larger set of imbalances. As long as non-US residents choose to hold and use dollars for trade and investment transactions, their demand for the currency keeps the dollar exchange rate at a level that increases the cost of US exports relative to competing foreign-made products. It also reduces the cost of imports relative to domestically produced goods. And the foreign sector's willingness to hold and invest dollars in American financial assets allows the US to continue to run up its tab with the rest of the world even as its trade deficit widens.

The accumulation of that form of red ink shows up on the other side of the US balance of payments accounts: the capital account. By any standard, the inflow of foreign capital measured by the capital account had become enormous in the 1990s and became a main support for US prosperity in that decade and into the new millennium. But US dependence on foreign capital creates an unsustainable foundation for economic growth, a fact that the Federal Reserve and successive US administrations have ignored. They have taken credit for ongoing economic growth during those years without acknowledging that foreign indebtedness has enabled the country to live beyond its means.

Commenting in 1971 on the role of dollar hegemony in the global payments system and how it would affect the trade deficit and economy of the US, the British economist Nicholas Kaldor predicted that it "would involve transforming a nation of creative producers into a community of *rentiers* increasingly living on others, seeking gratification in ever more useless consumption, with all the debilitating effects of the bread and circuses of imperial Rome" (Kaldor, 1971, p. 64).

One way in which dollar hegemony affects the US economy is through the accumulation of foreign exchange reserves held by other countries. Those reserves provide credit for the country in which they are invested as well as for the country that owns them, and their investment in US Treasury securities and the securities of government-sponsored enterprises (GSEs such as Fannie Mae and Freddie Mac) changed the allocation of credit in the US financial system. Augmented by enormous inflows of foreign private capital, these structural elements of the international monetary system contributed to the general prosperity the US experienced in the decade before 2008. But those good times were not, in fact, sustainable, because the mirror image of growing official and private foreign debt was the immense run up in domestic private sector indebtedness that set the stage for the crisis.

The dollar's role in the global system has had equally significant effects on other countries, precipitating crises around the world, beginning with the default and threatened default in 1982 of 15 lesser-developed countries that had borrowed dollar-denominated Organization of Petroleum Exporting Countries surpluses intermediated by US banks. While capital inflows increased growth and development in many countries in subsequent years, the costs of crises in the periphery of the global system contributed to the perpetuation of poverty and increasing inequality in many other emerging and developing economies.

Developments in the period before the 2008 crisis underscore the irrationality and inefficiency of the global financial and monetary systems. Beginning in 2004, increases in US interest rates sparked another round of carry trade transactions that brought a flood of foreign private investment into dollar assets, together with increases in inflows of foreign official investments as dollar reserves rose. The gross inflow through the US capital account was more than twice the amount needed to finance the trade deficit and other expenditures in the current account, and more than could be used to finance the borrowing binges of US households and businesses (US Department of Commerce, 2005).

As a result, the excess liquidity added to US financial markets was then exported through carry trades, using dollar borrowings to invest in higher-yielding assets in emerging economies. There, the inflow of dollars used to buy these countries' assets tended to be mopped up by their central banks in sterilization operations intended to prevent inflation and appreciation of their currencies. But, having accumulated additional dollar reserves in the process, the governments and central banks of emerging and developing countries invested them in dollar financial assets in the US and the Eurodollar market, setting in motion a sorcerer's apprentice scenario in which one response prompted another, and led to ever larger streams of cross-border flows and ever rising debt.

By amassing reserves, emerging markets were feeding the machine that generated the capital flows they were trying to guard against. They had, in fact, been doing this since 1999, when Asian and Latin American countries paid down bank debt and added to their deposits in the offshore markets, augmenting the amount of funding available for speculative activity in the international interbank market. By 2001, the build-up in foreign currency reserves as precautionary balances, to cover needed imports and protect against increases in the value of the dollar and dollar interest rates, led developing countries as a group to become net creditors to international banks. Their net creditor position was an outgrowth of their experience with volatile capital flows and illustrated one way that the international financial system undermined funding for development.

The main function of the need for the build-up in reserves was to enforce the export-led growth paradigm that required these countries to earn foreign exchange by reducing wages, in order to compete in selling cheap exports and then channel the surpluses they earned to rich financial institutions and economies.

The current, dollar-based international financial and monetary systems inflicted major damage through its role in feeding the unsustainable debt bubble in the global system that led to the 2008 crisis. In the US, for example, the amount of foreign investment in US financial assets rose in the 1980s and contributed 15 percent of total credit on average each year in the 1990s, peaking at 30 percent in 1998. Credit expansion fueled by foreign inflows resulted in unprecedented increases in the debt of all US sectors. Beginning with the Reagan administration, the debt of all US borrowers—federal, state, and local governments, corporations and non-corporate businesses, farms, households, non-profit organizations, and the financial and foreign sectors—doubled from $5 trillion in 1982 (the total accumulated debt since the beginning of the republic) to $10 trillion in 1990, and kept mounting through the years that followed. As the momentum accelerated in 2007, the year the crisis began, total outstanding US debt spiked to 352.3 percent of GDP (up from 255.3 percent in 1997), with particularly large increases in the debt of households and the financial sector relative to GDP (FRS, *Flow of Funds*, various issues).

Part V

In the US, one of the major losses brought about by deregulation was the abandonment of reliance on required bank reserves as a countercyclical lever to rein in and stimulate credit expansion and to perform as an effective monetary cushion for the financial system in a time of crisis. The alternative tool put in place in the 1980s was capital requirements—a rational response, in the wake of the Third World Debt Crisis, to the discovery that the major banks had not backed their offshore operations with capital and that, in 1983, the total capital of the nine largest banks could be wiped out if 15 highly stressed less-developed countries were to default on their dollar borrowings from those banks (Cline, 1983).

But the assurance that overlending could be prevented by requiring adequate capital backing for balance sheets proved wrong. Markets may punish individual institutions for unsafe behavior but, on a systemic basis, they behave pro-cyclically, willing and able to supply more capital in a boom when asset prices are rising but unwilling and unable to replenish capital when prices fall. And, of course, the value of any institution's capital appreciates in a boom but falls along with all other prices in a downturn.

In the bank-based system funded by deposits, and with a monetary cushion provided by required reserves held by the central bank, the pressure on capital tended to occur with a lag, giving banks at least a brief window of time to expand their lending into more profitable areas and to reduce non-performing loans as a share of assets and capital. The rules of the game in a market-based system are less forgiving: assets must be marked to market with "haircuts" taken against capital when prices fall; good assets must be sold to restore required capital ratios and meet margin calls for more collateral. Once the downward spiral begins, it moves very quickly, triggering downgrades in credit ratings and a loss of confidence that raises the cost of funding and lowers the firm's stock price. At that point, it is almost impossible for an institution to raise additional capital and regain its robust standing.

Therefore, designing an appropriate role for capital in a mixed bank- and market-based system is an issue that must be addressed in order to overcome the pro-cyclical effects embedded in the current system. Reliance on capital adequacy as the primary tool for macroprudential regulation of the banking system contributed to the development of the crisis; unfortunately, its continued centrality in the regulatory paradigm maintains the ongoing vulnerability to pro-cyclical market forces that produce crises.

Part VI

Outmoded national monetary systems also pose a major threat both to individual countries and to the global economy. That the Federal Reserve ignored the expansionary effects of foreign lending and made no effort to defuse the debt bubble becomes apparent in light of the excessive credit expansion in the years before the crisis, and its failure to warn the public of the level of risk. While central bank inaction was partly due to Fed officials' strong adherence to free market ideology, an equally persuasive argument is that, given the change in financial structure, the Fed was stuck with outworn tools that made it difficult to moderate or prevent the damaging rise in debt. Fed officials understood that meeting the central bank's obligation to prevent inflation and deflation required counter-cyclical actions but, even as they affirmed the continued effectiveness of monetary tools, former Fed chairmen acknowledged that those tools had become less powerful (Greenspan, 1993) and bore some offsetting risks (Bernanke, 2010).

A context for the argument that monetary tools have become counterproductive is provided by descriptions of how they were used during the crisis. In the initial response to the crisis, 62 percent of the Fed's total lending of $1.7 trillion was loaned to the 20 large banks it deals with in conducting the majority of its open market operations (Matthews, 2013). While these loans (at a median interest rate of 0.48 percent) may have been necessary to prevent a collapse of the financial system, they provided little relief for households and businesses, and their failure to reignite economic activity prompted the addition of quantitative easing (QE) to the toolkit.

Five years after the beginning of the 2008 crisis and following the third of its QE operations, the Fed had bought $3 trillion of US Treasury securities and MBS with relatively little increase in lending or economic activity to show for it. Of course, there tends to be a time lag before the effects of monetary policy show up, but this lag was longer than usual and the expected, eventual pick-up after any downturn was not occurring. Monetary officials in several countries—the US, the United Kingdom, and at the BIS—began to voice concerns about the limits of monetary policy. One, William White at the BIS, pointed out the dramatic change in financial structure that had occurred, noting that banking had been replaced by a "collateralized market system with the repo market at its heart" (White, 2013, p. 87).

The need for a new, inclusive reserve system builds on the reality of that observation. It recognizes that the old reserve system that imposed reserves on bank deposits was applicable only to banks, since banks alone can create deposits when they make loans. To regain systemic monetary influence will require imposing reserve requirements on all financial institutions. The structure that would make that possible would be one in which the Fed engages in repurchase transactions with all sectors of the financial system in a broad range of sound assets. To do so, the Fed would need to create reserves that would be posted on the liability side of financial institutions' balance sheets and posted as assets on the Fed's balance sheet. In the process of buying and selling assets through repo transactions, the Fed would add or subtract interest-free liabilities on the side of institutions' balance sheets that hold customers' funds and capital, thus enabling it to counter excessive losses or gains in either of those sources of funding. This would allow the Fed to act systemically in changing the supply of credit and restore its former role in conducting effective countercyclical operations.

The proposed system-wide reserve regime would overcome the procyclical pressures in the market-based system by allowing institutions to buy and sell reserves at face value, rather than be forced to sell assets as prices fall and "haircuts" deplete capital. It would also give all financial institutions direct access to the lender of last resort. For example, if mutual funds faced runs by shareholders, they could avoid selling assets by transferring them to the Fed under repurchase agreements and acquiring reserves needed to offset customers' withdrawals. Of course, the Fed would, as now, act in that capacity at its own discretion. But it would have a direct channel for action to replace the convoluted system used during the 2008 crisis, or in earlier years when it had to pressure banks to lend to other financial sectors to address their problems.

Part VII

Curbing the irrational forces of cross-border capital flows to moderate their excessive contributions to the expansion and destruction of debt is a necessary component of the effort to both stabilize global finance and ensure the potential for sustainable economic activity in the global economy that all nations need to protect and promote their own growth. Numerous proposals for additional issues of Special Drawing Rights (SDRs) by the International Monetary Fund (IMF) reflect widespread recognition of the need for reform. But dealing with the problem of the current system, in which the need for reserve creation is driven by the need for export-led growth, will require innovative structural arrangements.

One arrangement that would help meet this need would be the establishment of a closed-end, international investment fund under the Bretton Woods umbrella. The investment fund would issue its own liabilities in various national currencies and invest in private and public assets in emerging and developing countries. These investments would provide funds for infrastructure and other projects that require long-term financing. Selling shares in the proposed fund to private institutional investors, such as mutual and pension funds in both developed and emerging economies, would help provide to developing countries a buffer against the volatility of current channels for private cross-border flows. Shares in the fund would also provide assets for the investment of reserves by central banks and governments in emerging and developing economies. Given the multilateral guaranty by the fund backed by its Bretton Woods member countries, this channel for reserve investment would redirect export surpluses back into the countries that own them, rather than into the financial markets of strong-currency countries.

Still another, more critical, flaw in the current international monetary system must also be addressed: the means of payment. Creating a new international monetary system that would build on ideas developed at the time of the meetings at Bretton Woods, but not included in the institutional framework of that agreement, would meet that need. For example, using John Maynard Keynes' concept of an international clearing union, a public international clearing agency could be structured to hold the international reserves of countries; debiting and crediting their accounts through interactions with their national central banks would allow all countries to make international payments in their own currencies. Member countries' reserves would be backed by their government's securities and, with the permission of a majority of its members, the new agency would be able to buy or sell those securities to augment or reduce a country's reserves. This would allow the clearing agency, unlike the IMF, to engage in countercyclical strategies that would influence global liquidity and introduce an effective lender of last resort at the international level.

Given the inability and unwillingness of any other country or group of countries to accept the current account deficits that are inevitable for key currency countries, continuation of the current international monetary system depends on the ongoing successful economic performance of the US and its continued willingness and ability to remain the buyer of last resort for the global economy. However, continued US dependence on foreign savings to bolster economic performance has increased the vulnerability of the key currency. With holdings of dollar reserves by so many countries and in so large an aggregate amount, the threat is that a significant fall in the value of the dollar would sharply contract the value of global reserves. Such a decline in the value of reserves—like the one that occurred in the period 1928–32—would exert substantial pressure on national economies that would spread quickly throughout the global system.

Part VIII

In describing the ways in which changes in financial structure and regulation altered the US and global financial systems and how those changes contributed to an inexorable drift toward crisis, this brief analysis of the issues and problems discussed in the book concludes that the export-led growth imperative in the key currency system led to an unsustainable explosion in debt in the US and global economies and that the evolution of a privatized financial system operating in interconnected national and offshore markets with little or no public sector monetary or regulatory constraints contributed to the rise in debt to historically high levels over the last 30 years.

This final section gives evidence that dangerous levels of debt in relation to GDP in the US and global economies remain a threat to economic activity. It also notes the widening gap between what US residents own abroad and the US holdings of non-residents—a negative net international investment position that grew from 24 percent to 43 percent of GDP in the years from 2002 to 2016, as ongoing US trade deficits continued to be financed by foreign savings. America's high level of external debt makes it increasingly vulnerable to loss of confidence in the dollar as the key currency in the global system, as rising debt in the household and business sectors lower the level of growth in GDP on which that confidence depends, or because shifts in holdings of dollar assets become a means to express concern about the political environment. A significant fall in the value of the dollar would wreak havoc on financial markets around the globe. And, as noted, the fact that the aggregate level of international reserves held by emerging market and developing economies reached 24 percent of global GDP in 2016 exacerbated their vulnerability to a fall in the value of the dollar. A drop in the value of international reserves would cause immediate contractions in the economies of those countries.

In short, this book argues that the regulatory and monetary frameworks now in place have intensified rather than defused the threat of another crisis. Defusing that threat will require both regulatory and monetary reforms that will replace the debt-fueled, export-led growth models embedded in the global transactional framework, reduce pro-cyclical pressures introduced in the transition from a bank-based to a market-based system, and restore the potential for countercyclical initiatives needed to reinstate a stable financial system that can support sustainable economic activity in the US and global economies in the decades to come.

PART I

The unraveling of the 1930s-era framework

2. The euro market erodes US financial structure

In the early 1960s, United Kingdom (UK) banks began to accept deposits and make loans in United States (US) dollars in London; the branches of US banks in London quickly followed, creating what became an external market for national currencies that, in time, globalized world finance. The story of the beginning of the so-called Eurodollar market is a familiar one. It began when the Union of Soviet Socialist Republics deposited unspent dollars from loans received from the US during the Second World War. The Soviets deposited these balances in UK banks because they feared they would be confiscated if deposited in US banks. Given the strong demand for dollar loans in those years, the market grew as governments of other countries began to deposit into UK and US banks in London dollar reserves acquired as a result of US balance of payment deficits (Little, 1969).

The initial purpose of both the UK and US banks in making external dollar loans was to escape capital controls. In the case of US banks, the Voluntary Foreign Credit Restraint program was imposed in 1965 in recognition of the fact that an increased volume of lending to foreign borrowers from a growing number of banks in the US had become a major component of US payment deficits. In response, 12 American banks with branches overseas joined British banks in London in expanding the business of offering offshore dollar transactions. Since these transactions did not change the balance of payments accounts of either country, their operations were not prohibited by the Bank of England or the US Federal Reserve. Dollar deposits and loans were also used by UK banks to escape quantitative controls on the growth of credit and by US bank branches abroad to avoid reserve requirements, interest rate ceilings, and deposit insurance premiums. Although these were evasions of monetary controls, the central banks acquiesced as they thought operations in what came to be called the Eurocurrency market were unlikely to affect domestic credit conditions (D'Arista, 1976).

However, evidence of the balance-of-payments effects of the external market emerged as early as the mid-1960s as the Fed's actions in tightening credit in 1966 and 1969 pulled dollars out of offshore accounts for lending in New York. The Fed's loss of control over the credit supply led it to push interest rates to (then) historically high levels to dampen demand. What also became apparent was how different national economic sectors are affected when tight credit conditions attract sizable inflows of capital. In the 1969 credit crunch, borrowers who relied on small and regional banks without access to external sources of funds—particularly small businesses, the housing sector, households, and state and local governments—lost access to credit as domestic investors pulled funds from bank deposits and bought government securities. Banks with Eurodollar funding were able to continue lending to large corporate borrowers willing to pay rates higher than domestic interest rates to obtain or preserve access to credit (D'Arista, 1994a).

In the late 1960s, waves of capital flows into the US, and then into Germany, Switzerland, and other European countries, demonstrated how effectively the Eurocurrency markets could evade capital controls. In response to changes in interest rates, participants in the external markets changed the currency denomination of loans and investments outside national markets and invested the proceeds in financial assets issued in national markets. It also became clear that the measurable effects on exchange rates caused by the shifts in the currency denomination of loans and investments outside the national market were as great as the flows into or out of national markets or shifts in trade, but were more volatile. None of the governments of European countries or the US wanted to abandon fixed exchange rates, but the external market for their currencies made effective control over exchange rates impossible. As discussed in Chapter 12, recognition of the problem led the US to float the dollar in 1973 and end the Bretton Woods system (D'Arista, 1994a).

While little reliable information on the size of the Eurocurrency market was available in the 1970s, governments and central banks were aware of its rapid growth and several Federal Reserve Board governors expressed concern (D'Arista, 1976). The implications of its growth were seen somewhat differently by observers of international financial developments. Some argued that the creation and expansion of the Eurocurrency market were responsible for an extraordinary increase in international trade and investment and thus for a substantial rise in world prosperity. Others argued that the price paid for increased trade and investment was the loss of government sovereignty to the private international financial sector; that economic events, both domestic and international, were being determined less by public policy and more by private interests (D'Arista, 1976).

Moreover, some said that as central banks attempted to stabilize the exchange rate for their domestic currencies by buying and selling their own and other currencies, unrestrained money creation in the Eurodollar market contributed to worldwide inflation in the same way that excess money creation in national markets fuels domestic inflation. They noted that not only was there no countercyclical mechanism in the external market, but countercyclical measures employed in national economies tended to enforce a pro-cyclical pattern of events when individual countries tried to stabilize their economies. As discussed in greater detail in Chapter 17, tight money policies draw Eurocurrency funds into domestic markets in the form of loans, augmenting the liquidity the central bank is trying to mop up. Policies implemented to ease credit conditions induce an outflow of domestic funds that become Eurocurrency deposits. In either case, changes in interest rates produce results that are the opposite of those intended and national central banks experience a loss of monetary control (Hester, 1982; Blecker, 2002).

A further unforeseen consequence of the development of an external market was its effect on financial regulation. The credit crunch of 1969 led to the first of many steps to dismantle existing regulations: the removal of interest rate ceilings on large, negotiable certificates of deposit (CDs) to make them competitive with Eurodollar deposits and remove the incentive for transactions that shifted funds between the domestic and external dollar market. But this deregulation did not lessen flows. Instead, it created arbitrage opportunities between the two markets and increased flows between them. And when the euro markets took on the role of recycling the surplus earnings of Organization of Petroleum Exporting Countries (OPEC) in the mid-1970s, the cost of capital in US markets rose as US borrowers faced competition from Third World governments in accessing dollar loans (D'Arista, 1994a).

Because of its increasingly important role in recycling OPEC funds, the US government and central bank seemed unconcerned about the increased movement of funds to and from the Eurocurrency market in the 1970s. But it was a uniquely attractive market for US investors: freedom from exchange rate risk on their external dollar deposits added to the advantage of earning higher rates on external deposits not subject to reserve requirements and deposit insurance premiums.

The US government and central bank also seemed unconcerned about the degree to which outflows from the US fed liquidity into the external market. Rising inflation was attributed to the oil price increase and to overly expansive US monetary policy that was seen as a reflection of the government's decision to fight unemployment. By the end of the decade, however, the alarming fall in the dollar's value called attention to the possibility that "round tripping" of dollar deposits—the investment of dollars by US residents in unregulated deposits abroad and their reinvestment by foreign branches of US banks as loans to both domestic and international borrowers—had made the Fed's monetary operating targets obsolete and weakened its ability to control inflation. Also ignored was the fact that central banks' frequent interventions in the market had resulted in a build-up in their US dollar reserves and that the investment of these reserves in US government securities acted like an external mechanism for open market operations that flooded US credit markets and contributed to inflation (D'Arista, 2002).

In 1978, the Fed imposed reserve requirements on balances loaned by foreign offices of US banks to US residents. In the early 1980s, the Fed attempted to persuade other central bank members of the Basel Committee on Banking Supervision to join in imposing reserve requirements on all Eurocurrency liabilities. The failure of this effort left American banks at a significant disadvantage. Reserve requirements determine the ratio of total deposits that can be loaned out by a bank for profit. Since US banks were subject to reserve requirements on lending within the domestic market from both domestic and (from 1978 to 1990) offshore offices, while foreign banks were only subject to US reserve requirements if loans were made by offices located in the US, a new channel for inflows into the US opened in the 1980s: loans to US businesses from foreign banks' offices abroad (McCauley and Seth, 1992).[1] Foreign banks could and did lower rates on credits to US corporate customers, forcing American banks to expand lending to other, more risky domestic sectors such as commercial real estate and for highly leveraged transactions that financed changes in corporate control.

US banks were also experiencing a loss of competitiveness because their exposure to heavily indebted countries had lowered their credit ratings and raised their cost of funds. Moreover, in 1983, Congress had added a provision to the legislation increasing funding for the International Monetary Fund (IMF) that required US banking authorities to impose explicit capital requirements as a cushion against losses and as protection for the deposit insurance fund (D'Arista, 2002).

Along with other national banking systems operating with significantly lower capital requirements and lower funding costs, US banks reduced their traditional banking activities and reshaped their operations by securitizing loans to lower the need for capital, expanding their fee-generating, off-balance sheet activities in managing money and providing financial insurance against the interest and exchange rate volatility that was by then embedded in the system.

The Fed's response was to shift its regulatory approach. It led the effort to negotiate the capital adequacy standards adopted by the Basel

Committee on Banking at the Bank for International Settlements (BIS) in 1988 and promoted the adoption of a supervisory framework that placed responsibility for developing and monitoring internal controls on banks themselves. In 1990, it eliminated reserve requirements on domestic time deposits and reduced requirements on demand deposits from 12 to 10 percent (*Federal Reserve Bulletin*, 1990, table 1.15). Since capital requirements covered banks' consolidated operations and all external deposits were time deposits, the only cost advantage remaining for Eurodollar operations was the relatively small premium paid to insure domestic deposits.

Similar developments were underway in the national markets of other developed countries. The expansion of the euro markets continued to undermine the effectiveness of regulation in countries that relied on lending limits or liquidity requirements or other regulatory strategies designed to moderate credit expansion and promote stability in financial markets. Moreover, the ease of funding and lending in the euro markets made it clear that differences in regulation in national markets could affect banks' competitiveness in external markets and the competitiveness of national banking systems. As global developments increasingly affected conditions for attracting capital to, and retaining savings in national markets, the competitiveness of a country's banking system became more important. This form of competition intensified pressures for financial deregulation in tandem with increased economic competition in the global environment.

Pressures for liberalization came from many quarters—including the harmonization efforts of the European Community in later years—and had a strong ideological component. Nevertheless, concerns about monetary control, balance of payments positions, and the effects of changes in exchange rates initiated by external financial activity on the competitiveness of countries, as well as their banking systems, encouraged monetary authorities in industrialized countries to view a reduction in the cost advantages of the Eurocurrency markets as a means of reducing destabilizing capital flows. By the early 1990s, most of the regulatory restrictions on US banks that had made the cost advantages of the Eurocurrency markets attractive—interest rate restrictions, lending limits, portfolio investment restrictions, and reserve and liquidity requirements—had been reduced or eliminated, as had the controls on capital flows from domestic markets that were the original impetus for the creation of the external markets (D'Arista, 2002).

Meanwhile, the expansion of the external markets encouraged and supported the extraordinary increase in banks' trading activities. The largest, most active and globally integrated markets are the over-the-counter (OTC) markets for foreign exchange and financial derivatives. Bank dominance of those markets poses particularly difficult questions in terms of regulation because banks have imposed their institutional culture on these markets, adapting market practices to the style of portfolio lenders. Thus, as dealers in these markets, they "hold" instruments even if the portfolio in which they are held is "off balance sheet."

As the style of trading in which banks engaged became more pervasive across a wider spectrum of assets and institutions, the market system was pushed back, recreating conditions like those that prevailed in the US before enactment of the securities laws. OTC markets are opaque, not transparent; they do not conform to the concepts or requirements for disclosure necessary if investors are to make informed decisions. They are not public markets. There is no surveillance of trading practices and no system for routinely and continuously making information on prices and the volume of transactions available to the public. Above all, many of the instruments—OTC contracts, for example—are not readily tradable because the time periods for these contracts and the amounts covered are not standardized—a critical factor that undermines liquidity and contributes to concentrations of contracts within a relatively small circle of dealers.

These concentrations necessarily intensify when exposures must be hedged with new contracts because existing positions cannot be sold. Despite efforts to mitigate the potential repercussions of disruptions through netting agreements in derivatives contracts, these particular characteristics of OTC markets increase the potential that disruptions resulting from inaccurate assessments of credit or market risk will escalate into systemic crises. Moreover, derivatives contracts offered by banks have undermined the mutuality of the relationship between banks and their customers. Since transactions are profitable to banks when their customers lose, the assumption that the prosperity of the institution is linked to that of the customer—and vice versa—no longer applies.

The proliferation of non-public markets prompted regulators to privatize monitoring and surveillance at the level of the individual firm. Beginning in the US in the 1970s with the requirement that banks devise effective checking-in systems for recording foreign exchange transactions and positions (D'Arista, 1976), these requirements became a major component of the Basel Committee's core principles of regulation, and applied to all OTC trading markets in which banks participated. The weakness in this strategy was its emphasis on the individual firm. It reinforced lack of market transparency and increased the likelihood that, in the absence of effective external checks through clearing houses, systems for routing transactions that permit ongoing surveillance, or other forms of systemic oversight, gaps in firms' recording and monitoring systems would go unnoticed, resulting in large losses (Daiwa) or failure (Barings) for two major financial institutions in 1995 and increasing the potential for systemic repercussions.

But the threat of systemic repercussions was already in place as a result of the Eurocurrency market's major contribution to the transformation of financial structures: the expansion of the interbank market and its placement at the center of the transactional framework. The choice of the London Interbank Offered Rate as the primary pricing rate for the market and the daily fixing of that rate by the major banks—sometimes fraudulently as we now know—set the tone. But the interbank market already showed evidence of the interconnectedness that many now see as a major cause of the 2008 financial crisis.

In 1974, the failures of Franklin National Bank and Herstatt, a small German bank, revealed the linkages that had developed as banks relied more heavily on the market for liquidity. Franklin, heavily dependent on the interbank market, held over $1.1 billion of (mostly overnight) deposits of other banks in its London and Nassau branches, half of which (15 percent of its total deposits) were liabilities to the foreign branches of other American banks. Its failure, together with that of Herstatt, precipitated an 11.2 percent drop in the liabilities of US banks' foreign branches to other banks. Despite the Fed's open discount window, the scramble to protect funds in the interbank market drained liquidity (D'Arista, 1976).

In addition, both Franklin and Herstatt were in danger of defaulting on a large volume of foreign exchange contracts. The Federal Reserve Bank of New York took over Franklin's foreign exchange book, which was reported to have held $4 billion in contracts before the crisis. As Federal Reserve Board chairman Arthur Burns explained to US House Banking Committee Chairman Henry S. Reuss, "[The] failure of Franklin to perform on such a volume of international commitments would have undermined confidence in the foreign exchange market and tarnished the reputation of United States banks in general" (D'Arista, 1976, p. 185). There was also concern that, absent active intervention by the US lender of last resort, funds might move out of dollar balances and weaken the dollar.

The failure of Franklin National Bank demonstrated the degree to which domestic and international operations were integrated at US banks. It also made clear that regulators could not take a laissez-faire attitude toward the failures of large banks because a substantial portion of their uninsured liabilities are owed to other banks. It was suggested at that time that the implied guarantee against failure which seemed to be confirmed by the way Franklin was handled could encourage risk taking and unsound practices—an early acknowledgment of the moral hazard and "too-big-to-fail" problems that have continued to the present day (D'Arista, 1976).

As these developments illustrate, the shift to market-based systems both nationally and globally was initiated and supported by the creation of an external market. Other developments in the 1970s and 1980s that also contributed to this shift are discussed in the following chapters.

NOTE

1. This channel for inflows was not captured in US balance of payments data until the end of the decade.

3. Commercial paper guarantees and the emergence of a parallel banking system

The rising importance of money management and its requirements for ancillary services led to the marked increase in banks' trading activity in the 1970s and 1980s, which in turn became a driving force in structural change. Derivatives, standby letters of credit, and commercial paper guaranties are all innovative instruments devised by financial institutions to provide a privatized system of financial insurance to their customers. Banks are the major players in providing guaranties because they have the power to create deposits by making loans when the guaranty is activated.

While bank guaranties to loan to customers at some future date or in the case of some future outcome are part of banks' traditional business, the expansion of contingency lending in the 1970s assumed a volume and rate of growth that was unprecedented. Moreover, this growth was propelled by the strategy inaugurated in 1970 by the Federal Reserve itself to stem a crisis in the commercial paper market that occurred when the Penn Central Railroad defaulted on $83 billion of commercial paper and sound borrowers such as General Motors Acceptance Corporation, Ford Motor Company, and General Electric Capital Corporation were unable to roll over their outstanding issues.

The Federal Reserve opened the discount window and encouraged banks to lend to those companies and to other commercial paper issuers, but banks were not willing to lend without a more profitable form of encouragement. The encouragement that Walter Wriston of National City Bank had proposed in the 1960s was to grant permission for banks to issue large negotiable CDs exempt from interest rate ceilings in order to more actively manage their growth by engaging in what was called "liability management." After initial resistance, the Fed acquiesced to give banks the lending capacity to deal with the crisis since these CDs would be bought by money market mutual funds (MMMFs) as substitutes for the commercial paper that usually made up a substantial portion of their assets in addition to US Treasury bills (D'Arista and Schlesinger, 1993).

The Fed's solution for dealing with the 1970 crisis soon became institutionalized. Banks offered back-up credit lines (for a fee) that would be honored if the buyer was unable to issue commercial paper due to a subsequent loss of confidence in the market. The assumption was that, in a crisis, the Fed would assist in supplying funds needed to meet these contingency obligations and confidence would be restored.

But this back-up mechanism was introduced in a period when the business of banking was as yet relatively segregated from other financial functions. Passage of the Bank Holding Company Amendments in that same year opened demand for bank issues of commercial paper to fund new, "closely related to banking" affiliates which, under the new law, could not be funded by insured deposits. Bank-related commercial paper became the fastest-growing segment of the market; the volume of paper issued in the last half of the 1970s rose to historically high levels in relation to total credit flows. Because of their size, the size of their issues, and the fact that they were affiliated with federally insured institutions that enjoyed lender-of-last-resort protection from the Fed, the larger bank holding companies were able to raise funds at lower rates than both non-financial and other financial companies, and thus became the dominant issuers in the market (D'Arista and Schlesinger, 1993). But this could have impaired the perceived usefulness of the banks' guaranties to other commercial paper issuers since, in the event of a loss of confidence in the market, banks' impartiality in lending funds supplied by the Fed to non-bank issuers other than their own affiliates might be seen as less certain.

Moreover, a crisis of confidence in the commercial paper might have spilled over to the market for banks' negotiable CDs since these instruments were close substitutes and the inability of a bank holding company to roll over its commercial paper might have led to a loss of confidence in the bank. In that case, the possibility that the primary guarantors of commercial paper might be unable to meet their obligations would have blocked the channel the Fed had created to act as an indirect lender of last resort to this market and prevent a spillover into other credit markets.

An indication of the problems posed by combining the roles of issuer and guarantor within a bank holding company structure surfaced with the unfolding of the Continental Illinois Bank crisis in 1984. In that case, it was thought that the bank holding company might not be able to roll over its commercial paper because of the bank's inability to roll over its CDs. Given the State of Illinois' restrictions on interstate banking and limits on the number of a bank's offices within the state, Continental Illinois had grown by funding its operations with interest-sensitive, uninsured CDs and borrowings from other banks in the offshore market. At the time of the crisis, it had more uninsured than insured funding but, given the risk to the commercial paper and CD markets, the Federal Deposit Insurance Corporation (FDIC) acted to shore up the holding company as well as the bank, in effect extending government insurance coverage to the commercial paper market (Jackson, 1985).

The FDIC's action in 1984 raised—and still raises—the question as to whether attempts to insulate banks' deposit-taking activities from other lines of business can be a successful strategy for protecting taxpayers in a crisis. Overlapping activities and funding in the same markets increases the risk for systemic crises affecting the financial sector as a whole. Moreover, guaranties on commercial paper give some of the protection afforded by deposit insurance to instruments that are especially subject to a systemic loss of confidence because they are unsecured promissory notes.[1] Reliance on this protection resulted in a larger share of funds of households, businesses, and state and local governments being moved from banks to MMMFs and, in the 1980s, led to the emergence of a parallel banking system that undercut bank lending and the growth in deposits.

The parallel banking system emerged in the 1970s with the introduction of MMMFs that began to buy commercial paper and became a source of funding for finance companies. The parallel system performed its bank-like intermediation by dividing funding and lending between two separate entities, each of which dealt directly with the public through only one side of its balance sheet, and grew rapidly in the 1980s when banks were facing pressure from the removal of deposit rate ceilings and the Fed's determined efforts to fight inflation by raising interest rates to an historical high of 20 percent.

The collapse of the savings and loan industry at the beginning of the decade cost taxpayers over $500 million. Failures of more than 1000 banks between 1985 and 1990 pushed the FDIC's Bank Insurance Fund into insolvency and forced it to borrow $90 billion to continue operations. Loss of confidence in depository institutions encouraged households, businesses, and state and local governments to shift holdings from banks to MMMFs and MMMFs, in turn, used the inflow to increase funding for finance companies by buying their commercial paper. In addition to those companies that loaned to households and businesses, others established mortgage companies that created an unregulated parallel housing finance system in competition with thrifts (D'Arista, 1994a).

By the end of the 1980s, finance companies ranked as the largest set of unregulated intermediaries in terms of their aggregate assets (FRS, *Flow of Funds*) and the size of individual companies (Moody's, 1990), and had a larger impact on credit markets than did other unregulated intermediaries. Making the same kinds of loans as banks to businesses and households and funding those loans with commercial paper held directly by businesses or MMMFs in which businesses and households invest, finance companies functioned like banks with little or no regulatory oversight and almost no regulatory costs. For example, they were not subject to capital or reserve requirements, limits on loans to individuals or related borrowers, or limits on transactions with parents or affiliates. Their operations were not subject to the demands of the Community Reinvestment Act, Glass-Steagall restrictions, or restrictions on operating across state lines. By lowering their cost of funds and charges on loans, finance companies used their advantage over banks to fuel their growth and profitability.

The competitive advantage of finance companies is reflected in the jump in their assets from 15.8 to 26.1 percent of banks' assets between 1980 and 1992, and the even larger increase in their commercial paper issuance from 8.0 to 24.2 percent of banks' time and savings deposits over the same period. Their impact on banks' credit flows was no less striking. Banks held 39.1 percent of total credit market debt in 1980 but their share fell to 26.5 percent by 1992. By 1992, finance companies' share of business loans—once the major assets of commercial banks—had risen to two thirds of the share held by banks (D'Arista and Schlesinger, 1993). By issuing billions of dollars in guarantees for commercial paper, banks had nurtured the growth of their rivals while increasing their own exposure to risk.

Some saw the rise in the parallel system as a benefit, in that it gave small businesses wider access to credit (Quint, 1991) and household savings access to higher interest rates and wider investment opportunities (Sellon, 1992). But a number of serious public policy concerns emerged such as the possibility that ownership of large finance companies by major non-financial companies would make markets susceptible to concentration and anticompetitive practices.[2] There was also concern that finance companies' costing advantages would increase the risk to the FDIC by weakening bank portfolios (Zuckerman, 1991). Another important concern was that the shrinkage of the banks' role in credit markets would undermine Federal Reserve leverage in transmitting monetary policy, making it more difficult to prevent disruptions and manage crises while giving access to the public sector lender of last resort to unregulated entities (D'Arista and Schlesinger, 1993).

As the 1990s progressed, however, growth in lending for housing brought an increase in mortgage companies, in assets held by government-sponsored enterprises (GSEs) and federally related mortgage pools, and in mortgage-backed securities (MBS). A number of finance companies were also mortgage lenders, but the growth of the sector as a whole declined since these mortgage lenders, like banks, sold rather than held mortgages as the process of securitization shifted a growing share of housing finance to the securities markets. Thus, the development of the MBS market dampened the growth of the parallel banking system that relied on commercial paper issues to fund portfolio lending to businesses and consumers.

NOTES

1. Moreover, commercial paper was not classed as a security under the Securities Act of 1933 and not subject to the protections under that Act on the grounds that it was issued in large amounts and thus bought only by sophisticated investors.
2. Among the major industrial companies that owned finance companies in the 1980s were General Motors, General Electric, Chrysler, Ford, Xerox, ITT, Westinghouse, IBM, AT&T, Whirlpool, and Textron. Other top finance companies were Sears Roebuck Acceptance Corp., Transamerica Finance Group, and American Express Credit Corp.

4. ERISA moves savings into securities markets

After passage of the Employee Retirement Income Security Act (ERISA) of 1974, pension and mutual funds became the fastest growing US financial sectors and, by 2005, as households shifted the majority of their savings from deposits into mutual fund shares and pension fund reserves, they had become the largest holders of US financial assets (D'Arista, 2006). The growing dominance of these two channels for saving effectively transformed the US financial system, eroding the once central role of bank deposits and loans in favor of marketable instruments. Policymakers have come to realize that changes in the value of financial assets held by these institutions are now a powerful influence on spending and investment decisions by households and businesses and that those changes are an important factor in altering the pace of economic activity.

How to anticipate those changes and mitigate unwanted outcomes by bringing institutional investors under a regulatory framework appropriate for their post-ERISA role and under the influence of the monetary authority remains an area ignored in most policy and academic discussions. The financial system continues to operate under a monetary and regulatory regime designed for a par-value, bank-centered system that no longer offers protection for investors or borrowers even as the now more dominant market-based system has increased risk to all borrowing and investing sectors. Even more importantly, through changes in households' net worth, the movement of savings into securities markets outside the countercyclical influence of the central bank has created a set of pro-cyclical impacts with large effects on economic stability and growth.

The number of US pension funds grew during the Second World War as a form of deferred compensation and in the 1950s when many companies joined industry leaders such as General Motors Corporation in establishing defined benefit pension funds which typically were not backed by holdings of assets. Bankruptcies in the difficult economic climate of the early 1970s drew attention to the lack of pre-funding as many workers lost promised benefits. ERISA's requirement for funding was the principal purpose for and safeguard in the legislation. It was also the primary spur for the rapid growth in pension fund assets over the decade that followed. In addition, it created a new and strong demand for securities issues such as corporate stocks and bonds and US Treasury bonds—the principal assets in which pension funds invest (D'Arista, 1994a).

In addition to these private pension funds, publicly funded plans outside the social security system, such as retirement funds for state and local government employees and federal government employees, also grew in size and importance after passage of ERISA. Rapid growth in US investment company assets is linked to the growth of pension funds, but it began almost a decade later, as mutual funds became the recipients of a rising volume of retirement savings channeled into defined contribution plans.

The requirement to fund pensions and the initial choice of corporate stocks and bonds as the principal assets held by the funds were seen as contributing to a higher level of capital formation in the 1970s than would otherwise have occurred. But by the 1980s, concerns were raised that the management of funds was concentrated in too few hands and that managers overseeing the funds of several or many clients faced conflicts of interest when sales of stocks for one client's fund would affect the value of the outstanding stocks of another client. Moreover, concentrations of stocks in large funds resulted in buying and selling in large blocks and contributed to volatility in prices and the need for hedging (D'Arista, 1994a). Some feared that the concentration and conflicts of interest inherent in pension fund management made a mockery of corporate governance. To avoid conflicts of interest, managers often refrained from voting shares of a company held in one or more funds to avoid conflicts of interest. Another reason not to vote the shares of a company held in more than one fund under management was to avoid losing a company whose shares were to be voted. In addition, managers were thought to contribute to "short-termism"—buying and selling stocks to show quarterly gains in order to enhance the appearance of their performance, rather than holding stocks for long-term gains (Monks, 1985).

Yet another major concern that surfaced in the 1980s was that a rise in the value of stocks allowed the employer/sponsor to reduce contributions to the fund. Some employers/sponsors even used increases in stock value to recapture surplus funds in pension plans for other uses. Companies with surplus funds in pension plans also became attractive targets for hostile takeovers during the heightened merger activity in that decade. And, finally, some analysts made the point that pension funds created an inherent conflict between the economic functions of securities markets to fund long-term investment for capital formation and the fiduciary responsibility of fund managers to minimize risk for current and future retirees (Monks, 1985).

In a larger economic context, however, the increasing importance of these public and private funds is due not only to their role as repositories of benefits for current and future retirees, but also to their added weight and influence in financial markets. By year-end 2005, total assets of US private and public pension funds and individual retirement accounts (IRAs) had risen to $12.2 trillion—an amount comparable to the nation's annual output and 26 percent of the $47 trillion US financial assets market (FRS, *Flow of Funds*). It is now widely believed that the institutionalization of saving through payroll deductions and tax incentives is needed to supplement social security benefits; that perception prompted an even more rapid growth in IRAs after the mid-1990s.

As noted, the change in channels for household savings not only reduced the traditional role of banks and their share of total financial assets, it also transformed the business of banking. Institutional investors' growing appetite for securities provided an additional incentive for banks to securitize assets rather than hold them in portfolio. Moreover, as their diversification requirements expanded demand in capital markets, pension, and mutual funds contributed to the rise in assets of the housing-related GSEs, such as Fannie Mae and Freddie Mac, and federally related mortgage pools, as well as the group of asset-backed issuers that included private mortgage companies, finance companies, and other non-bank lenders (FRS, *Flow of Funds*). As a result, the US capital markets became the primary arena used by both businesses and consumers for investment and borrowing.

Data on the rise in money management as a dominant activity in US financial markets, outstripping banks in terms of their relative shares of holdings of financial assets, is discussed in the analysis of concentration in Part II (see Chapter 9). In fact, the expansion of institutional investors as a group has been rapid in all Organisation for Economic Co-operation and Development countries and in emerging economies as well. Their dominance in both national and global markets has raised concerns about their effects on financial stability, on the implementation of monetary policy and crisis prevention strategies, and on capital formation and corporate governance. In 2005, the IMF noted that institutional investors are subject to the same credit risks as banks but more susceptible to market risks. And because they tend to be large institutions, their decisions "make markets" (IMF, 2005, September, p. 65). As a result, relatively small changes in the portfolios of such institutions may increasingly affect global financial markets. Moreover, unlike financial markets dominated by banks, capital markets tend to "transmit changes in risk appetite, credit assessments, or perceived economic fundamentals more broadly, much faster, and more directly" (p. 67).

Another concern about the effect of the expansion of institutional investors was raised by the BIS in its 2002 *Annual Report*, which noted "the inherent pro-cyclicality of market-based financial systems" (BIS, 2002, p. 151). Markets supply more funds at lower cost in a boom and ration access (and raise costs) in a downturn. Bank-dominated systems that are subject to central banks' quantitative monetary tools, such as reserve and liquidity requirements and lending limits, have, in the past, been able to serve as conduits for countercyclical policy aimed at moderating the spikes and troughs inherent in market-based systems. In bank-based systems, central banks can generate and supply credit in a downturn and ration credit in a boom by imposing costs and limits on lending. This aspect of pro-cyclicality—the erosion of monetary control—is discussed in Part VI, but there are other ways in which systems dominated by institutional investors contribute to the problem.

In the 2001 downturn, for example, constraints on investment and employment were prolonged as large corporations struggled to cover shortfalls in their defined benefit pension plans. In the US, these plans had been net sellers of assets after 1994 when stock prices were rising, relying on appreciation to cover their growing liabilities to beneficiaries, and did not resume net purchases until 2003. All other US pension plans remained net purchasers of assets in the same period, with the largest net acquisitions by IRAs. As stock prices fell, all plans suffered losses but defined benefit plans had the largest losses and experienced the slowest recovery (D'Arista, 2006).

As pressure to meet funding requirements escalated, companies were forced to divert income into pension investments rather than the ongoing operations of the firm. In some cases, perceptions about the impact of funding obligations on balance sheets and future growth depressed stock prices and led to downgrades in credit ratings that resulted in higher borrowing costs. Comparison of the losses of various types of plans suggests that, because of their investment decisions, the corporate sponsors of defined benefit plans not only exacerbated the pro-cyclical impact of the downturn on their own net worth, but on that of their employees and beneficiaries as well (D'Arista, 2006).

The downturn in 2001 and the subsequent financial crisis in 2008 had equally severe effects on the pension funds of state and municipal employees and retirees, as most of these also tend to be defined benefit funds. The loss in value of assets meant that, in a period of falling local government revenues, a substantial share of taxes had to be diverted to restoring the value of pension funds rather than increasing state and local investments in education or infrastructure, or providing other services that might have stimulated job creation and other economic benefits.

Another characteristic of the shift to market-based systems is the pro-cyclical nature of the wealth effect on household balance sheets. While the face value of households' holdings of bank deposits remains constant over the business cycle, the value of their credit market instruments and corporate equities—held directly or indirectly through pension and mutual funds—fluctuates, rising during a boom and falling in a downturn. Spending tends to increase as these assets appreciate in value and decline as they depreciate. Thus, to the extent that increases in households' marketable financial assets have, over time, augmented the wealth effect, their influence in amplifying booms and busts has grown to be a critical factor in determining economic growth.

For example, one way asset bubbles and their collapse caused damage in both advanced and emerging market countries was through losses in pension fund and retirement accounts invested in marketable securities. In the US, the bubble in stock prices accounted for a phenomenal 71 percent rise in households' net worth and an 86 percent increase in the value of pension fund reserves between 1994 and 1999, constituting a "wealth effect" that contributed to rising consumption and declining personal savings. After the market break, net worth fell 6.4 percent from year-end 1999 to 2002 but pension fund reserves fell 12.3 percent (FRS, *Flow of Funds*). While the percentage losses were small relative to previous gains, the IMF reported that the retreat in equity prices had produced a negative wealth effect equal to 70 percent of households' disposable income (IMF, 2002).

The Federal Reserve's efforts to counter these effects with ample provisions of liquidity and low interest rates provided the conditions for households to refinance debt and use appreciating equity in real estate to finance continued consumption. In addition to pushing up the prices of homes, low interest rates contributed to a rebound in stock prices in 2003 that raised net worth (12.2 percent) and pension fund reserves (16 percent) (FRS, *Flow of Funds*). But the policy response entailed a further increase in household debt that many observers, including the BIS (2003), believed would aggravate any eventual downturn.

These examples of pro-cyclical developments point to yet another important consequence of the changes in channels for savings. As the IMF observed, increasing the exposure of individuals to direct rather than indirect forms of risk has made the household sector the "shock absorber of last resort" in the financial system (IMF, 2005, April, p. 5). That view was validated when the net worth of households and non-profits dropped by over $10 trillion from 2007 to 2008.[1] Their net worth did not regain

2007 levels until 2012. From 2011 to 2016, however, it rose by more than $25 trillion to $90.2 trillion, driven largely by the rise in prices of corporate equities held directly and indirectly (in pension funds) by these sectors and a recovery in real estate values (FRS, *Flow of Funds*).

The unprecedented volatility of changes in the net worth of households from 2007 to 2016 is a clear indication of the increased vulnerability they face in a market-based financial system. Proposals comparable in effect to deposit insurance that would protect savings held in pension funds and IRAs remain a critical item on the agenda for future reform efforts. Such proposals are needed to promote financial stability and growth as well as prevent severe disruptions in the lives of families.[2]

NOTES

1. The net worth of these sectors was $66.5 trillion in 2007 and fell to $56 trillion in 2008 (FRS, *Flow of Funds*).
2. One proposal to accomplish this goal is offered in Chapter 11.

PART II

Deregulation and financial innovation create the context for crisis

5. An overview of financial restructuring and its consequences

The immense scale of intervention by the United States (US) Federal Reserve and Treasury to shore up a collapsing financial system in 2008 is unprecedented in US history. The actions taken underscore the nature of the problems with which they were dealing: the interconnectedness of institutions and markets around the world; the overall lack of transparency in institutions, markets, financial activities, and assets; the incredible leverage that had increased the exposure of financial institutions in relation to their capital, and the innovations that, without analysis of their effects, transformed the financial system in ways that made it much more profitable and added much more risk.

Deregulation has been blamed as the cause of many of these problems and it clearly played a large role in creating the conflicts of interest and lack of transparency that developed in the decades after the 1980s. Deregulatory actions of particular importance include the exemption of mortgage-backed securities (MBS) from registration and disclosure, the repeal of the Glass-Steagall Act, and the authorization of multipurpose financial holding companies. On the other hand, the successful strategies developed by banks to evade capital and reserve requirements by securitizing loans, moving investments and derivative contracts off their balance sheets, and relying more heavily on borrowed funds to expand their activities rather than on deposits, created equally destructive problems because they contributed to an immense expansion of debt for both financial institutions and their customers.

The collapse of the Madoff Ponzi scheme dealt a heavy blow to confidence in the US Securities and Exchange Commission in particular, and the effectiveness of US regulatory authorities in general. But the other equally substantial problem that became apparent as institutions failed and markets froze was the avoidance of oversight responsibility by the Federal Reserve. Before March 2008, the Fed had not moved to acquire information about the interconnectedness and cross-exposure to risk among counterparties in the enormous credit risk transfer markets where collateralized debt obligations (CDOs), credit default swaps (CDSs), and other complex over-the-counter (OTC) derivatives were traded (Sorkin, 2009). That, in turn, underscores their larger failure: the complacent conduct of business as usual based on old assumptions about the effectiveness of regulatory and monetary strategies—despite glaring evidence of a paradigm shift in the structure of financial markets. As Hyman Minsky warned in the 1980s,

> The Federal Reserve has to be concerned with the effect of the changing structure of financial relations ... [It] must guide the evolution of financial institutions favoring stability enhancing and discouraging instability augmenting institutions and practices ... [and] needs to recognize its responsibility for the normal behavior of all finance. (Minsky, 1986, pp. 349, 359)

As discussed in Chapter 4, the major change in structure that the Fed seems to have ignored was the shift from a bank-based to a market-based system. Banks ceased to be the dominant holders of credit market assets as household savings moved from banks to pension and mutual funds.[1] Securitization—inaugurated by Fannie and Freddie, the government-sponsored enterprises (GSEs)—took off in the 1980s after passage of the Secondary Mortgage Market Enhancement Act of 1984 exempted privately originated pools of mortgages from registration and disclosure. The next stage of securitization—the growth in asset-based securities that bundled car loans and other consumer receivables—succeeded in moving a rising share of household debt, as well as savings, to the capital markets, and making a larger share of outstanding credit subject to regulation applicable to market-based institutions.

In its 2002 *Annual Report*, the Bank for International Settlements (BIS) warned that market-based systems were inherently pro-cyclical. The full meaning of that warning became abundantly clear when the collapse of Bear Stearns was followed six months later by the bankruptcy of Lehman Brothers and the bailout of AIG, followed in turn by massive infusions of aid and asset guaranties for Citigroup and Bank of America. These developments were the result of the Fed's failure to recognize that the potential for a systemic crisis had been intensified by the web of interconnections among financial institutions and sectors, and that all institutions—including banks—were now subject to the pro-cyclical rules of the market system to which Bear, Lehman, and AIG were subjected.

The collapse of AIG illustrates how the rules of the market system affected—and still affect—the larger institutions in the global financial system. The tipping point for AIG was its role as a major counterparty in derivatives markets—the various trillion dollar, non-public, non-transparent markets in which the more important institutions in all sectors have become interdependent through the process of buying and selling various forms of financial insurance to one another. Having been allowed to develop outside the framework of exchange or clearinghouse structures, OTC derivatives contracts pose a systemic risk because they were not designed to be traded. Existing positions, tailored to the needs of a particular client, must be hedged by buying or selling even more contracts, pushing up the nominal value of outstandings to many multiples of the value of the underlying assets, and increasing interdependence (and the potential domino effect) within the global system.

When the Fed turned down AIG's request for a loan the week before it had to be bailed out, AIG warned that if Lehman—one of the ten largest parties in the $62 trillion market for CDSs—went down, then AIG would also be vulnerable. The systemic effects that threatened AIG were due to its sizable share of outstanding CDS contracts and resulted from the downward pressure imposed by the decline in prices for the assets backing the contracts. As prices fell, additional collateral had to be posted, followed by a write-down in asset values that required charges against capital. The decline in capital triggered a drop in credit ratings, raised the cost of what little credit AIG could obtain, and sank its stock price, making it difficult to raise the capital it needed to remain viable. Once in such a downward spiral, there is little hope of recovery and the bailout was needed to prevent—or, as it turned out, to slow—the fall of the next domino.

The chapters that follow in this section describe some of the more important changes in financial structure and the innovative practices that contributed to conditions that led to the crisis. They do not dwell on the exotic products that served as fuses for the explosion, since many excellent analyses of these products are readily available (Epstein and Crotty, 2009; Sorkin, 2009; Cassidy, 2010). The purpose here is to provide an overview of changes that resulted in the dissolution of the old system without having created a coherent framework of regulation and oversight for the system that replaced it.

NOTE

1. Between 1977 and the end of 2007, the assets of all depository institutions plummeted from 56.3 percent to 23.7 percent of total financial sector assets, while the assets of pension funds and mutual funds rose from 21 percent to 37.8 percent. Other sectors that gained shares of credit market assets over this period were GSEs and federally related mortgage pools (from 5.3 percent to 13.2 percent), asset-backed securities issuers (from 0 percent to 7.3 percent), and security brokers and dealers (from 1 percent to 5.3 percent) (FRS, *Flow of Funds*, various issues).

6. Securitization

Securitization is arguably the most important financial innovation in terms of moving the process of supplying credit from portfolio lending to the capital markets. It was an early response to changes in regulation and the drift toward a market-based system that occurred in the 1970s and 1980s. The innovative nature of securitization was the creation of mechanisms to package pools of loans and issue securities against them to sell in the capital markets.[1] It was a mechanism that came about as a response to a crisis in the early 1970s when the GSEs—Ginnie Mae, Fannie Mae, and Freddie Mac—were called on by Congress to support savings institutions and small banks by buying their low-interest rate mortgages when a dramatic spike in interest rates associated with Eurodollar inflows was draining their deposits while at the same time shoving their portfolios underwater (see Chapter 2).

By the end of the 1970s, another spike in interest rates caused by inflation forced Congress to enact the Monetary Control Act of 1980, repealing the 1930s legislation that had imposed interest rate ceilings on bank and thrift deposits. The 1930s Act set interest rates 0.5 percent higher for thrifts than for banks to encourage deposits in savings institutions that were restricted to making loans for residential mortgages. The higher interest rate ceiling for thrift deposits had been an effective strategy to allocate savings to housing, and had created a stable market for mortgages by allowing savings institutions to hold long-term, fixed-rate loans in portfolio.

Put in place when depository institutions held a dominant role in credit markets, this structural framework not only supported housing but also augmented the role of banks and thrifts as effective channels for transmitting monetary policy initiatives by supplementing the Fed's efforts to control credit through open market operations and changes in reserves. When the Fed bought or sold Treasury bills in open market operations, it pushed the interest rate on those securities above or below the interest rate caps on banks and thrifts, which would have expanded or constrained lending through increases or decreases in the supply of deposits.

By ending interest rate ceilings, the Monetary Control Act of 1980 ended the ability of thrifts to hold the mortgages they made at a time when they faced a high and volatile interest rate environment for deposits. In an effort to preserve their traditional mode of operation, they offered adjustable rate mortgages that shifted the interest rate risk to the home buyer; these proved to have only limited popularity. Moreover, the safety valve provided by the GSEs in 1970 could not protect them from the second and larger spike in interest rates at the end of the decade. The industry continued to sink under a legacy of long-term low-interest rate mortgage loans even though, by 1983, MBS issued by the GSEs accounted for 20 percent of outstanding residential mortgages (FRS, *Flow of Funds*). The following year, total trading in mortgage-related assets reached $1.6 trillion—more than the dollar value of trading on world stock exchanges—and expanded further as the decade progressed (D'Arista, 1994a).

A further boost to securitization was given by the Secondary Mortgage Market Enhancement Act of 1984 which facilitated the expansion of the private market for MBS. Banks had joined thrifts in supporting the legislation because the "originate and distribute" model removed the uncertainty in portfolio lending caused by the removal of ceilings on interest rates and was seen as a way to increase profits by bypassing the constraints of reserve requirements as well as the new capital requirements that had been introduced the previous year. Investment banks were already earning large fees for packaging and selling securities backed by pools of mortgages and they, too, strongly supported the legislation. In this way, the channel for mortgage finance shifted from a purely institutional framework to one that melded it to a market framework and linked a growing number of financial sectors.

While the House and Senate Banking Committees approved the 1984 legislation with little objection, the Securities Subcommittee of the House Energy and Commerce Committee had reservations.[2] Members objected to exempting private issues of MBS from registration and disclosure, arguing that relying on the assessments of a few nationally recognized rating agencies was an inadequate substitute. Proponents argued that the exemption was needed to allow private issues to compete with the exemption given to Fannie and Freddie because of their status as GSEs. Two of the witnesses before the subcommittee—Preston Martin, the vice chairman of the Federal Reserve Board, and Henry Kaufman, the prominent Wall Street economist—also opposed the exemption. In addition, they warned that loosening the link between creditors and borrowers would encourage inadequate loan evaluation. Kaufman characterized securitization as permitting a drift "toward a financial system in which credit has no guardian" (Kaufman, 1985).

Having authorized entry by private financial institutions into the market for securitized products, Congress allowed it to develop without the most basic safeguards that apply to other securities markets. As noted, MBS were exempt from registration and disclosure and, as a substitute for due diligence, issuers were required to obtain ratings for MBS issues from statistically recognized rating agencies. The fact that the rating agencies earned fees from the issuers created an embedded conflict-of-interest regime that, in time, removed any trace of due diligence from the MBS market. Another notable omission was the absence of a requirement that MBS be traded on organized exchanges so that information on the volume and price of transactions would be available to investors—an omission that, in the autumn of 2008, exacerbated the crisis because the absence of information augmented the uncertainty that froze market activity. In addition, the absence or nonexistence of capital backing along the chain from origination to issuance became yet another barrier to the renewal of trading.

Attracted by the laissez-faire nature of the market, new, unregulated originators such as mortgage brokers became major players because they could originate loans and sell them without having to raise capital to hold them in portfolio. Banks and savings banks also increased their lending for housing because securitization allowed them to earn fees for originating and servicing the mortgages without having to raise the capital that would have been required to hold them in portfolio. In the 1990s, securitization expanded to include car loans and consumer receivables and, together with MBS, issuance and trading of asset-based securities came to dominate capital markets and credit flows. Between 1977 and 2007, the fourfold increase in the share of total credit market assets accounted for by GSEs, mortgage pools, and asset-backed securities issues was a major factor in the 33 percent drop in banks' share over the same period (FRS, *Flow of Funds*). At that point, the traditional bank-based system so carefully crafted in the 1930s had come to an end.

By 2004, the regulatory concerns raised 20 years earlier appeared to have been validated. The absence of capital restrictions on banks' securitization exposures and the unregulated status of many mortgage originators resulted in undercapitalization of what had become the largest US credit market. As the market developed, most MBS carried high ratings and continued to do so even as the volume of sub-prime mortgages increased. Credit rating agencies, issuers, and investors appear to have believed that securitization could actually diminish the risk of sub-prime mortgages when pooled (Pollin, 2009). However, as the crisis unfolded, the absence of disclosure concerning the pool of mortgages that backed these securities contributed to the severe disruption in confidence within the financial system, exacerbating the credit crunch. Moreover, without needed information about individual loans, efforts to negotiate loan workouts became much more difficult than in the past (Crotty and Epstein, 2008; Stiglitz, 2008).

The role of the sub-prime mortgage scandal in the financial crisis is now a well-recognized outcome of the loose regulatory environment in which securitization developed, as are the laxity and conflicts of interest inherent in the behavior of the rating agencies. But those are not the only ways in which the unfettered growth of securitization caused damage. The diversion of so large a share of credit flows into the market for MBS created a housing bubble. It also ensured that MBS were held and traded by all financial sectors, all of which inevitably experienced distress when loss of confidence caused trading to dry up and prices to fall. But in the build-up of the bubble, large profits were made by financial institutions and rising house prices gave a boost to household savings. Then, when the bubble burst, homeowners experienced a double whammy: their net worth fell because of the drop in the value of their homes and fell further as the value of MBS in their pension and mutual funds declined.[3] In addition, the lack of disclosure about the underlying mortgages in the securitized pools dealt a third blow to households because barriers to loan workouts exacerbated the rate of foreclosures.

While the Dodd-Frank Act addressed many of the problems that precipitated the financial crisis, the implications of securitization for systemic structure and stability were not acknowledged or addressed. Failure to do so perpetuates the threat of the continued unraveling of traditional safeguards for securities markets. Also ignored in discussions of the additional reforms needed to promote stability are the effects of this innovative financial technique on credit flows and changes in households' net worth. Some of the proposals offered to reform the securitization process in the aftermath of the crisis are discussed in Chapter 10, together with other needed reforms to restore the stability of financial activities and markets.

NOTES

1. Securitized debt differs from debt securities in that debt securities are issued directly by a single borrower and, in the case of non-financial corporate bonds, backed by tangible assets, while securitized debt is issued by financial intermediaries and backed by pools of loans to multiple borrowers.

2. The report of the Subcommittee on Telecommunications, Consumer Protection and Finance also warned that MBS were crowding out corporate borrowers, that they had already exceeded gross issuance of corporate bonds by 60 percent in 1983, and that the capital markets would continue to be dominated by MBS.
3. For data on the impact of the 2007–2008 financial crisis on households' net worth, see Chapter 4.

7. Weaving the web of interconnectedness

The implosion of the US financial system in 2008 was initiated by a drop in housing prices that set off price declines in markets for financial assets related to housing, including markets for financial products that had been invented to insure against declines in asset prices. But the rapid spread of that implosion across almost all sectors of the system was the result of the growth in reliance by financial institutions on borrowing from and lending to other financial institutions. The development and expansion of this source of funding led to what came to be known as "interconnectedness," a web of relationships that could cause the missteps of a few to create tripwires that would fell others. The repeal of Glass-Steagall in 1999 wrote "finished" to a systemic structure that reliance on intersystemic funding had already ended. Gone was the compartmentalized system crafted in the 1930s that had prevented problems originating in one sector from spilling over into others, and that had permitted the Federal Reserve to act through a dominant and insulated banking system to put out fires in other sectors.

At the heart of the threat posed by the interconnected system that emerged in the 1970s and 1980s was the extraordinary growth of the financial sector's indebtedness to other financial institutions rather than to non-financial investors. Increased access to credit within the financial sector made it possible for financial institutions to raise higher levels of debt than would have been possible if they had relied on funding provided solely by the income and savings generated by the real economy. Given the increased availability of credit, they were able to raise their leverage ratios and the levels of speculative trading for their own accounts. The rising profits and compensation that resulted masked the growing vulnerabilities embedded in intersystemic funding that led to the crisis.

Tighter links among institutions and the rise in speculative activity depended on growth in the markets for repurchase agreements (repos), reverse repos, commercial paper, and euro market borrowing. These were the primary sources that provided funding for trading by banks for their own accounts.[1] Repos figure prominently in the rise and fall of the leverage linked to speculative activity since the securities used as collateral for repo transactions can be borrowed and the funds acquired can be used to raise more cash to buy more securities. As the search for profits by banks and other financial institutions took them further away from traditional services to non-financial customers and the scale of proprietary trading for their own accounts increased, rapid and excessive growth in both their borrowing as a share of total credit flows and their claims on and liabilities to other financial institutions ensured that problems in one group of institutions would spill over into others, and set the stage for the crisis to come.

The pyramidal process began as banks, investment banks, and hedge funds pledged assets on their balance sheets to back short-term borrowing in the repo and commercial paper markets and used the proceeds to buy additional assets.[2] These additional assets were usually purchased to take advantage of differences in short- and long-term interest rates and were held off balance sheet in the institutions' trading accounts. The larger the amount borrowed, the larger the position and the higher an institution's profits. Larger positions could reap sizable profits even when margins were thin.

The excessive rise in an institution's debt might have raised questions from regulators and investors if they had not been hidden temporarily[3] or permanently in off-balance sheet accounts. Nevertheless, the rising demand for collateral should have been noticed. It fueled demand for US and European government debt instruments and contributed to the rise in sub-prime mortgage lending to increase the supply of MBS for collateral.[4] The growth in issues of synthetic assets also fed what had become an insatiable demand for backing for short-term borrowing. As the pyramidal nature of the process created a hollow system increasingly dominated by speculation and removed from real economic activity, the addition of synthetic assets as collateral turned balance sheets into pure froth.

The critical market practice that led to interconnectedness emerged in the so-called external or euro markets in the 1970s. The collapse of Franklin National Bank in 1975, which threatened major losses on interbank deposits for US bank branches in London and, as discussed in Chapter 2, prompted the Fed to take over its foreign exchange contracts as well as lend to its creditors, was just a small dress rehearsal for the events of 2008, which were caused by funding strategies that relied on borrowing by financial institutions from other financial institutions.

A further indication of the damage caused by interconnected funding strategies was provided in the aftermath of the default on Russian government debt and the collapse of Long-Term Capital Management

(LTCM) in 1998. In the 1990s, intersystemic borrowing within the external markets was used to finance the burgeoning carry trade. Carry trade transactions involve borrowing short term at low interest rates to invest in higher-yielding longer-term assets. While these strategies were also conducted in domestic markets, the major share of activity occurred offshore in those years. The most important channel, the yen-dollar carry trade, developed in response to Japan's efforts to counter recession with low interest and exchange rates. Investors borrowed yen to buy higher-yielding dollar or euro or emerging market assets. Converting borrowed yen into dollars or other currencies further depressed the value of the Japanese currency, caused the currency in which the investment was made to appreciate, and produced gains from both differences in interest rates and currency appreciation.

When LTCM collapsed, the turmoil in the market prompted a flight to safety that raised the price (and depressed the interest rate) on US Treasuries, erasing the profitability in yen-dollar carry trades and forcing banks and other speculators to unwind positions at a loss. While there was (and still is) little information on the scale of proprietary trading, the fact that the yen gained 7 percent in value against the dollar in one day in October 1998 and rose an additional 10 percent by the end of the year demonstrated how large the positions had become (FRS, 1998). Losses dampened the activity for a while but, as the BIS and the International Monetary Fund (IMF) reported in 2002, the volume of carry trade activity accelerated as institutions took larger positions to compensate for the low interest rate environment adopted by the major central banks that year. The IMF warned that carry trades contributed to herding and magnified the risk of large movements in prices and shrinking market liquidity if positions had to be reversed (IMF, 2004, April). It also urged regulatory scrutiny of the complex, risky, and largely unsupervised credit risk transfer markets for instruments such as CDOs and CDSs, where the notional value of outstanding contracts globally had risen by 44 percent to $1.6 trillion in the first half of 2002 (IMF, 2004, September), and repeatedly warned that international markets had become an arena for speculation.

The build-up in borrowing within the financial sector was not limited by law. While the National Bank Act of 1865 restricted loans to individual non-financial borrowers to a given percentage of a bank's capital, there was no similar restriction on loans to financial borrowers. Moreover, the original Basel Capital Accord did not subject commercial banks' proprietary trading positions to capital requirements, because it was assumed that these transactions were short term and bore little risk. Despite concerns and warnings by international authorities, the Fed and the Comptroller of the Currency adopted a posture of benign neglect toward these practices as they expanded in both the domestic and offshore markets during the 1980s and 1990s. Moreover, an explicit boost to borrowing was given with passage of the 1999 legislation (Gramm-Leach-Bliley) that repealed Glass-Steagall and gave banks permission to borrow in order to fund traditional and non-traditional activities. At that point, the market for securities repurchase agreements took off, rising from about $1 trillion in 2000 to $4.3 trillion before the collapse of Bear Stearns in March 2008. As early as 2003, funds borrowed under securities repurchase agreements were a larger share of US banks' liabilities than checkable deposits (FRS, *Flow of Funds*).

The failure to limit banks' exposure to other financial institutions—a breach of a centuries-old banking practice that had limited loans to individual borrowers as a prudent tool of diversification—increased their lending and reduced the amount of their funding subject to reserve requirements. But it also increased funding for other sectors, including investment banks, hedge and private equity funds, and mortgage brokers, and, because of banks' dominant role in repo markets, opened a channel that allowed banks' non-financial sector savings to become indirect sources of funding used by many non-banks in other financial sectors. As a result, the repo market propelled growth in the financial sector as a whole, with total sector debt rising from 63.8 percent to 113.8 percent of gross domestic product (GDP) over the decade ending in 2007 (FRS, *Flow of Funds*). US national income and product accounts show that financial corporations' profit rose from an historical average of about 10 percent to reach a record level of 40 percent of total corporate profits in 2001–2003, falling back to about 30 percent in 2007. Both the rising scale of debt and profitability of the financial sector in those years suggest that its growth came at the expense of growth in the real economy.

US banks were not the only institutions with outsized exposures to debt. After the crisis, the Bank of England noted that the balance sheet of its banking sector had grown threefold from 2000 to year-end 2007 (Bank of England, 2009), and the collapse in Iceland revealed that the assets of its three largest banks amounted to over ten times the country's GDP (Wade, 2009). Leverage had bloated the global financial system out of proportion to the real economic activity that would be needed to sustain the debt it had created. As James Crotty noted:

> It is not possible for the value of financial assets to remain so large relative to the real economy because the real economy cannot consistently generate the cash flows required to sustain inflated financial claims. It is not economically

> efficient to have such large proportions of income and human and material resources captured by the financial sector. (Crotty, 2009)

An additional outcome was that the growing importance of financial activity as a source of profits, and the increased reliance on other financial institutions to fund that growth, weakened the link between the financial sector and the real economy. As a foundation for financial opportunity, economic activity had become less important. The profitability of the largest institutions no longer depended on the growth and profitability of their non-financial customers. Moreover, the assumption on the part of the largest institutions—that they were using their own rather than other people's money—undermined their sense of fiduciary responsibility. Given the profits generated, financial institutions had a powerful incentive to ignore the possibility that rapid growth built on rising leverage was unsustainable and to not question the process that propelled that growth.

The BIS argued that the run-up in debt of both financial and non-financial sectors in the period 2000 to 2004 reflected excess liquidity created by central banks in the major industrial countries (BIS, 2004). Others asserted that the housing bubble was fueled and speculation was encouraged by the Fed's maintenance of negative short-term interest rates after 2002. There is abundant evidence to support both arguments, but it is also true that financial institutions themselves played a significant role in enabling the explosion of debt that took place in this period. While liquidity expansion and debt creation are typically under the influence of central banks, the ability of the largest institutions to implement strategies that monetized debt through a pyramidal process of borrowing in short-term wholesale markets allowed them to become less dependent on central banks to create the liquidity they needed to expand growth and profitability.

As the scale of leverage grew, the risk to systemic stability posed by leveraged position taking intensified with increased concentration in the global financial system. Derivatives contracts were another key channel for dangerous interconnectedness. As a stark example of the problem, the *Financial Times* reported that when Lehman was placed in bankruptcy in September 2008, that bank alone was counterparty to 6500 different institutions and corporations across 1.2 million derivatives transactions. Overall, Lehman's US arm was a counterparty to $100 billion derivatives transactions. Moreover, a full two years after its collapse, only one third of these transactions had been unwound (Sakoui, 2010). More generally, institutional concentration in the derivatives markets was itself a channel for interconnectedness. By 2010, five of the largest OTC derivatives dealers accounted for 95 percent of the US and half of the global market. But, ironically, the greatest degree of concentration occurred in the markets for credit derivatives and structured products such as collateralized debt obligations—instruments designed to disperse risk. For example, the BIS triennial survey of June 2004 revealed that 42 percent of the notional value of CDSs represented contracts between reporting dealers (BIS, 2005a). Given that a handful of banks in the US and other advanced economies dominated these markets, the fact that this limited number of dealers accounted for *both* sides of a substantial percentage of these contracts ensured that, as proved to be the case, liquidity in derivatives and their underlying markets would drastically shrink when any one of these institutions was compelled to unwind its positions.

Lack of transparency in the markets for assets used as collateral for borrowing contributed to the growing level of uncertainty that spread throughout the global system in the fall of 2007. As discussed, the tipping point for the collapse of the paper pyramid was the slowdown in the housing market and the beginning of a dip in prices. Weakening prices precipitated margin calls on MBS collateral[5] and required charges against capital. Eroding capital undermined the creditworthiness of institutions, making it difficult and expensive to fund existing positions and forcing asset sales.

Interconnectedness accelerated the process as the need to preserve capital and uncertainty about counterparties' positions dried up the supply of short-term funding provided to financial institutions by the major sources of that funding: financial institutions themselves. In the wake of the Lehman bankruptcy, the collapse of the short-term wholesale markets—the epicenter of the credit freeze—intensified the downward spiral of falling asset prices as funding for buyers of assets that had to be sold disappeared. The immediate threat to the major institutions' capital positions revealed the inadequacy of capital to prevent or cushion the implosion caused by the extraordinary level of systemic interdependency that had developed over the preceding decade (Gorton and Metrick, 2009).

NOTES

1. Banks' pyramidal borrowing in the repo market made possible the expansion of trading for their own accounts in domestic and foreign assets and in markets for synthetic assets such as CDOs. Repo borrowing also expanded the volume of proprietary trading for investment banks and hedge funds.
2. On "rehypothecation" and the shadow banking system, see Singh and Aitken, 2009.

3. For purposes of reporting, repos were often hidden off balance sheet temporarily at the end of the month. They were also systematically and permanently hidden in certain off-balance sheet transactions and as funding for off-balance sheet conduits.
4. This process began with the 2005 bankruptcy code amendments that expanded the special treatment of repos from Treasury-backed repos to repos backed by mortgages and other securities (Taub, 2010).
5. Selling assets to meet calls for additional collateral is another powerful channel for the spread of contagion. During the LTCM crisis in 1998, for example, a large share of the good assets that were sold were Brazilian bonds, with the result that Brazil suffered a crisis unrelated to developments in its own economy and financial markets.

8. Opaque markets and opaque balance sheets

Financial innovation has contributed to the growth of institutions, markets, and activities that have greatly undermined the amount and quality of information needed to maintain confidence and promote liquidity in the US financial system. The threat to asset values has been exacerbated by the spread and growth of non-transparent, OTC markets for securitized assets and derivatives, by the growth of underreported and undercapitalized off-balance sheet positions and by the increasingly important role played by highly leveraged, non-transparent institutions such as hedge funds and private equity funds in credit and derivatives markets.

Americans hear daily—even hourly—about developments in the stock markets but, before the financial crisis, most had never heard of the much larger markets for asset-backed securities including MBS, or for contracts that derive their value from changes in exchange rates for foreign currencies, or changes in interest rates or the prices of commodities or credit obligations. Moreover, few are aware even now that there is much less information about these much larger, global markets than there is for the stock market. In the market for CDSs, for example, outstanding contracts on underlying assets were valued at over $62 trillion in 2007—more than the total value of all the actual financial assets in the world (BIS, 2008).[1] Nevertheless, information on these markets is based on reports on outstanding contracts at a specific time and is collected with a lag. Information on the volume of trading is particularly difficult to assess. But reports for 2002 estimated that the average large dealer entered into 1900 transactions and made over 22,000 settlements on a *weekly* basis (Cornford, 2008).

As the subprime crisis unfolded, the absence of information on declining values undermined the process of price discovery in many of these markets and led to a halt in trading. Lack of information on trading volume increased uncertainty and amplified suspicions about the exposure of counterparties. As noted, it was the CDS market that proved to be the tipping point for Bear Stearns, Lehman Brothers, and AIG (Morgenson, 2008).[2] Questions about the size of their holdings and the value of the collateral behind them drove down their stock prices and made counterparties unwilling to provide the credit they needed to survive.

In the aftermath of the Bear Stearns sale to JPMorgan Chase, the April 2008 report of the Financial Stability Forum noted that there had been longstanding concerns about the operational and settlement infrastructure for derivatives markets. Proposals for reform included requiring that all derivatives be registered and traded on exchanges (Crotty and Epstein, 2008) or establishing a central clearing house for settlements that would obtain information on clearing house members' capital and the value of collateral backing contracts.

Such proposals were not new, but they had been vigorously opposed by banks on the grounds that the standardized contracts required for exchange trading (settlement dates and amounts in particular) were limitations that disadvantaged customers, compared with the advantages of OTC trading. OTC trading involves bilateral deals that can be tailored to the specific needs of the customer.[3] It is because of these advantages that OTC contracts are so attractive and also why they cannot be traded. The seller of the contract can only hedge the position by buying another contract from another dealer, who must then buy a contract to hedge her position—a chain that, as noted, results in the extraordinary growth in the aggregate nominal value of outstanding derivatives contracts that is far greater than the total value of the underlying financial assets on which these contracts are based.

The structure of the OTC derivatives markets increases their contribution to systemic risk. The inability to trade these bilateral contracts tends to concentrate the market in the hands of relatively few dealers. Although the value at risk—based on estimates of the changes in price likely to occur between the dates contracts are sold and settled—is relatively small, other than in times of crisis, it is nevertheless a very large share of the capital of the largest parties in OTC markets. Moreover, the susceptibility of these markets to a halt in trading and the requirement that collateral against contracts be marked to market can abruptly multiply exposure in a crisis. Dodd-Frank initiated the process of increasing the share of derivatives contracts that will be traded on exchanges. Since failure to restructure the OTC markets is not an option, the need to preserve these provisions of the legislation is a priority.

The treatment of contingency contracts is another current and future area of concern. Contracts such as letters of credit have long been a standard part of banks' menu of services to customers. But a wider variety of financial insurance came into play in the 1970s when, as discussed in Chapter 3, banks began to offer guaranties for commercial paper to shore up the market for funding the activities of their own holding companies, as well as to earn fees from finance and non-financial companies. By the early 1990s, banks backed over $100 billion of the commercial paper issued by the 15 largest non-bank finance companies, and their role in insuring financial assets expanded further as the decade progressed.

In the 1990s, the entire panoply of bank guaranties became something of a parallel or shadow banking system. The largest US banks held a volume of contingent liabilities on their books rivaling the actual volume of their loans and other assets. Estimates of total commitments and contingent liabilities issued by domestic institutions were as high as $5.6 trillion as early as 1991 (D'Arista and Schlesinger, 1993). As the shadow system developed, additional off-balance sheet products and entities—CDOs and structured investment vehicles (SIVs), for example—were created to expand the range of guaranties for financial assets; off-balance sheet holdings exploded. Although the system purported to substitute private guaranties for public support, it created an explicit channel through which buyers of these contracts could gain access to the public sector lender of last resort and, as it turned out, to the taxpayer as well.

But the OTC derivatives markets call attention to another problem area in the market-based US financial structure that emerged in the 1960s and 1970s. Tailoring derivatives contracts to the particular needs of individual customers is based on concepts derived from portfolio lending and, in fact, these markets were developed by the primary portfolio lenders: commercial banks. But as their holdings of contracts for derivatives grew, banks moved them and other contingency contracts off balance sheet where the absence of reporting requirements made it possible to ignore the insufficiency of the capital needed to cover such large exposures.

Like all contingency contracts, OTC derivatives held by banks cannot be classified as assets or liabilities on banks' balance sheets until they are settled and the result can be classified as either a loss or a gain. Banks used that glitch in the balance sheets of portfolio lenders to justify the practice of holding them off balance sheet in trading accounts.[4] The movement of banks into the business of marketing and trading OTC derivatives during a period when the process of deregulation was sweeping away traditional regulatory barriers was not challenged.

That fact should not, however, lead to the assumption that this is a "normal" banking activity. There is no economic or systemic reason why derivatives should be sold by banks. As the entry of large investment banks into the business in the 1980s suggests, dealing in derivatives is not tied to the traditional deposit-taking and lending activities of banks or to the payments system. It is, in fact, so esoteric an activity that, as noted, only five institutions accounted for 97 percent of the market when the crisis erupted in 2008 (Office of the Comptroller of the Currency, 2008). The remaining 8000 US banks did not sell derivatives or trade them for their own accounts.

Equally questionable was the assertion that dealing in derivatives is part of banks' role as intermediaries, that they help meet the hedging needs of their customers. Data from the Commodities Futures Trading Commission and the BIS discussed during consideration of the Dodd-Frank legislation showed that sales and trades with commercial end users accounted for only 8 to 9 percent of the OTC market. Over 90 percent of contracts involved transactions between dealers or with other financial institutions. And, in the end, the events of 2008 made a mockery of the frequently voiced assertion that derivatives were invaluable in shifting risk to those most able to bear it—unless, of course the assumption was that those most able to bear it were taxpayers.

The way in which banks' off-balance sheet holdings contributed to the crisis was described by Timothy F. Geithner, then president of the Federal Reserve Bank of New York, in testimony before the US Senate Banking Committee (Geithner, 2008). He said that the pull-back of many of the traditional providers of the asset-based commercial paper, used by banks to fund off-balance sheet positions, forced banks to provide other financing for these positions or take them onto their balance sheets. As banks' cost of raising unsecured funding shot up and maturities shortened, their scramble for funding helped spread the crisis to other financial institutions and markets, with particularly adverse effects on the commercial paper market and the holdings of money market mutual funds (MMMFs). What ensued, Geithner concluded, was the classic pattern in financial crises: margin calls, sales of assets to meet the calls, further downward pressure on asset prices, and additional margin calls and falling prices that exacerbated the downward spiral.

As the crisis unfolded, there were no calls for outlawing off-balance sheet holdings from the various groups active in shaping regulatory decisions, including the Basel Banking Committee at the BIS, the Financial Stability Forum, and the Group of Thirty.[5] Others writing on financial reform made the argument that placing all assets on balance sheets and requiring the same capital backing for these products would remove one of the incentives for large financial institutions to maintain their excessive focus on providing credit insurance rather than on extending the credit needed to support economic activity (Crotty and Epstein, 2008; Lewitt, 2008). Others pointed out that the Spanish authorities allowed banks to have SIVs but required them to have the same capital backing as other assets, rather than the slightly lower requirements permitted by the Basel II agreement on capital adequacy (Cornford, 2008).

Moving these positions onto balance sheets where they would be subject to reporting requirements would greatly increase the transparency of the financial system. Subjecting these positions to the same capital requirements as other assets would help ameliorate the extreme under-capitalization of banks' holdings of derivatives and other contingency contracts. However, as discussed in Chapter 10, provisions that deal with interconnectedness enacted in Dodd-Frank could, if implemented, shrink off-balance sheet positions in the process of addressing the larger concern: that extending financial guaranties to other financial institutions is an inherently hazardous activity that facilitates the spread of systemic crises.

Meanwhile, the lack of transparency created by the shadow banking system is reflected as well in the lack of supervision of and information about large and significant players, such as hedge funds and private equity firms. Hedge funds are viewed as potentially destabilizing because so little is known about the overall nature and scale of their activities, how leveraged they are, and how concentrated their holdings may be. Despite calls for regulation of hedge funds after the collapse of LTCM in 1998, they continued to operate without registration and reporting requirements even as their share in trading and investment grew substantially larger in the years that followed.

Proposals for regulating hedge funds and/or private equity firms included the recommendations of the Fisher II working group of the BIS that hedge funds report market, liquidity, and credit risk (Griffith-Jones et al., 2007) and, from the Group of Thirty, that regulators establish appropriate standards for capital, liquidity, and risk management for all systemically significant private pools of capital that employ substantial amounts of borrowed funds. In a series of recommendations dating back to 2006, a committee of the European Parliament requested that the Parliament's commission on hedge funds and private equity submit legislation by November 30, 2008 that would regulate these entities to ensure appropriate capital requirements, require registration and authorization of funds' managers, and impose limits on leverage (European Parliament, 2008).

While the European Union committee joined others in calling for more information about these entities, it also argued that "new and better regulation of hedge funds and private equity cannot be isolated from the need for better regulation of other financial actors"; that the increased interdependence of all financial firms "requires a coherent and consistent approach to regulation" (European Parliament, 2008, p. 16). Their proposals are consistent with the view that all firms should be subject to the same regulatory framework applicable to other financial firms involved in the same activities[6]—including, in the case of hedge funds, collateral and margin requirements as well as capital requirements and limits on leverage. Their report provides what many would regard as the basic standard for forging a regulatory framework that can address the problems and concerns about the global financial system in place in the 2000s. But the implementation of that standard has not yet begun.

NOTES

1. Total outstanding derivatives contracts stood at $596 trillion at year-end 2007.
2. AIG's holdings of CDSs amounted to about $500 billion in mid-2007 and generated $250 million a year in premiums up to that point. By the end of September 2007, however, it recognized a $352 million unrealized loss on its CDS portfolio and by the end of June 2008, the total losses on its derivatives operations reached $25 billion.
3. The International Swap Dealers Association had developed standardized documentation for OTC derivatives contracts—an important reform for defusing legal risks—but the amounts and terms of OTC contracts have not been standardized.
4. Trading accounts are a common balance sheet structure for investment banks that are backed by capital. The requirement that holdings be marked to market on a daily basis, with deductions to capital for losses, provided a degree of soundness regulation for investment banks that was not required for banks as their trading accounts ballooned. Moreover, as investment banks moved into providing financial insurance through contingency contracts, those contracts were not included in the capital and mark to market requirements that applied to accounts involved in trading underlying financial assets such as stocks and bonds.
5. The Basel Banking Committee is composed of central bank members of the BIS. Formed after the collapse of the international monetary system in the 1970s, it assumed an oversight role in monitoring international banking markets and, in the 1980s, setting capital requirements for banks.

   The Financial Stability Forum consists of representatives of the ministries of finance, central banks, and financial regulators of 12 countries (Australia, Canada, France, Germany, Hong Kong, Italy, Japan, Netherlands, Singapore, Switzerland, United Kingdom, and the US), of multilateral institutions (IMF, World Bank, BIS, and Organisation for Economic Co-operation and Development), of some more specialized international bodies (Basel Committee on Banking Supervision, International Association of Insurance Supervisors, International Organization of Securities Commissions, Committee on Payment and Settlement Systems, and Committee on the Global Financial System), and of the European Central Bank.

   The Group of Thirty is a private non-profit consultative group that evaluates the international repercussions of decisions taken by public and private sectors. The current chairman of the group is the deputy prime minister of Singapore. Paul Volcker is chairman emeritus.
6. Others who advocated comprehensive functional regulation include D'Arista and Schlesinger, 1993; D'Arista and Griffith-Jones, 2001; and Williams, 2008.

9. Growing concentration leads to "too big to fail"

In the past, structural and regulatory efforts to promote competition within the US financial services industry and ensure access to credit stressed the need to prevent the concentration of financial resources. Beginning in the 1970s, changes in financial structure made these restraints obsolete, and increases in institutional and asset concentrations helped drive the process of restructuring. Failure to restrict institutional concentration began to impair the market system itself, since markets work best when decision making reflects different viewpoints and perspectives. Reducing the number of independent decision makers in the system increased the potential for "one-way" markets. The dominant position and market power of a few large institutions in each financial sector contributed to the spread of destructive, lemming-like behavior in all sectors.

Even without the damaging effects of the 2008 financial crisis as evidence, failure to curb concentration undermines systemic efficiency in a number of ways. For example, as the number of institutions declines, so does the number of alternative sources of capital and credit. The result may be an uneven distribution of credit that rewards some sectors at the expense of others. Rising levels of institutional concentration may make it harder for the financial system to assist the development of small, innovative companies and processes that would mature in time to ease the disruptions caused by declining older firms and methods.

Fewer institutions may also lead to increased volatility in secondary markets for traded assets. With the growth of institutional investors' share of securities markets, the size of single transactions tended to grow larger and have greater impact on markets. As a result, the demand for instruments and vehicles to offset wider swings in prices increased, but risk also increased as the number of counterparties for hedging contracts shrank.

Meanwhile, the implications of institutional concentration for the conduct of monetary policy were—and are—almost totally ignored in discussions of these issues. Over time, the largest individual financial institutions grew to be somewhat insulated by the size of their transactions relative to the size of the market. The market power and growing interdependence of these institutions and markets undermined the central bank's effectiveness as a stabilizing force in the pre-crisis years, when the size of the Fed's aggregate transactions in a given time period diminished proportionately relative to the share of the largest institutions. Thus, as the size of failures rose, along with their monetary and social costs, the ability of the central bank to protect customers of financial institutions weakened and the burden forced on taxpayers ballooned.

The rate of growth of large US financial institutions accelerated in the 1960s as they expanded their international reach and their share of financial activity at home. Concern about the trend toward financial concentration grew as well, intensifying in the mid-1980s as the potential failure of one large US bank, Continental Illinois, threatened to cause ripple effects throughout the system. The Federal Reserve justified its loans and other support for this big bank's holding company by arguing that its collapse could weaken other financial institutions that held loans to and accounts with Continental Illinois. Regulators also worried that closing the bank would strain the resources of the Federal Deposit Insurance Corporation (FDIC) if it were required to cover the deposits of the bank's non-financial customers. They also worried about the potential effect on the commercial paper market and bank guaranties for commercial paper if Continental Illinois' holding company defaulted on its borrowings and the bank could not meet its contingent guaranties to other issuers (D'Arista, 1994a).

"Too big to fail" became a common term of reference for the dilemma posed by the expansion of big banks in the 1980s, but many analysts saw a broader trend extending to other sectors as well. While most of the focus was on banks, their analyses called attention to the number of institutions that accounted for more than half of the total resources of any given financial sector. By that measure, the level of concentration was already unacceptably high in the mid-1980s. Less than 1 percent of the total number of banks, securities firms, and life insurers accounted for half of the total resources of those sectors. Property casualty insurers and thrifts were only slightly less concentrated, with 2 percent of the former and 4 percent of the latter accounting for half of their sectors' resources (D'Arista, 1994a). Despite widespread recognition that some institutions were "too big to fail," the trend toward concentration increased over the next two decades and intensified as "supervisory mergers" and "purchase and assumption transactions" became the preferred methods of handling failing depository institutions. Box 9.1 on the change in institutional concentration between 1984 and the crisis in 2008, when the number of institutions that were considered “too big to fail” required massive infusions of funding by the Federal Reserve and Treasury, illustrates the remarkable increases that occurred in this period.

BOX 9.1

Banks
In 1984, the top ten US banks accounted for 26 percent of the total assets of the sector, with 50 percent held by 64 banks and the remaining 50 percent spread out among the remaining 11,387 smaller institutions. The Federal Reserve reports that about 11,500 mergers took place from 1980 through 2005, averaging 440 a year and reducing the total number of banks to 7500 (Mester, 2007). By mid-2008, five banks had become the dominant institutions in the market in terms of total assets and as holders of 97 percent of the total amount of notional derivatives such as interest and exchange rate swaps, CDOs, and CDSs (Office of the Comptroller of the Currency, 2008).

Securities firms
The most concentrated financial sector, mergers beginning in the 1980s reduced the number of firms in the securities industry. At year-end 1984, the top ten firms (0.12 percent of the 7800 firms registered) accounted for 41 percent of the sector's capital, 47 percent of total revenue, and 55 percent of underwriting profits (D'Arista, 1994a). By year-end 2008, most of these ten firms had been acquired by or had become bank holding companies or, in the case of Lehman Brothers and Bear Stearns, had failed.

Institutional investors
With the shift of household savings to the capital markets after the passage of the Employee Retirement Income Security Act in 1975, money management became a dominant activity in financial markets and, by the 1980s, almost all sectors were participants in managing investments. While life and property-casualty insurers invest premiums as providers of insurance, the management of assets of pension funds and retirement accounts is distributed among life insurers, banks, securities firms, and mutual funds. Nevertheless, asset management is concentrated among a relatively small number of firms given the size of the assets involved. For example, in 1984, only 37 institutional investors managed half of the $1.2 trillion of assets of beneficiaries at a time when 64 banks accounted for half of the $1.4 trillion of banking assets (D'Arista, 1994a). By year-end 2007, institutional investors held $25.3 trillion, or 43.7 percent of total financial assets, compared to $13.7 trillion, or 23.7 percent held by banks (FRS, *Flow of Funds*). Subsequent analyses of concentration in this sector and of the distribution of assets in their holdings is insufficient, but asset concentration is as much a matter of concern as the relatively small number of institutions that manage these investments.

While banks' role in channeling savings into economic activity has diminished, a high level of concern about bank concentration is warranted given this sector's role in the payments system and the safety net that backs that system. The FDIC was created in 1933 to restore confidence in banks and promote economic growth by protecting depositors and ensuring the efficient circulation of the nation's money supply. The remarkable success of this agency in restoring and maintaining confidence was, however, undermined in 1980 by the removal of interest rate ceilings. As discussed above, when the level of rates banks and thrifts had to pay to attract deposits soared above returns on outstanding loans, bank and thrift failures escalated and the decade became disastrous for the deposit insurance funds. From 1980 through 1992, more than 4500 federally insured depository institutions failed, with assets of more than $630 billion and at a cost of about $130 billion to the insurance funds and taxpayers (Barth and Brumbaugh, 1993). Although the federally assisted mergers and acquisitions that were part of the strategy for managing the crisis sharply reduced the number of institutions affected, the crisis itself and its cost undoubtedly relaxed concerns about the rising level of concentration.

At the same time, other developments contributed to undermining existing restrictions on bank size. The major legal restrictions were the 1927 McFadden Act that gave states the right to prohibit out-of-state banks from opening branches in their states, and regulations imposed by the Federal Reserve that limited a member bank's share of total deposits in a given metropolitan area. The intent was to provide multiple sources of bank credit to prevent the concentration of financial resources, promote competition, and ensure access to borrowers.

But these restrictions became meaningless in the 1970s as banks set up credit card operations and loan production offices nationwide, and gathered a larger share of non-deposit liabilities in money markets at home and abroad. The irrelevance of the prohibition on interstate branching was pointed out repeatedly using the example of the New York banks that could set up branches in every continent across the globe, but not in New Jersey. The pressure from banks to end the restrictions was rewarded in 1992 when 34 states changed their laws to allow nationwide banking and the remaining states followed shortly thereafter.[1]

Beginning with the Bank Holding Company Act Amendments of 1970, the expansion of banks into other financial activities also contributed to concentration in the sector. Being able to engage in non-traditional businesses at home and abroad gave larger institutions an advantage in terms of growth that their smaller competitors did not have. For example, smaller banks could not raise the capital to set up leasing, factoring, or mortgage banking affiliates or establish foreign branches or compete in attracting foreign borrowers. In addition, the largest banks were already engaged in a variety of other activities in their overseas offices, including securities underwriting and trading, before passage of the Gramm-Leach-Bliley Act in 1999 that repealed the Glass-Steagall Act and further widened permissible activities for banks.

Meanwhile, the Basel capital adequacy standards adopted in 1988 reflected a shift in regulatory views on the appropriate means for curbing bank concentration. Those who advocated using capital adequacy standards in place of quantitative regulations as the primary regulatory tool assumed that market forces would effectively curb the growth of banks and bank credit by providing capital to sound institutions while withholding it from the less sound. In effect, the issue of restraining bank concentration was turned over to the market. But, aware that regulatory authorities would not let the largest institutions fail, the market tended to favor those institutions, providing them with a disproportionately larger share of additional capital and contributing to increases in institutional size and concentration.

Not everyone agreed that market forces could or should moderate concentration. Like former FDIC chairman William Isaac, some argued that stronger antitrust laws should be applied to banks to ensure that there were plenty of alternative means of gaining access to bank credit (Brownstein, 1983). But the Treasury and other regulators favored consolidation of the more than 12,000 banks operating in the US in the early 1980s to encourage efficiency and economies of scale. It was not that the "too big to fail" problem was ignored. It was, in fact, accommodated in the FDIC Improvement Act of 1991 by authorizing federal regulators to rescue large banks and cover their uninsured deposits if their failure would create serious risk to the US banking system.

Missing in that legislative response was concern about the serious risk posed by the build-up throughout the financial system of asset concentrations related to mortgage lending. In addition to institutional concentration, restraining asset concentration is a problem that must be addressed to restore systemic stability and avoid further crises. As demonstrated in the crises that afflicted Japan and emerging market countries in the 1990s, and the US and other advanced economies in the 2000s, asset concentrations can trigger collapses in financial systems that halt growth and distribute losses throughout financial and non-financial sectors.

Requirements for diversification are a traditional means of dealing with the problem. In the US, making diversification a necessary component of soundness regulation was first embodied in provisions of the National

Bank Act of 1865 and its requirement that loans to a single borrower be limited to no more than 10 percent of bank capital. Requirements for diversification were also included in holding limits on investments in stocks of individual corporations by insurance and investment companies. Moreover, as part of the New Deal reforms, margin requirements were imposed to prevent the excessive use of credit for purchases of stocks, in view of recognition that leverage had fueled the rapid build-up in stock prices that led to the crash of 1929.

Margin requirements limit the amount of credit that can be used to buy stocks and are an effective tool for dealing with asset concentrations because they apply to all investors, financial and non-financial. Former Fed chairman William McChesney Martin raised margin requirements to contain the bull market that developed in the 1960s, and former Fed chairman Arthur Burns used them again in the 1970s. During the chairmanship of Alan Greenspan, however, the Fed left the requirement at 50 percent. As the boom in technology stocks got underway at the end of the 1990s, it was widely argued that raising the margin requirement would have moderated both the bubble and the bust that followed.

But margin requirements do not apply to other classes of assets. There are no limits on how much can be borrowed to buy MBS, for example, nor are there holding limits on the amount that can be held by institutional investors. The absence of these restrictions helped create the asset concentrations at the heart of the 2008 crisis. Moreover, limits on banks' loans to individual borrowers as a percentage of capital do not apply to all systemically important lenders. And, as discussed above, banks, too, have been able to avoid capital restrictions on both individual and aggregate lending to other financial institutions. Moreover, securitization allowed banks to originate, distribute, and service a rising volume of residential mortgages and consumer loans without raising additional capital or infringing on restrictions limiting loans in relation to capital.

The absence of uniform restrictions on asset concentrations made it possible for a rising share of total credit used to finance residential mortgages to create the potential for a housing bubble. Part of that bubble was inflated by the growth in subprime lending, but it was the overall concentration in lending for mortgages that was the driving force behind the bubble. The originate and distribute model was supposed to lead to asset and risk disbursement and diversification, but it led, instead, to a concentration of assets that increased risk. For a while, the rise in housing prices kept pace with the escalation in outstanding mortgage debt and pushed up the value of households' net worth. But with the run-up in household debt from 66 to 100 percent of GDP over the decade ending in 2007, the debt burden increased both the strain on families and the fragility of the financial system (FRS, *Flow of Funds*).

The small business sector was one of the many casualties of the concentration in credit flows to housing. Increases in direct bank lending to small businesses all but collapsed after 2001, but banks restructured credit flows to those borrowers by allowing the use of their homes as collateral (FRS, *Flow of Funds*). This channel for lending was more profitable for banks since loans for housing could be securitized and sold rather than held on their balance sheets. For small business owners, there was little choice other than to borrow against the inflated value of their residences. But, as house prices dropped, they lost that source of financing and many struggled to save both their businesses and their homes.

NOTE

1. The relaxation of restrictions on interstate banking fits into the time frame associated with the deregulatory policies of the 1980s but, as discussed in Chapter 2, the real drivers of deregulation, well before the Reagan and Thatcher administrations, were changes and practices inaugurated in the unregulated euro market. Deregulation, in this and many other cases, was a ratification of those changes.

10. Regulating the post-crisis system

Regulatory strategies in the post-crisis era must take into account the system now in place. It is not possible to turn back the clock. Efforts to reinvent the compartmentalized system envisioned in Glass-Steagall—despite its many merits—are irrelevant. Glass-Steagall was applicable to a system dominated by many large, medium-sized, and small banks, engaged in the traditional intermediation activities that were then their mission: accepting savings deposits and the checkable demand deposits that channeled payments throughout the economy, and providing short-term working capital for businesses and loans to households. Other sectors also had specific and important missions in this compartmentalized framework: providing short- and long-term credit and investments for consumers and households (thrifts, credit unions, finance companies, and securities firms); financing commercial mortgages and making medium- and long-term loans for businesses (insurance companies); underwriting securities for capital formation (securities firms), and managing many kinds of risk for all sectors (insurance companies) (D'Arista, 1994a). While it will not be possible to return to a world in which these missions are assigned to particular financial sectors, it is important that existing and new regulatory strategies make sure they are adequately covered by the institutional structure of the system.

Underlying the need to ensure an adequate structure to serve the many financial requirements of an advanced and growing economy is the belief that regulation matters. The international fairs in Ghent and Bruges in the fifteenth century reflected the importance of the role of regulation in their recognition of the need for confidence and fairness (Braudel, 1982). These markets and others throughout Europe in that period operated under the patronage of a sovereign charged with overseeing the standardization of weights, measures, and the value of money. In the case of a national economy, commitment to a fair and effective financial system requires a regulatory framework that reflects a much larger mandate: the understanding that failure to transform financial capital into economic activity impedes growth—and, conversely, that lack of growth weakens the economy and the value of the financial investment behind it.

Beginning in the twentieth century, there was also recognition that regulation was necessary to protect the transmission belt for monetary policy and that financial stability is critical for effective policy implementation and to maintain public confidence in making the financial transactions that sustain economic activity. And, finally, regulation provides the norms that ensure fiduciary responsibility recognizing that credit decisions are so critical to the well-being of the economy that making those decisions is a quasi-public responsibility.

Reflecting those beliefs, the objectives of regulation include: channeling financial resources into productive uses; promoting soundness to prevent institutional failures and financial crises; preventing conflicts of interest, fraud, and the concentration of financial resources to ensure the impartiality of credit decisions and promote fairness; making sure all credit-worthy borrowers have access to credit; and ensuring balanced credit flows. These are not objectives that can be accomplished by relying on market forces. Only government can perform that role in its capacity to represent the people, businesses, and institutions who use and rely on the financial system for the conduct of their economic lives and whose economic well-being depends on its effectiveness and stability.

The good news about Dodd-Frank is that its passage into law in 2010 fully recognized the importance of government regulation. But, other than the sections in the act that deal with interconnectedness by limiting banks' lending to other financial institutions in relation to capital, it fails to correct many of the regulatory flaws made glaringly apparent by the unfolding financial crisis. The following discussion deals with the major areas of concern described in the preceding chapters—securitization, interconnectedness, proprietary trading, leverage, and concentration—and provides an overview of reform proposals offered at the time of the crisis.[1] Two critical areas in need of reform, the financial safety net for households and monetary policy tools, were not included in discussions of Dodd-Frank and are examined in Chapter 11 and Part VI.

SECURITIZATION

It is difficult to believe that originating, pooling, and securitizing mortgages, car loans, and other forms of consumer credit will not remain major activities in US credit markets and that securitized assets will not be held by almost all institutions in the US financial system. Calls for reforms in this area attest to a widespread assumption that securitization will continue. ***Higher capital requirements*** appear to be a one-size-fits-all solution to any area that has been identified by the financial crisis as needing reform (US Department of the Treasury, 2008; Financial Stability Forum, 2008; Group of Thirty, 2009; IMF, 2009) and concern about adequate capital for banks' exposure to MBS was addressed in the Basel II requirements.[2]

The widespread losses on MBS and related derivatives throughout the financial system suggest that higher capital ratios should also be applied to exposures of other financial institutions such as finance companies, brokers, and hedge funds that originate and/or trade and hold securitized products. Failure to do so would not only give those institutions a competitive advantage over banks in terms of profitability but, equally importantly, would fail to address the systemic implications of an undercapitalized MBS market. So far, the focus has been on banks, but requirements for capital coverage for all securitized exposures should be made uniform and applied to all institutions that originate, underwrite, or hold them.

The Financial Stability Forum (2008) proposed reforms that would provide *disclosure and greater transparency* at each stage of the securitization process. Crotty and Epstein (2008) and, in 2009, a Bank of England report, argued for disclosure about the underlying assets in the pool so that the risk of each underlying mortgage could be examined. Given the size of losses on securitized assets experienced by pension funds and other pools of household savings, it seems reasonable to argue that MBS issuance should not be permitted to go forward without insisting on the same requirements for disclosure that apply to the issuance of all other securities. That level of disclosure is needed for investors and to ensure that mortgage borrowers can be identified in order to facilitate workouts if needed. The opaque character of the pools of mortgages backing MBS intensified the problems in establishing value as house prices fell and impeded efforts to help homeowners renegotiate mortgages and avoid default.

Other proposals offered during consideration of Dodd-Frank—which, like those discussed here, were not part of the legislation enacted—included a requirement that securitization products be simplified and standardized and that transactions be documented to the extent possible. That would go a long way toward increasing transparency of both the instruments and the market, but not far enough. Nevertheless, accomplishing those objectives would make it possible to move toward the next critical step: requiring that MBS and other securitized products be traded on exchanges to provide real-time information about prices and the volume of trading. A market economy cannot function efficiently if investors are confronted with trading arrangements that obscure what is happening in the market for a given product. To obtain all the information that investors need to evaluate investment decisions, they must be able to make transactions in regulated markets that are open and accessible.

Improved lending standards is another area of reform that must be addressed. Allowing lenders to relax (or even ignore) loan-to-value ratios and borrowers' ability to repay ensured that securitized assets would develop into the toxic assets they became. The systemic threat posed by securitization will not be lessened until more stringent and prudent standards are reinstated and enforced at the level of origination. Comprehensive regulation of institutions and the oversight of the Consumer Financial Protection Bureau created by Dodd-Frank will help accomplish that objective.

As Dodd-Frank moved toward enactment in 2010, some argued that mortgage originators should be required to retain a meaningful share of the credit risk they were packaging into securitized and other structured products (Group of Thirty, 2009). Referred to as "skin in the game," it was seen as a way to improve due diligence. A more specific proposal on the subject was offered by economist Joseph Stiglitz, who proposed that the share of the loan held by the originator match the amount put down by the borrower—no less than 20 percent for each, unless the government guaranteed the mortgage (Stiglitz, 2008). This 40 percent minimum would, in effect, provide a form of insurance for the pooled loan that would insulate it from a decline in the price of the home. If prices fell, both the lender's and the borrower's equity might be wiped out, but a loan work-out could reduce that share of the principle without altering the amount of the mortgage held in the pool.

Addressing the need to protect these securities using strategies such as those involving "skin in the game" is undeniably a priority for reform, given the amount of MBS held throughout the financial system, their impact on the values of pensions and household savings, and thus their influence on changes in spending and economic activity. But recognizing that these securities need to be protected raises another issue that must be addressed: the role of privileged assets such as MBS in credit allocation. However worthy the objectives that have supported the institutions and strategies that favored financing for housing, the rapid build-up in credit to any one sector of the economy is unsustainable. Thus, quantitative restrictions at the level of origination as well as limits on holdings applicable to all institutions are reforms that would have beneficial macroprudential influences.

As a final comment on securitization, it should be noted that because securitized assets are so inherently complex, opaque, and impossible to monitor as currently packaged and traded, attempts to impose new rules on the process are likely to produce only modest repairs at the margin. But securitization is a structural development that must be watched with ongoing attention, using discussion of the reform proposals that have been offered as part of the process of assessing developments as they occur. However, as is likely with any important structural change, new, unintended consequences will surely emerge. In this way, the failure to address problems associated with securitization will lead to new systemic threats in the future.

INTERCONNECTEDNESS

Sections 608, 619, and 611 of the Dodd-Frank Act are arguably the most important reforms put in place by the legislation. They amend sections of four other essential federal financial statutes[3] to take into account the expansion of transactions among financial institutions and changes in the kinds of transaction that channel credit flows. One of the critical reforms provided by these amendments is their extension of previous limits on loans to non-financial borrowers under these acts to include borrowers that are unaffiliated financial institutions.[4] The other critical reform is that the amendments address changes in the kinds of transaction that have evolved in lending to both financial and non-financial borrowers to incorporate a broader definition of what constitutes credit exposures.

The new definitions of credit exposures made subject to limitations include:

- all direct and indirect advances of funds under an obligation for repayment or that are repayable from specific property pledged by or on behalf of the person receiving the funds;
- national banks' contingent liabilities such as contractual commitments to advance funds (to the extent specified by the Comptroller of the Currency); and
- derivatives transactions, repo and reverse repo transactions, and securities borrowing and lending.

In addition, an amendment to the National Bank Act provides a broad definition of derivatives that includes contracts, agreements, swaps, or options based on the value of, interest in, or quantitative measure of events or occurrences related to commodities, securities, currencies, interest rates, and indices of other assets.

In other words, limits on the exposure to any client or affiliate in relation to a bank's capital will be based on an aggregate of all such transactions. Thus, the most important effect of these provisions will be to rein in the number of transactions between banks and other financial institutions, and their credit exposure to any one financial institution. And, by enlarging the list of transactions that constitute credit exposure, they also reduce the risk posed to banks by the increased use of transactions with non-financial customers outside the previous limits on loans.

Limiting exposures to derivatives and contingent liabilities related to any one customer, financial or non-financial, will reduce the immense volume of banks' off-balance sheet liabilities and retard their future growth. In addition, limits on banks' credit exposures to other financial institutions will shrink the short-term wholesale funding markets. Other positive outcomes likely to be produced by these provisions include:

- shrinking the debt of the financial system (and the economy as a whole) as a share of GDP;
- reducing leverage and proprietary trading as funding in the repo markets becomes less available;
- reducing the size of the largest institutions that rely on wholesale funding for trading activities;
- raising the share of deposits subject to reserve requirements as sources of funding in credit markets and restoring the potential for Federal Reserve control over the supply of credit; and
- tightening the link between finance and the real economy by reducing the flow of credit to financial borrowers relative to flows to non-financial sectors.

Because these provisions are amendments to existing acts, they did not require studies before implementation or discretionary rule making by regulators, and were scheduled to become effective one year after enactment of the Dodd-Frank Act.[5] The failure of institutions to adhere to the limits and the failure of regulators to enforce them would result in clear violations of the law.

But time for implementation is long past and these rules appear to have stalled, eroding their potential effectiveness in reining in the abuses that the largest institutions believe are critical for their profitability. Introduced in March 2010 by Senator Christopher Dodd with little fanfare, despite the radical nature of the reforms they provided, these provisions were not widely discussed. The focus of debate was elsewhere, and it is still the case that many interested parties are unaware of the existence of this powerful set of reforms and have not acted to ensure their implementation. Moreover, given a deregulatory bias on the part of the majority members in the committee with jurisdiction in the US House of Representatives, a move toward implementation is certain to prompt the introduction of weakening amendments. At the time of writing, the outlook for these provisions is uncertain.

LEVERAGE AND PROPRIETARY TRADING

One major incentive for the build-up of leverage was the relaxation of restrictions on capital requirements for investment banks in 2004, which led to debt-to-equity ratios that no one questioned until Bear Stearns collapsed in March 2008 with, in common with its competitors, a ratio of 30 to 1. Moreover, as revealed by the collapse of LTCM in 1998, hedge funds probably had—and still have—ratios much higher than those of investment banks and their leverage can have major effects on asset prices around the globe if, as it seemed at that time, it took only a dollar of capital to place bets on $100 of assets. With ratios of 20 to 1, the larger banks seemed to be less leveraged than other institutions, but those ratios applied only to on-balance sheet holdings and not to off-balance sheet conduits and positions (Albrecht, 2009).

It was banks' off-balance sheet proprietary trading accounts that reflected the scale of their leverage. When financial institutions trade for their own account rather than for customers' accounts, they are said to be engaged in proprietary trading. A long-standing component of investment banking activity, proprietary trading became a major and large-scale activity for commercial as well as investment banks in the decade before the crisis. In the case of commercial banks, the incentive to engage in trading for their own accounts grew out of their efforts to increase profits by minimizing the amount of capital proscribed under the Basel I capital adequacy requirements. Since assets acquired through trading were assumed to be temporary holdings in connection with lending operations, the amount of capital backing required was minimal.

Even though the BIS had warned (in 2002) that proprietary positions involving carry trade activity had accelerated and that institutions had increased their leverage and were taking larger positions to compensate for the low interest rate environment adopted by central banks, US regulators seem to have been unaware of the actual scale of trading by banks and the size of their off-balance sheet positions. In January 2009, the Group of Thirty, under the leadership of Paul Volcker, proposed that strict capital and liquidity requirements be imposed on the proprietary trading activities of systemically important banking institutions (Group of Thirty, 2009). Stricter capital requirements would reduce the amount of borrowed funds that institutions could use to leverage their positions and increase profitability. Liquidity requirements would limit mismatches between the maturity of assets and liabilities involved in trading, and make carry trades less profitable. In testimony before the House Committee on Banking and Financial Services on September 24, 2009, Volcker expressed the view that a heavy volume of proprietary trading by commercial banks should be prohibited and that the distinction between "proprietary" and "customer-related" trading should be maintained by the active use of capital requirements.

The Volcker provisions enacted in Dodd-Frank limit proprietary trading, limit banks' connections with hedge funds and private equity funds, and contain provisions for implementing strengthened capital, liquidity, asset, and liability rules for investments and practices that promote excessive risk. Both the Volcker Rule and the provisions dealing with interconnectedness described above are major reforms that should rein in the excesses that led to the crisis. But the key, as with all aspects of the Dodd-Frank Act, will be rigorous enforcement and vigilant oversight. This can only occur if there are data available to assess the impacts of these rules and if there are expert and committed observers—economists, bloggers, analysts, and congressional staffers—to monitor and analyze the implementation process.

CONCENTRATION AND "TOO BIG TO FAIL"

Limits on institutional and asset concentrations must be given priority status in shaping ongoing reform proposals. At stake is what is termed the macroprudential function of financial structure and regulation in performing this sector's key role in promoting growth in a national economy. The breakdown in that role during the financial crisis requires that its causes be addressed to ensure it will not be repeated. The following discussion proposes guidelines for reforms that should be considered in meeting that objective. While raising capital requirements is one of the strategies that can play a role in limiting the size of institutions, it is not discussed here since that is already the preferred response. And while this author argues that strengthening capital requirements cannot solve many of the key problems revealed by the crisis (see Chapter 23), relaxing capital requirements will create problems, especially when there are no other strong regulations in place.

One of the important elements in crisis management strategies since the 1980s has been to encourage or permit the take-over of fragile institutions or their assets by supposedly stronger acquirers. While this option may be necessary in some cases in the short term, it is one that intensifies the potential for systemic risk in the future. Many of the mergers that occurred should have been unwound when the crisis was over and, going forward, all institutions should be made to conform to new limits on institutional concentration.

In the aftermath of the crisis, the Group of Thirty's recommendation to limit the share of deposits held by banks nationwide was a start, but Congress needs to develop new strategies to limit the size of all financial institutions, not just banks, and take into account the size of their operations worldwide. Some of the measures and principles that should be included in these strategies are:

- *Limits on the total size of the financial sector in relation to the size of the national economy.* While financial institutions that are domiciled in one country may have operations worldwide, it is the central bank in the home country that is responsible for providing liquidity to its financial sector and the taxpayers of that country that must fund the bailouts. As Crotty (2009) has argued, the capacity to perform those critical functions is determined by the proportional relationship between the size of the financial sector and the output of the economy in which it is based.
- *Limits on the size of individual institutions.* One basis for setting the limits must be the size of the financial guaranty programs—the FDIC, the Securities Investors Protection Corporation, and state programs to protect insurance beneficiaries. "Too big to fail" could be defined as any institution whose failure would cause a substantial depletion of the resources of the guaranty programs and thus put taxpayers at risk.
- *Reinstating or adopting competition policies that place limits on de novo expansions as well as mergers and acquisitions.* The objectives of such policies are to increase the number of decision makers in the system, provide many alternative means for borrowers to gain access to capital and credit, promote diversity in financial services, and ensure that those services meet local needs. Measures of their success would be their ability to prevent a contraction (and promote an increase) in the number of institutions that account for half the total assets of a given financial sector or, in terms of conglomerates, of the financial sector as a whole.

To meet these objectives, regulatory agencies must be given authority not only to prevent excessive expansion but to break up institutions if they reach a size that exceeds either the policy guidelines or any specific numerical limits Congress might impose. The enactment of Glass-Steagall in 1933, which required the break-up of institutions that engaged in both commercial and investment banking, provides the precedent for such policies.

- *Limiting asset concentration.* Imposing margin requirements on all financial assets (including derivatives and commodities) bought on credit would be an effective way to stop the development of bubbles in the future. But Congress must amend the law both to broaden the range of applicable assets and to ensure that the Federal Reserve responds to an expansion in holdings of any type of financial asset, including equities, by raising the margin requirement. The Fed should also be directed to raise and lower margin requirements to restrict or stimulate credit flows to various sectors of the economy. An alternative approach would be to use transaction taxes to achieve the same objectives.

The guidelines and proposals outlined above draw on existing restrictions and objectives that have defined competition policy for the financial sector in the past. While some might need to be revised to take into account the changes in financial structure that have occurred over the past 50 years, the underlying strategies they embody remain viable means to accomplishing the necessary task of limiting financial concentration.

CONCLUSION

This discussion of proposed reforms exemplifies the proverbial closing of the barn door after the horses are out. But since they are out, there is no doubt that the flawed framework through which they galloped must be dealt with. It is not clear that we know all the gaps and, taking that into account, the main thrust of this discussion has been to raise issues about the underlying objectives for reform efforts. What is clear is that developments before and after the crisis have changed the structure of the financial system and that those changes have altered the relationship between financial institutions and both regulatory and monetary authorities, and between finance and the real economy.

To deal with those changes in ways that will restore financial stability, this discussion argues that regulations must be clarified and strengthened; must apply to all institutions engaged in a given function in the same way, and must be structured to overcome the pro-cyclical bias imposed by the rules and practices of a market-based system. It supports the view that there must be a new focus on systemic stability in addition to institutional soundness and, as provided in Dodd-Frank, a new emphasis on consumer protection. The final, critical element needed to ensure stability and protect consumers of financial services is an overhaul of existing financial guaranties and the protection of beneficiaries of pension and retirement accounts. Proposals to address those faults in the system are offered in Chapter 11.

NOTES

1. Reform proposals dealing with opaque markets and off-balance sheet positions are discussed in Chapter 8.
2. There was, however, subsequent concern that, given developments in 2008, ratios might not be high enough and higher requirements were included in Basel III (Cornford, 2008).
3. These include the Federal Reserve Act, the National Bank Act, the Home Owners' Loan Act, and the FDIC Improvement Act.
4. Section 610 is the amendment that extends limits on national banks' loans to individual non-financial borrowers in relation to their capital to financial customers—a class of customer not previously subject to these limits. It also amends the Home Owners' Loan Act to extend these limits to savings associations. Section 609 amends section 23A of the Federal Reserve Act to broaden the definition of credit exposures (included in Section 610) under existing limits on transactions between a bank and its subsidiaries and affiliates. Section 611 amends the FDIC Improvement Act to provide consistent treatment of derivatives transactions to state laws governing lending limits of state banks.
5. Sections 609 and 610 took effect at the end of July 2011—one year after the transfer date—and Section 611 took effect 18 months after the transfer date.

11. Mending the financial safety net for savers

Federal deposit insurance for commercial banks and savings institutions was authorized in the 1930s after decades of debate and experimentation with state programs. The success of these funds in restoring confidence in depository institutions after the wave of bank failures in the early years of the Depression was seen by economists as one of the most important structural changes in the banking system and a fundamental contribution to US monetary and financial stability. The growing perception of deposit insurance as the cornerstone of financial stability and its record in providing protection at minimal cost led to the creation in 1970 of federal insurance funds for credit unions, and more limited funds for securities firms and state guaranty funds for insurance companies (D'Arista, 1994a).

As discussed, providing financial insurance for other financial institutions became a major activity of the largest private institutions in the decades after the 1970s—a development that suggests that the financial sector itself recognized the implications of structural changes underway and that those changes had increased the need for protection. But none of the innovative products introduced in the decades before the crisis increased protection for the majority of savers. Deposit insurance was, and still is, in place in the US and other countries, but the shift in personal savings from banks to pension and retirement funds has greatly reduced the ratio of coverage for total savings.

The fact that the majority of household savings are no longer covered by financial guaranties has important implications for systemic stability because it has undermined the high level of confidence in the system that deposit insurance once provided against runs on banks. Savers' confidence is also undermined by the fact that the institutions that hold and make decisions about the investment of their funds are less regulated than banks. Losses during the financial crisis in the value of funded pension and retirement plans and mutual funds had—and will continue to have—important consequences for changes in aggregate demand and economic activity. Allowing the individual saver to absorb the impact of shocks from financial disruption in a market-based system may cause macroeconomic repercussions that could be avoided if a larger segment of household savings were protected by a financial guaranty system tailored to the current reality of where and to whom savers entrust their funds. To address this new reality, we begin this chapter with a proposal for reforming the financial guaranty program and continue with proposals to improve the governance of pension and retirement funds.

CREATING A NEW FINANCIAL GUARANTY PROGRAM FOR INDIVIDUAL SAVERS

One way to provide more effective coverage for personal savings would be to replace current financial guaranty programs with a system that protects individuals rather than institutions. In such a system, the insurance fund would cover personal accounts, identified by social security numbers, held in one or more federally regulated financial institutions. Total coverage for individual savers would be limited to a certain amount even if spread across several institutions, and records of individuals' or households' aggregate savings would be maintained by the insurance fund.[1]

The insured individual would pay the premiums for insurance under this system. Premiums would be collected from the interest or gains on covered assets, offset by a full tax deduction, and paid directly to the insurance fund by the institutions in which they are held. The premium would amount to 10 percent of annual earnings on assets (about 50 cents for every 5 dollars of earnings) until the fund reached the desired level. Thereafter, a premium of 1 percent of earnings would probably be more than adequate in a system covering all savers and their retirement plans. Insurance reserves would be invested in government securities and the system would be compulsory to ensure that all savers are covered, that reserves are adequate and that liability for losses is fairly distributed.

The system might begin with coverage limited to $250,000, as it is now under deposit insurance, but with automatic adjustments for inflation. Individual savers could choose the accounts they want covered if, as noted, the total amount covered was within the maximum allowed. A given account might include full or partial amounts held in savings deposits or certificates of deposit, in MMMFs, or in an individual retirement account (IRA) or other pension or retirement account. The saver would have the option to change the mix of accounts covered on an annual basis to reflect changes in anticipated needs, such as saving to buy a house or paying for a child's education.

This basic framework could be elaborated or modified in a number of ways. For example, it could better reflect the needs of savers by increasing the amount of coverage for accounts held in more than one name or for heads of household based on the number of dependents. Small savers could be given additional advantages, such as a waiver of premium payments on aggregate accounts under a given amount or a sliding scale for premiums based on gross income. To emphasize the protection of pension and retirement funds, the ceiling for coverage of assets held in such plans could be raised for individuals as they approach retirement age.

Some argue that moral hazard is inherent in any financial guaranty scheme (Davis, 2001), but the proposal to insure individual savers is one that confronts the moral hazard involved in insuring institutions: it can accommodate failure. For example, if an institution did not take the necessary steps to improve the quality of assets or address other problems and appears unlikely to do so, it would no longer be permitted to advertise that the individual accounts it holds are insured and it would be required to notify customers that accounts held there would not be covered after a certain date. While this would certainly create runs on individual institutions and result in failures, savings would move to other institutions before losses could occur. In this way, a generalized loss of confidence in the financial system would be avoided by an explicit assurance that institutions that are permitted to accept insured accounts are considered sound by regulatory authorities.

A more difficult and equally important problem to be addressed involves protecting transactions balances that constitute the nation's payment system. The extension of guaranties to MMMFs during the financial crisis raised critical questions about the amount of coverage needed and who should be covered. The current level of coverage is clearly inadequate and has made the insured, non-interest-bearing demand deposit offered by banks less attractive than transaction accounts that pay interest.

But the reality is that all transactions accounts must be covered regardless of the amount. The current limit on coverage is wholly inadequate in the case of employers, whether they are large or small businesses, state and local governments, or the many non-profit organizations active in community life. While we grapple with the problem of "too big to fail," the reality is that the failure of even a small bank can cause a major disruption if it holds the balances that make possible the economic activity of the community in which it is located. A community bank that holds deposits used to pay the bills of a local hospital cannot be allowed to default on those deposits since it would mean salaries could not be paid, supplies could not be purchased, and patients could not be cared for.

Obviously, any institution offering transactions accounts of whatever nature should be regulated in the same way that banks are regulated and, as now, be prohibited from paying interest on these accounts to discourage their use as savings accounts. All such institutions should report the aggregate amount of transactions accounts they hold daily to the Federal Reserve and bear the level of scrutiny required to assess the value of the assets in which they invest these accounts. The proposal for monetary reform offered in Part VI would solve some of the problems posed by the need to protect the payment system because all institutions would hold reserves created by the Fed and those reserves would be supplied to, and removed from, the liability side of their balance sheets. The Federal Reserve would, in effect, become the guarantor of the payment system.

IMPROVING GOVERNANCE OF PRIVATE PENSION FUNDS

The current framework governing private pension funds raises concerns about how plan sponsors and money managers meet their fiduciary responsibilities to beneficiaries. For example, the employer-sponsor of defined-benefit plans pools funds that include both the delayed compensation of employees and beneficiaries, as well as its own contributions. The employer-sponsor is entitled to assume responsibility for making decisions as to how the funds will be invested and by whom, how much will be paid for management fees, and who is to make corporate governance decisions about voting shares held by the plan. Under current US law, the status of beneficiaries is the same as that of nineteenth-century widows and orphans—that is, their rights as owners are subordinated to the decisions made by the fiduciary. The decisions taken by the fiduciary are assumed to be the same as those a "prudent man" would take in making decisions about his own affairs.

While labor unions play a role in administering some pension plans, most defined-contribution plans are also administered by employers. Defined-contribution plans convey more explicit ownership rights to beneficiaries than do defined-benefit plans. The account is held directly in the beneficiary's name and she has some choices as to the types of assets in which to invest as well as some ability to move or withdraw funds. However, since most defined-contribution plans are pooled to increase portfolio diversification, the individual beneficiary must accept the employer's choice of manager and forego the right to engage in managing the pool or actively participate in corporate governance decisions. Holders of IRAs and Keogh plans do make individual choices about the financial institutions in which they pool funds to ensure diversification of assets but, having selected an institution, they too become subordinate to the investment and corporate governance decisions of that institution's management.

In short, the majority of private pension and retirement plans are funneled into an institutional mix of money managers where the rights of owners of pension assets are shifted without any clearly defined, across-the-board rules governing the conduct of those managers (Blackburn, 2003). In this environment, managers feel free to charge exorbitant fees without regard to performance (Baker, 2003), and—as ably documented by the many analysts of Enron, WorldCom, and subsequent frauds and collapses—their investment and corporate governance decisions are frequently distorted by conflicts of interest, as discussed in Chapter 4 on the Employee Retirement Income Security Act (ERISA).

Given the level of actual and potential abuse, the framework for private pension and retirement plans needs to be restructured to remove conflicts of interest from the system. One improvement would be to allow owners of defined-contribution plans and IRAs to organize their own investment pools, select their own directors and managers, set fees and investment policies, and determine strategies for the exercise of corporate governance. There is precedence for pooling beneficiary-owned defined-contribution funds in the mutual structure of TIAA-CREF, the insurance fund that covers teachers and employees of non-profit organizations. These new funds need not be related to the workplace. They might instead be organized around geographic areas or specific investment goals or, as in the case of TIAA-CREF, particular types of work or professions. Nevertheless, they would still be subject to oversight by the Department of Labor and the IRS, as ERISA plans are now. Moreover, if individual accounts were federally insured as proposed above, the insurance agency would also have an oversight role.

The primary objective of the proposed mutual structure for defined-contribution plans is to increase pension asset owners' involvement in investment and corporate governance decisions, as well as to set appropriate fees for services, including the salaries of managers and analysts. But such a structure would also eliminate the fundamental and ineradicable flaw inherent in the current system as discussed in Chapter 4: the conflicts of interest that arise when institutional investors who manage more than one defined-benefit or defined-contribution plan avoid the risk of losing a plan sponsor as a client by not selling holdings of that company's stocks or bonds to protect beneficiaries of other plans.

Another problem that must be solved involves the issue of size in cases where there is market domination by very large individual funds or by managers entrusted with large numbers of funds. As discussed in Chapter 7, money management is the most concentrated financial sector. Wider price swings and one-way markets are two possible results of these types of concentration. Moreover, state government funds in populous states that cover many workers manage such large amounts of money that they find it difficult to make investments in small businesses—a major obstacle in channeling savings to a sector whose needs for credit are critical for expanding jobs and funding innovation. For these reasons and others discussed in Chapter 4, increasing the number of decision makers in the market is another important macroprudential aspect of pension fund reform. Creating a mutual structure for beneficiaries to manage defined-contribution and IRA pension assets would help begin that process.

NOTE

1. This would require modifying the reporting system to include all principal amounts in addition to current reports on interest income, and fair market value of IRA accounts that are already submitted to the Internal Revenue Service based on social security numbers.

PART III

The advent of globalization

12. Dollar hegemony

Part II dealt with the issues and outcomes of deregulation and financial innovation in a national setting, discussing reform proposals that primarily apply to financial institutions and regulators based in the United States (US). But, as Chapter 2 argued, the development of offshore markets in the 1960s and 1970s was one of the more powerful influences on changes in domestic financial structure and regulation. Much of the actual unwinding of existing regulations and many of the innovative strategies discussed in Part II were developed by offshore markets. Regulatory relaxations in the domestic market were often responses that validated what had already occurred in global financial markets.

The advent of globalization, however, was not limited in its powerful effects to alterations in financial structure and regulation. Those changes occurred in the context of a major shift in the international monetary system and were instrumental in shaping the structure of the global economy that emerged in the 1970s. Part III deals with two critical contributions to the emergence and growth of globalization—dollar hegemony and the investment of foreign exchange reserves—and conclude with an overview of developments in international financial markets in the 1990s that contributed to earlier crises outside the US and culminated in global recession in 2009. We begin with dollar hegemony because it was the critical element in the evolution of globalization and remains the foundation for global integration.

Acceptance of a national currency, the US dollar, as the primary means of payment in the global economy meant that other countries had to earn dollars to buy oil, other commodities, inputs for manufactured goods, and other goods and services that they needed to import from others. This resulted in a system based on the requirement for export-led growth for all economies other than the US. Given that US consumers could always pay in the currency earned or borrowed in their own economy, the US market became the desired outlet for exports from the rest of the world. And, being the preferred buyer of last resort for the rest of the world allowed the US to live beyond its means. It could do so because some of the dollars other nations earned by exporting to the US were saved as foreign exchange reserves and invested in dollar assets held in US financial markets. The net inflow from those investments provided an ample supply of credit to US buyers of goods produced abroad.

This particular paradigm created by the central role of the dollar in global payments has become increasingly fragile. It is an international payments system that depends on continued growth in the US economy as the necessary underpinning for confidence in the dollar. But because the US economy has become dependent on foreign savings to maintain growth and sustain its ability to buy the imports that generate those savings, the continuation of the current system depends on the ability of the US economy to support its immense and growing net debt to the rest of the world, a level of net debt that increases quarterly when, as continues to be the case, the US Commerce Department's Bureau of Economic Analysis reports yet another deficit in America's balance of payments.

The US balance of payments accounts were—and are—at the heart of an inescapable move toward globalization. They measure the nation's transactions with the rest of the world and are a critical indicator of sources and uses of funds in the global economy. The US became a debtor nation in 1989 and its chronic trade deficits—the measure of how much more it buys from foreign countries than it sells to them—matter to Americans because, by reducing opportunities to sell more goods at home and abroad, they diminish demand and output in the home economy.

For some, trade deficits are viewed as a reminder that the domestic jobs cut by selling fewer exports tend to be in high value-added sectors, while the jobs that have replaced them tend to be relatively low paying. Most observers acknowledge that the US trade deficit is a problem, but attribute the cause to anticompetitive practices such as export barriers, currency manipulation, and dumping by America's trading partners. Despite its vigor and persistence, the ongoing political debate over trade almost always casts the trade deficit as a stand-alone phenomenon.

In fact, the trade deficit stems from a wide set of causes—in particular, as noted, the dollar's key currency role in global payments and investment—and represents a larger set of imbalances. As long as non-residents hold and use dollars for trade and investment transactions, their demand for the currency keeps the dollar exchange rate at a level that increases the cost of US exports relative to competing foreign-made products. It also reduces the cost of imports relative to domestically produced goods. But since non-residents are willing to hold and invest dollars in American financial assets, the US can continue to run up a tab with the rest of the world even as its trade deficit widens.

The accumulating red ink simply shows up on the other side of the US balance of payments accounts, the capital account. By virtually any standard, the inflow of foreign capital measured by the capital account had become enormous in the 1990s and became the main support for US prosperity in that and the subsequent decade. But US dependence on foreign capital creates an unsustainable foundation for economic growth which the Federal Reserve and successive US administrations have ignored. They have taken credit for surges in economic growth during these years without acknowledging the role of foreign indebtedness in enabling the country to prosper by living beyond its means.

It is true, however, that a larger role for the dollar was inevitable given the reality of American economic power at the end of the Second World War, when the US accounted for 60 percent of world output, owned 60 percent of the world's gold reserves, had modest import requirements, and was able to produce much of what the rest of the world needed to resume post-war economic growth. US officials saw dollar hegemony as a way to increase the potential for US businesses and financial institutions to penetrate other markets and expand overseas operations. They also realized that the ability to freeze dollar accounts in US banks or in foreign banks operating in the US would add to the tools available to execute geopolitical strategies (Gisselquist, 1981).

As the dollar's role in cross-border payments came to dominate developments in both the US domestic and international financial markets, criticism of what has been called the "exorbitant privilege" accorded the US currency has been heard consistently from non-US public and private sources. Only a few American academics and non-profit organizations have raised concerns about how dollar hegemony affects the US and global financial systems and the economies of the US and the rest of the world. In the case of the US, policymakers consistently ignored evidence that capital flows initiated by dollar hegemony played a large role in promoting US growth in the 1990s and 2000s by supporting rising and unsustainable debt levels for both financial and non-financial sectors, and facilitated the 2008 crisis by expanding the liquidity that fed speculative activity. A discussion of how these developments evolved is necessary to understand not only how they contributed to the crisis but how they have eroded American financial and economic sovereignty despite—or because of—the use of the dollar as the world's transactions and reserve currency.

As might be expected, the story begins in an earlier decade. The defining moment was the Nixon administration's decision in August 1971 that the US would no longer pay out gold to other countries in exchange for dollars. Pressure from other countries to convert holdings of dollars into gold and the Bank of England's need to convert $700 million into gold to alleviate pressure on sterling threatened a run on the dollar in that year that would have greatly lowered its value and closed foreign exchange markets. The Smithsonian Agreement negotiated at that time included a devaluation of the dollar (from $35 to $38 for an ounce of gold) and upward revaluations of other currencies. But that agreement failed to prevent another, larger run on the dollar in February 1973 that prompted $10 billion of intervention by central banks to stabilize foreign exchange markets. The dollar was devalued again (to $42.50) and allowed to float (Dam, 1982).

There were several important byproducts of these years of monetary turmoil. Intervention by central banks to support the value of the dollar (or prevent the appreciation of their own currencies) resulted in a massive increase in foreign exchange reserves in the period 1970–74—an increase of 65 percent in 1971 alone (Dam, 1982). The outcome of these actions was an unprecedented increase in international liquidity that ignited ongoing inflation in the US and other countries throughout the 1970s. Another far-reaching outcome was that public sector influence over international monetary developments was substantially eroded as control of the international payments system and balance-of-payments financing shifted from national central banks to transnational private banks. The result was precipitous growth in the external (Eurocurrency) markets and a rising volume of cross-border capital flows that dwarfed the volume of trade.

Commenting on the dollar crisis in a series of articles published in the *Times* of London, the British economist Nicholas Kaldor described what he saw as the inevitable effects of the dollar's role on the American economy:

> The persistent large deficits in the United States balance-of-payments—given the universal role of the dollar as the medium for settling inter-country debts—acted in the same way as a corresponding annual addition to gold output … So long as countries preferred the benefits of fast growth and increasing competitiveness to the cost of participating in financing the United States deficit (or what comes to the same thing, preferred selling more goods even if they received nothing more than bits of paper in return), and so long as a reasonable level of prosperity in the United States (in terms of employment levels and increases in real income) could be made consistent with the increasing uncompetitiveness of United States goods in relation to European or Japanese goods, there was no reason why any major participant should wish to disturb these arrangements …
>
> [But] as the products of American industry are increasingly displaced by others, both in American and foreign markets, maintaining prosperity requires

> ever-rising budgetary and balance-of-payments deficits, which make it steadily less attractive as a method of economic management.
>
> If continued long enough it would involve transforming a nation of creative producers into a community of *rentiers* increasingly living on others, seeking gratification in ever more useless consumption, with all the debilitating effects of the bread and circuses of Imperial Rome. (Kaldor, 1971)

As it turned out, what Kaldor foresaw in 1971 aptly describes what deepened slowly over many years into the situation that still characterizes the American economy of today. As already noted, the US became a debtor nation in 1989. A decade later, at year-end 1999, its negative net international investment position reached 16 percent of gross domestic product (GDP). In the years before the downturn in 2002, it absorbed about 70 percent of global current account surpluses. By 2003, the country's net external debt had reached 24.1 percent of GDP and continued to rise in 2005 as the current account deficit reached 6.4 percent of GDP. A more worrisome measure of US vulnerability, however, was the stock of foreign investors' holdings of *marketable* instruments—US Treasury securities, stocks, bonds, and bank liabilities. These holdings—$6.78 trillion, or 62 percent of GDP at year-end 2003—are readily bought and sold in the uniquely deep US financial markets and even a small run-off in foreign holdings would inevitably exert upward pressure on US interest rates that could slow growth and undermine confidence in the American economy and its currency (US Department of Commerce, *Survey of Current Business*, various issues).

To conclude that America bought time for a continuation of its role as monetary hegemon leads one to ask why it did so and for whom. The obvious US beneficiaries were financial institutions. Non-financial corporations protested that the effects of the rise in the value of the dollar in the 1980s had undermined their competitiveness. But seeing no effective effort to address their concerns, many large American companies moved offshore to take advantage of a more favorable exchange rate position by selling into the home market rather than producing in it.

However, it is likely that the continuation occurred to some extent without conscious design—that these same countries (and others added to the list over the years) also participated in maintaining it for the reason Kaldor states: that it was a method of economic management that offered them fast growth and increasing competitiveness. But, as he suggested, it is a method of global economic management that cannot be sustained.

Many other non-US observers, however, continued to see dollar hegemony as a privilege. In its June 2005 *Annual Report*, for example, the Bank for International Settlements (BIS) noted that US external debt accumulation is limited by the fact that the rest of the world bears the exchange rate risk. Emerging economies that borrow in dollars suffer exchange rate losses when the home currency depreciates but US external assets benefit from exchange rate gains when the dollar depreciates. They argue that this effect, which some characterize as "debt relief," helps restrain the rise in the ratio of US net international liabilities to GDP.

Of course, if the dollar were to appreciate, the restraint on external debt growth could disappear or reverse as its increased value attracted more foreign savings. And, even with the valuation changes the BIS cites that shrink the net investment position, the dollar value of foreign-held assets as a share of US GDP continued to rise more rapidly than the rate of US output growth into the new millennium.

In a speech at a conference sponsored by the *Economist* and the CATO Institute in November 2003, Federal Reserve Board chairman Alan Greenspan addressed the issue of dollar hegemony, noting that the dollar's status as the world's primary reserve and transaction currency enlarged the capacity of the US to incur foreign debt relative to other nations. He acknowledged that having one's currency used as a store of value was both a blessing and a curse—a blessing because it encourages foreign investors to finance growing consumption and investment in the currency's country of issue and a curse because it can leave the issuing country overly dependent on foreign inflows, vulnerable to shifts in market sentiment, and isolated as the main source of demand growth.

At worst, Greenspan continued, the "curse" can expose a primary reserve currency issuer to the kind of damage England endured in its post-Second World War sterling crises. Recounting these episodes, he called attention to the severe pressure that post-war liquidation of foreign balances exercised on Britain's domestic economy. But he blamed the severity of that experience on one-time factors (notably a delay in removing wartime controls), implying that the dethroning of the pound holds few actionable lessons for prolonging—or managing a bloodless transition from—the reign of the dollar.

Instead, the Fed chair conjectured that market forces might someday spontaneously generate a new international monetary system in which the euro and other currencies share the dollar's role if the unrestricted advance of globalization were allowed. While he did not develop this idea in detail, the notion that an increasingly privatized international financial system could efficiently sort out the imbalances it helped create seems Panglossian at best.

Greenspan's conjecture also overlooked an extremely relevant piece of recent history. During the 1970s, a wider group of currencies did, in fact, account for larger shares of global reserve holdings. But the private sector's use of these currencies as stores of value proved highly disruptive as speculative movements ravaged the exchange rate stability needed for the expansion of trade. These disruptions reinforced Europe's desire to adopt a single currency. And they helped transform international banks from lenders to providers of financial insurance against the increased volatility of currency values and interest rates they themselves had created.

Meanwhile, in 2004—the year after Greenspan's assurance that dollar hegemony posed no immediate threat to the US or global economies—a net inflow of foreign investment pushed the ratio of total foreign holdings of US assets to 106.6 percent of GDP, up from 97.0 percent at year-end 2003 (US Department of Commerce, *Survey of Current Business*, various issues). This enormous inflow of foreign funds added to the run-up in US financial and non-financial sector debt and asset prices and set the stage for the crisis to come. And even after the Great Recession that followed the financial crisis, when prosperity in America and the rest of the world remained threatened by debt and job and wage deflation, there was no discussion of the need to change the destructive international monetary system that continues to weaken all participants in the global economy.

13. Foreign exchange reserves

Official foreign exchange reserves function as a keystone for the global monetary system. They provide a mechanism for countries to adjust the surpluses and deficits that constantly occur as individuals, firms, and government entities make payments to one another in the course of international trade and investment transactions. The majority of those payments are made in dollars, euros, yen, and pounds sterling, and most recently the renminbi, with smaller amounts in the currencies of other developed economies. Countries that do not issue these key currencies must acquire them in order for their citizens and companies to conduct most types of international transactions.

Foreign exchange reserves are created as these individuals and companies deposit payments denominated in key currencies in a domestic bank which subsequently redeems the funds for local currency with the nation's monetary authority. The central bank now owns a deposit with the foreign financial institution that issued the check and it usually invests that deposit in a reserve currency country's least risky debt securities in order to earn a return.

For example, foreign central banks invest their dollar reserves primarily in US Treasury bills and bonds and, before the 2008 crisis, the securities of US government-sponsored enterprises (GSEs) such as Fannie Mae and Freddie Mac. Reserves denominated in euros are invested in government securities issued by European Central Bank member countries such as Germany, France, and Italy. In this way, reserve holdings provide a source of credit for the country in which they are invested and backing for credit generated by the central bank of the country that owns them.

Because the largest share of international reserves is denominated in dollars, the US has become the main user of this credit source. By year-end 2003, foreign central banks and other foreign official entities had invested 69.2 percent ($2.1 trillion) of total reserve balances in US dollar assets. About half of that amount was held in domestic financial assets—an outstanding loan equivalent to 9.5 percent of US GDP at that time. Their ongoing purchases of government debt reduced the fiscal burden for US residents and permitted a larger share of domestic savings to flow into private financial assets (BIS, *Annual Report*, various issues; US Department of Commerce, *Survey of Current Business*, various issues).

Indeed, the stockpiling of dollar reserves was another factor that, in the 1970s and subsequent decades, set in motion an additional demand for securities in preference to US bank deposits. As the investment of dollar reserves held by other countries in US financial assets absorbed a larger share of government securities, US investors bought substitutes of similar maturity and size issued by GSEs like Fannie Mae and Freddie Mac and by private companies. In time, this was another of the many forces that fueled demand for mortgage-backed securities and helped create the housing bubble.

Meanwhile, the US holds a very small amount of foreign exchange reserves. Ironically, universal acceptance of the dollar as a transaction currency and store of value tends to constrain US chances to accumulate foreign exchange. Since the American end of almost all international trade and investment transactions is conducted in dollars, US citizens and non-financial firms acquire very little foreign currency. In addition, the Federal Reserve discourages holdings of balances denominated in foreign currencies in US domestic markets. Most of the small amount of foreign exchange reserves the Federal Reserve holds has been accumulated by intervening in foreign exchange markets and initiating swaps with other central banks.

Exports and capital inflows provide the major means for building international reserves. In all countries except the US (again, the dollar's dominant status makes the US exceptional), international reserves rise when export sales bring in more foreign exchange than the nation needs to pay for imports or service foreign currency denominated debt. Countries also accumulate reserves when their central banks exchange domestic currency for the foreign capital that flows into their national economies in the form of bank loans, purchases of securities, or direct purchases of companies or real estate.

In some cases, like the pre-1997 expansion of East Asian economies, huge trade surpluses and surging capital inflows can quickly ramp up the amount of international reserves. But Asia's 1997 financial crisis provided a cautionary lesson in how quickly these build-ups may dissipate in the face of massive outflows of foreign portfolio capital or when foreign creditors abruptly call in or fail to roll over foreign currency denominated loans.

Reserves also fall if nations use them to finance a trade deficit or to defend the value of a currency in foreign exchange markets. As discussed in Chapter 16, the experience of many Latin American countries in 1998 and 1999 provided a classic example of official reserves contracting sharply in response to multiple pressures.

The manifold uses of foreign exchange reserves explain why most countries need to hold them and why investors examine those holdings when assessing country risk in non-key currency nations. Stocks of international reserves provide crucial information about the ability of borrowers to service debts denominated in foreign currencies and the capacity of producers to purchase equipment, imported intermediate inputs, fuel, and other commodities. In developing and emerging market countries, holdings of official international reserves as assets on the central bank's balance sheet also influences the availability of credit, and gains and losses of reserves became increasingly important in the 1990s and early 2000s in determining trends in employment, income, and growth in affected economies. In 1999, for example, positive and negative changes in reserves exceeded 15 percent in 13 out of 23 emerging economies and topped 30 percent in four countries (IMF, 2000).

But while the gyrations of a dollar-denominated international reserve system dramatically jeopardized the financial stability of developing and emerging economies in the 1990s and early 2000s, their growth had seemingly little effect on developments in the US economy. America's expanding current account deficit did not discourage the ongoing flow of exports to the US or foreign investment in US financial assets. Other countries continued to be willing to sell goods for dollars due to America's enormous consumer market and the flourishing consumer credit system that helped US buyers purchase foreign goods. In addition, interest differentials among the major reserve currencies generally favored investment in dollar financial assets from 1994 onward.

Given the enormous inflows of foreign capital, it would be remarkable if the US had not experienced a run of general prosperity during the 1990s. But the external factors that contributed to the good times were not, in fact, sustainable; the mirror image of the growing official and private foreign debt was the immense run-up in domestic private sector indebtedness that set the stage for the 2008 crisis.

14. An overview of developments in global financial markets in the 1990s

Throughout the 1980s and 1990s, proponents of financial liberalization argued that lifting restrictions on international capital movements, deregulating national financial markets, and integrating those markets globally would spur economic growth worldwide and benefit developing nations in particular. On the surface, at least, part of that promise appeared to have been fulfilled by the beginning of the 2000s. Rising volumes of capital flows propelled the external and domestic debt of many countries to historically high levels and coincided with robust rates of economic growth.

Between 1995 and 2002, world output grew by 10.6 percent at market exchange rates (in US dollars). Measured by purchasing power parities—a weighted average of the price of goods and services across countries—the rise in world output totaled a spectacular 42.3 percent, far eclipsing growth in the preceding decade. Moreover, developing nations had assumed an advancing role in the global economy—a trend reflected in their growing share (38.1 percent) of global output. Much of the increase in these countries' aggregate share reflects the expansion of developing Asia, which contributed almost a quarter of global economic growth by year-end 2002. China's share (12.1 percent) was only three percentage points smaller than the euro area (15.7 percent), while India's share (4.8 percent) had surpassed that of the United Kingdom (3.1 percent) (IMF, 2003b).

Beneath the surface, however, global economic developments told a more complicated, less flattering story about unrestricted capital flows and decontrolled finance. For one thing, the large emerging economies that had expanded most impressively—China and India—had consciously resisted some of the main policy prescriptions associated with liberalization. For another, stark inequities continued to pervade the global system. Developing countries' share of world exports (20.3 percent) amounted to a little over half their share of global GDP. And the fact that 78.2 percent of the world's people lived in these countries underscores the gross disparity in output and income that persisted between the haves and the have-nots (IMF, 2003b).

Moreover, in the aggregate, the countries that most urgently needed external investment to flow through their borders in order to finance development had become net exporters of capital. In the wake of the 1998 Asian financial crisis, developing countries began a massive build-up of foreign exchange reserves to protect themselves in the event of future crises. Led by Africa and developing Asia, these countries enlarged their reserve holdings by 98.4 percent between 1995 and 2002, thereby increasing their reserve coverage as percentages of imports, external debt, and debt service requirements (IMF, 2003a).

At the same time and for similar reasons, private investors from developing countries substantially increased their deposits in foreign banks. These actions produced a major shift in the global makeup of capital flows. By the end of 2002, emerging economies as a group supplied a larger share of net outflows (–$125.2 billion) than the euro area (–$120.5 billion) and they contributed 23.7 percent of the net inflow to the US (IMF, 2003).

To be sure, not all emerging economies transformed themselves into net exporters of capital. Most African, Latin American, and Central and Eastern European countries continued to rely on capital inflows to finance current account deficits and support growth. In the Western Hemisphere, for example, developing nations' reserves fell far short of keeping up with expanding external debt between 1995 and 2002 (IMF, 2003a).

Still, these exceptions to the rule did not substantially alter aggregate flows of financial resources from the poor to the rich. And with their emergence as net creditors to the US, developing countries had a direct stake in the global system's most egregious imbalance: America's ballooning current account deficit.

By year-end 2002, America had become the global economy's dominant importer of both goods and capital. Net capital inflows to the US in that year amounted to $528 billion and absorbed a staggering 75.5 percent of total net capital outflows from the rest of the world. By contrast, shares of the other six largest net capital importers ranged from just 2.8 percent for Australia to a mere 1.4 percent for Portugal (IMF, 2003).

In 2002, the US current account deficit reached –$480.9 billion, or 4.7 percent of GDP. As the US deficit swelled, so did the number of countries in surplus and the amounts of their reserve holdings, thus deepening already substantial distortions in the global economy. The largest current account surpluses were posted by Japan, Germany, and China and they accounted for 37 percent of net capital exports as well (IMF, 2003a).

Over time, the net capital inflows that financed America's current account deficits left the US with a mounting stock of outstanding liabilities to the rest of the world. In 2002, its net foreign liabilities rose to $2.8 trillion or 25 percent of US GDP (US Department of Commerce, 2003). In absorbing such a disproportionate share of global savings, the US had become a borrower of first choice and buyer of last resort whose influence extended far beyond its commanding 21.1 percent of world output.

Of course, other nations have reinforced this influence through their reliance on exporting to US markets and acquiring dollar-denominated financial assets as the price of admission to those markets. By continuing to emphasize export-led growth, both emerging and advanced economies have perpetuated the US role as locomotive for the global economy. And in the decade before the 2008 crisis, their capital inflows provided the strong, ongoing stimulus that kept that locomotive on track.

Fortified by these inflows, US growth rates strengthened in the second half of the 1990s, reaching levels from one to one and a half percentage points higher than the US average in the years from 1985 through 1994, and outpacing growth in other G7 countries (IMF, 2003a). This superior performance appeared to confirm the unique potential of the American economy and validate public policy choices (notably the maintenance of positive interest rate differentials and a strong dollar) that precipitated ever-larger current account deficits.

PART IV

Building toward crisis in the global economy

15. Concerns and warnings

Despite America's superior economic performance in the 1990s, its halting recovery from a brief economic contraction at the beginning of the new millennium cast some doubt on assumptions about the benefits of globalization. A pick-up in household borrowing sustained United States (US) demand for imports in 2002 and thus bolstered growth in Asia's developing countries, but the global economy displayed relatively little forward movement. As growth slowed in the euro area and Japan, developing countries in the Western Hemisphere fell into recession as they lost access to capital flows (IMF, 2003a).

As a result, questions about the sustainability of US external deficits were raised and it seemed increasingly clear to some that America's relative economic and financial strengths might not be actually commensurate with its outsized role in the global system. Those concerns were expressed in the 2003 *Annual Report* issued by the central bank members of the Bank for International Settlements (BIS) and by Federal Reserve Board chairman Alan Greenspan in November 2003 at a conference sponsored by the *Economist* and the Cato Institute.

After describing how developments in the US drove the global economy in the 1990s, the BIS *Annual Report* chronicled a remarkable decline in the saving rate of US households that made America increasingly reliant on global savings while at the same time accounting for a disproportionate share of global demand growth. The report linked rising US external debt to a variety of domestic imbalances, including rapid credit growth, asset price increases, and overextended balance sheets. Given these developments, it argued that the build-up in US internal and external debt would reverse and thereby limit both US consumption and the export potential of other nations. Indeed, it warned that countries' continued pursuit of export-led development would actually inhibit global growth and that, in the current low inflation environment, problems of more generalized inflation might emerge. In addition, the BIS noted that slower growth had already reduced *potential* growth rates in Europe and Japan, diminished demand for imports in those countries, and could further complicate America's efforts to readjust external balances.

At the November 2003 conference, Greenspan addressed many of the same issues, acknowledging that the persistent US current account deficit was a growing concern because it added to the stock of outstanding external debt that could become increasingly more difficult to finance. In Greenspan's view, the question was whether the deficit would defuse benignly, as it did (temporarily) in 1986, or force a troublesome resolution (Greenspan, 2003).

While aspects of Greenspan's remarks were discussed in Chapter 12, further analysis is warranted in the context of the urgent warnings expressed by the BIS in this period. The former Fed chairman attributed widening imbalance in the US and global economy to increased layers of financial intermediation that made it easier to diversify and manage risk but that, at the same time, facilitated an ever rising ratio of domestic liabilities (and assets) to gross domestic product (GDP). However, rather than bemoan these imbalances, he lauded the growth of international financial intermediation for creating an ever larger class of investors willing to break away from the inhibitions of "home bias" (i.e. investing their funds in domestic assets) and thus move such a large share of the world's savings to America.

One of the striking aspects of Greenspan's speech, however, was what he didn't say. Describing the build-up of record payment imbalances, the head of the world's most powerful central bank did not acknowledge that US monetary policy may have helped spark capital inflows well in excess of the amount needed to finance US current account deficits by maintaining interest rate differentials between the dollar and other key currencies that placed the dollar at an advantage in terms of expected rates of return. He also failed to explain why the Fed had failed to sterilize some portion of the inflows, continuing its benign neglect in conducting monetary policy as if there were no inflows and no external market for dollar assets and liabilities. A casual observer hearing the chairman's remarks might have concluded that Fed decisions played no role in creating the global imbalances which, Chairman Greenspan acknowledged, were a source of some concern.

As for correcting the imbalances, Chairman Greenspan thought the reluctance of foreign investors to accumulate additional US debt and equity claims would likely serve as the restraint on the growth of US imbalances. He didn't explain what might trigger that reluctance but implied it would form the first stage of a relatively painless process in which market forces would incrementally defuse the worrisome build-up of the current account deficit and net external debt as long as globalization was allowed to proceed and create an ever more flexible international financial system.

By contrast, the BIS report was more prescriptive in terms of policy. Anticipating the possibility of a financial crisis and recession and addressing the problems of deflation and lagging demand (and, by inference, payments imbalances), it endorsed the idea that monetary authorities should use unconventional means to provide liquidity when interest rates reach the zero bound. It recommended that central banks use any asset—preferably financial and beginning with long-term bonds—to supplement their balance sheets in an effort to prevent or contain deflation. However, it also cautioned that central banks would be taking a private sector risk and could experience large losses which might need the adoption of a framework for central banks to share these losses with governments.

Other BIS prescriptions included encouraging Europe and Japan to undertake structural adjustment and urging central banks to respond more effectively to the aftermath of booms. Its report chastised the US and Japan for adopting poorly conceived and/or ineffective fiscal stimulus and again noted that America's household saving rate must climb to help shrink the current account deficit. In addition, it breezily suggested that the shift towards a service-based economy in the industrial world should accelerate given the growth and rising productivity of emerging economies.

16. Crises in the periphery of the global system

The context for concerns about the sustainability of the global system at the beginning of the new millennium was yet another of the ongoing series of crises that had plagued emerging and developing countries over the previous two decades. The crises that struck the periphery of the global system started in the 1980s as deregulation and monetary instability began to cause problems that left national governments and central banks defenseless in response to increasingly large international capital inflows followed by equally sizable outflows. As a result, growth and rising productivity in emerging economies had come at a heavy cost.

The first of these crises began with Mexico's default on its debt to international banks in 1982; the second was the rapid outflow of foreign money from Mexico in 1994 after a period of heavy inflows from 1990 through 1993; the third was the East Asian crisis as, again, heavy foreign inflows reversed into outflows in 1997–98; and the fourth was what was called the "synchronous" crisis of 2002 when the bursting of stock market bubbles in developed countries spilled over into emerging market economies already weakened by two decades of crises that brought sporadic growth followed by financial and economic collapse.

LATIN AMERICA'S LOST DECADE: 1982–90

The crisis that began in 1982 was the outcome of the strategy for recycling Organization of Petroleum Exporting Countries (OPEC) surpluses after the oil price increase in the mid-1970s, a strategy that was the result of both public and private sector decisions to place the surpluses in international banks for lending to what were then called lesser-developed countries. The effect was to make these countries the new locomotive for the global economy. The expectation was that their growth would increase exports from industrialized countries and even out the increased cost of the hike in oil prices. But that strategy was upended by the second oil price increase at the end of the decade, and the sharp rise in dollar interest rates as the US fought inflation and the falling value of the dollar; it became clear that the now heavily indebted middle-income countries could not roll over their debts at the higher rates and shorter maturities on offer from their creditors. The most burdensome element was the realization that the foreign exchange needed to service the debt accumulated in the 1970s and any additional borrowing would have to be earned and could only be earned by exporting to industrialized countries with strong currencies.

Foreign lending dried up as it became clear that the most heavily indebted developing countries—most of which were in Latin America—could no longer serve as expanding markets for industrialized countries' exports but would have to export their way out of debt. Not only did the strategy not provide the outcome anticipated in terms of channels for trade, it had put international banks at risk—especially US banks, which had been the major recipients of OPEC surpluses and the major lenders to Latin America. Recognition that defaults by these countries could greatly erode the capital of the nine largest US international banks was a factor in the Congressional decision to add to legislation funding the International Monetary Fund (IMF) in 1983 an explicit capital requirement for banks (Cline, 1983). But the surplus funds of OPEC countries were also at risk and part of US government strategy was to encourage those countries to move funds into the US and invest them in Treasury bonds and mortgage-backed securities issued by the government-sponsored enterprises (GSEs), Fannie Mae and Freddie Mac.

The Latin American debt crisis caused private and public international financial institutions to focus on the need for developing countries to expand export capacity as a sign that a country was regaining creditworthiness. The IMF instituted conditions for multilateral credits that suppressed demand in these countries to induce falling imports so that export surpluses would service debt and result in external adjustment. Consequently, the export-led growth strategy emerged in tandem with immense negative resource transfers. Over the years from 1983 through 1989, negative net outflows from Latin America amounted to *minus* $116 billion as heavily indebted countries used all foreign exchange earned from exports to service external debt (IMF, 1995).

The debt crises of the 1980s and 1990s moved export capacity to the center of development policy despite little evidence that strong currency countries other than the US were willing to accept the current account deficits needed to ensure their success. Moreover, given the debt overhang, rising exports could not and did not spur growth in the heavily indebted countries in the 1980s. But the export-led growth strategy also failed to inhibit the expansion of external debt. The total external debt of developing countries continued to grow, rising from about $1 trillion at the beginning of the 1990s to $2 trillion in 1999. While the decline in debt as a share of exports of goods and services, from 198.2 percent to 160.9 percent between 1991 and 1998, attests to the success of the strategy in raising the volume and value of exports, the ratio of debt service payments to exports for all developing countries rose from 22.4 percent to 24 percent over the same period. For developing countries in the Western Hemisphere, however, debt service as a percentage of exports rose from 39.3 percent to 45.7 percent (IMF, 1999).

THE MEXICAN CRISIS OF 1994–95

As noted, Mexico's inability to service its debt in 1982 had inaugurated the first crisis involving developing countries and it inaugurated the second as well. Capital inflows and outflows had continuously destabilizing impacts on the Mexican economy throughout the 1990s. Prompted by recession and lower interest rates in the US and other Organisation for Economic Co-operation and Development (OECD) countries in 1989–90, international capital moved back into the developing world in search of higher returns. But, in the years 1990 through 1993, most of the inflow to Mexico was in the form of portfolio investment in stocks rather than through bank loans, creating a new dynamic in terms of its financial and economic effects and new challenges for policy responses.

The shift in the channel for flows to developing countries reflected the change in investment patterns in the markets of industrialized countries. As discussed in Chapter 4, the institutionalization of savings—that is, the choice of pooled funds held by pension funds, life insurance companies, mutual funds, and investment trusts as repositories for the majority of savings—increased the share of funds invested in securities and enhanced the role of institutional investors compared to that of depository institutions. And this shift was taking place in other OECD countries as well as in the US. In fact, the slowdown in international bank lending after the 1982 debt crisis had encouraged the growth of the Eurobond market as a source of financing for corporations and governments of OECD countries; this became an increasingly attractive substitute for more expensive domestic bond markets in some industrialized countries.

Portfolio investment in Mexico and other developing countries became possible when many of these countries began to relax exchange controls and open their capital accounts at the end of the 1980s and the beginning of the 1990s. It was enabled by the response of institutional investors who saw international diversification as beneficial and increased investments in newly created emerging market mutual funds. These funds accounted for about 30 percent of new international investment by US mutual funds during the period 1990–94, while pension funds also contributed to the flow, investing through mutual funds or directly for their own accounts (D'Arista and Griffith-Jones, 2001).

As noted, capital inflows to Mexico initially were largely in the form of portfolio investment in stocks. As the market boomed, appreciating stocks used as collateral for bank loans set off a domestic credit boom that peaked in 1994 after stock prices had already begun to decline. Thus, while there is a strong association between a rise in credit and in stock prices, the volume of foreign investment in stocks was the cause of both the credit boom and the asset bubble in Mexico (Griffith-Jones, 2001). For example, capital inflows to Mexico rose to 192 percent of domestic credit flows in 1993. This was—or should have been—a whole bouquet of red flags signaling the dangers ahead: in particular, the collapse of the banking system after the 1994 crisis imploded the value of stock used as collateral to back new bank loans in this period. As a result, the instability generated by capital flows in both stock and credit markets inhibited growth in credit and market infrastructure and left a lingering legacy. At year-end 2001, outstanding credit as a percent of Mexico's GDP was 23 percentage points below the level in 1994. Moreover, total outstanding credit ($153.3 billion) was significantly lower than Mexico's external debt of $232 billion (D'Arista, 2003).

In the case of Mexico, it is clear that monetary policy did not and could not offset the adverse effects of capital flows. Given that portfolio flows provided the primary channel for inflows in the early 1990s, that direct investments augmented that channel in the latter part of the decade, and that the supply of domestic credit was too small to use as a fulcrum to sterilize inflows or offset outflows, the central bank had no tools to stabilize financial markets and support demand-led growth. Only the export sector could thrive since it could earn US dollars to buy needed imports and repay debt used to finance production.

While the export-led growth strategy was effective in expanding the size of the economy, it required the Bank of Mexico to maintain high interest rates to attract foreign inflows and maintain an exchange rate much lower than the fixed rate in the earlier years of the decade to ensure that prices of exports remained competitive in the global economy. Again, this was a policy that constrained non-export sectors by raising the cost of capital, credit, and imports and driving up prices for a more limited supply of goods produced in domestic markets for domestic consumption.

Meanwhile, the resumption of net inflows into Mexico in 1997 did not augment the supply of domestic credit. Much of the inflow was denominated in dollars and invested in the export sector. Given the net decline in the flow of credit in 1994 (46.5 percent), outstanding credit as a share of GDP fell to 24.7 percent in 2001, the year in which the next crisis period emerged (D'Arista, 2003).

THE MONETARY AND FINANCIAL CONSEQUENCES OF NAFTA FOR MEXICO

On top of the setbacks resulting from the 1994–95 crisis, the monetary and financial repercussions of the adoption of the North American Free Trade Agreement (NAFTA) in 1994 created additional, serious, ongoing disadvantages for Mexico. The removal of capital controls and the opening of these financial sectors to foreign financial institutions were integral parts of the agreement. Their adoption contributed to the contraction in domestic credit that caused increased reliance on external borrowing, impeded growth in many non-export sectors, and undermined domestic demand. Mexico became more dependent on exports for growth and on its major—almost exclusive—trading partner, the US, as a market for its products.

The increase in trade among the NAFTA economies in this period was often cited as evidence of the agreement's success. Total exports within the group rose from $239.6 billion in 1990 to $685.6 billion in 2000. US exports to its NAFTA partners climbed from 28.3 percent to 37.2 percent of its total exports over the decade, while Canada's rose from 74.6 percent to 87.3 percent and Mexico's from 79.4 percent to 89.5 percent of their total exports over the same period. But the rise in Canada's exports to Mexico—from 0.39 to 0.51 percent of its total exports—and Mexico's exports to Canada—from 0.49 to 2.04 percent of its total exports (World Trade Organization, 2001)—suggest that NAFTA increased Canadian and Mexican dependence on the US and inhibited diversification of their markets even within the trading bloc itself.

More importantly for Mexico, however, was the fact that the gains in trade did not translate into comparable gains in growth. GDP growth was stronger (and inflation lower) before the peso crisis in 1995. For the period 1994–2000, Mexico's real average annual rate of growth of 3.6 percent was below that of the US and Canada and inflation averaged 24 percent (IMF, 2002a). Moreover, the value of Mexico's external debt jumped from 25 to 58.3 percent of GDP in 1995 and ended the decade above 40 percent, with debt service payments averaging around 3 percent of GDP for most of the period (IMF, 2002b).

The instability generated by the impact of capital flows on the growth and contraction of Mexican credit markets suggests that any effort to develop a robust financial system would have been likely to fail. Indeed, the collapse of credit in Mexico coincides with the increase in foreign ownership of financial institutions. This increase was greatly facilitated by provisions in NAFTA. Access to the financial markets of other parties was a primary issue in the agreement affecting finance. Responsibilities were placed on the host country to provide the same treatment and opportunities for financial institutions domiciled in other NAFTA countries as those afforded its own domestic institutions.

Mexico was given a transition period during which it could limit the share of total assets and capital of foreign financial institutions. During this period, it could request consultations to determine the existence of threats to the Mexican market and payments system if ownership by foreign banks reached 25 percent of the aggregate capital of all banks in Mexico. But any actions it took could be challenged by Canada or the US. Also, during the four years after the end of the transition period, Mexico could freeze group capital limits once (for a period of only three years) if capital limits for foreign financial institutions—25 percent for banks and 30 percent for securities firms—had been reached.

While there are important safeguards in the agreement,[1] Mexico was left with few options for implementing them. The pattern of lending by foreign banks did not support the development of domestic credit and the kinds of policies the Mexican government and central bank might take to increase access to credit and stimulate its growth would tend to have limited acceptance by foreign financial institutions or their governments. If the supply and availability of credit remained inadequate to expand demand-led growth, Mexico would remain dependent on export-led growth and on US markets for exports.

In 2001, for example, growth slowed in the US and Canada and real GDP contracted by –0.3 percent in Mexico. Domestic credit shrank by an amount equal to almost 1 percent of Mexico's GDP (IMF, 2003a). A net capital inflow of $22.3 billion was the only source of new credit as the dominant foreign banking sector shunned lending in pesos in favor of lending US dollars and euros from their home offices abroad. The export sector continued to borrow since it could earn external currencies to repay credits. For other sectors, the cost of borrowing was prohibitive and the volume of goods and commodities produced for domestic consumption fell. Thus, even as the value of Mexico's exports to the US declined, its dependence on the trading relationship—and on external dollar-denominated borrowing—intensified, exacerbating its position as a client state tied to its northern neighbor.

CRISES SPREAD: ASIA (1997–98) AND THE "SYNCHRONOUS DOWNTURN" OF 2002

When the Asian crisis erupted in 1997 and spread to other continents in 1998, funding channels that had previously brought in abundant capital in the aggregate to emerging economies essentially shut down within a matter of months. During 1998, cross-border loans to these countries fell by –$83.6 billion, effectively canceling the $76.7 billion net inflow in 1997, and fell an additional –$41.7 billion in 1999 while their international bond issuance declined by half. In Thailand, where the crisis originated, international bank credit plummeted by –$61.5 billion between 1997 and September 1999. As funding was withdrawn in Korea and other crisis countries (including Russia with a drop of –$12.8 billion), the effects reverberated throughout Asia with loans to China decreasing by $20.1 billion over the same period (BIS, 2000).

As borrowers in Asia and Latin America spent much of 1999 paying down their bank debt, lendable funds piled up in the external interbank market and eventually sparked a new round of speculative activity. According to the BIS, this activity included financing hedge funds and carry trade currency bets. Consequently, after the Asian and Russian crises, cross-border lending decisively shifted to developed countries even as flows moderated following the disruptive collapse of Long-Term Capital Management in 1998 (BIS, 2000). Between year-end 1996 and the third quarter of 2001, outstanding cross-border and foreign currency claims of BIS reporting banks on developed countries rose by $3.8 trillion or 76 percent, despite a –$315 billion drop in claims on Japan. Meanwhile, aggregate flows to developing countries suggest that 1998 was more the beginning than the end of contraction for most of these countries (BIS, 2002b).

But the international banking market faced a new crisis as banks severely contracted their cross-border lending by –$108.6 billion in the second quarter of 2001 and ventured to loan only $4.3 billion in the third quarter. Against the backdrop of US recession and the September 11 attacks on New York and Washington, they reduced exposure to other banks and to Japanese and emerging market borrowers while modestly increasing investments in euro-area government securities and in debt issued by US GSEs such as Fannie Mae and Freddie Mac (BIS, 2002b).

The abrupt contraction between the first and second quarters of 2001 illustrates the pronounced pro-cyclical nature of the international banking market. During good times, banks inevitably ratchet up cross-border loans. But as the effect of debt build-ups gradually becomes more evident, caution and retrenchment inevitably follow the surge of over-lending. While that pattern had recurred repeatedly in emerging economies, the second quarter in 2001 was clearly a reaction—as the BIS had warned—to the risks accompanying excessive credit expansion in Europe and the US.

In fact, a new, distinct crisis began when large declines in major stock markets in the second and third quarters of 2002 reverberated throughout the global economy. Between May and July, the US S&P 500 lost 26 percent of its value; the London FTSE 100 lost 26 percent, Germany's DAX 30 percent, and Japan's TOPIX 11 percent. As discussed in Chapter 4, the drop in the US market produced a negative wealth effect equaling 70 percent of households' disposable income—the first sizable and widespread impact experienced by the US economy in the wake of a financial crisis since the turmoil of the 1970s (IMF, 2002).

Meanwhile, capital flows to emerging market countries—already weak in the first quarter of 2002—slowed further and then reversed in the second quarter as investors pulled money out of emerging-market mutual funds, depressing equity values in almost all countries except China, Indonesia, and Thailand. The second-quarter slide in the stock markets of emerging economies began with a crushing sell-off in Brazil, which hit the rest of Latin America particularly hard and resulted in sinking exchange rates for the Argentine, Brazilian, and Mexican currencies (IMF, 2002).

The exchange rate shifts that occurred in the wake of the slide in stock values in emerging economies had a substantial impact on their external deposits in BIS-reporting banks. During the first quarter of 2002, Asian businesses, households, and governments resumed their net placement of strong-currency deposits abroad while their counterparts in Latin America and the Middle East withdrew large amounts. Despite the volume of these withdrawals—and despite an aggregate decline in emerging economies' deposits that began in the third quarter of 2001—developing countries as a group remained net creditors to international banks, as they had been since the Asian crisis erupted in 1997–98 (BIS, 2002a).

At the end of March 2002, the external deposits of all emerging economies exceeded their debts to banks by $212.7 billion—mostly due to Asian borrowers' crisis-borne decision to use balance of payments surpluses to pay down debt and build up precautionary balances in foreign currencies—providing vivid evidence of just how little cross-border lending had contributed to development. Portfolio investment in developing countries also fell as investors became more selective and narrowed what had been the primary channel for inflows during the emerging market boom of 1990–94.

Brazil was hit particularly hard by developments in this period. Its currency, the *real*, lost half its value between April and July 2002 and its sovereign debt spread—the amount of interest charged above an indicator such as the rate on US government securities—rose by 24 percent. Since nearly one third of Brazil's domestic debt was linked to the exchange rate, the *real*'s steep depreciation drove the value of domestic and external debt to levels that could not be serviced without dragging the economy into depression. Debt restructuring was clearly needed to conserve earnings in order to finance ongoing economic activity. It was also needed for the creditors holding the debt since international banks' outstanding external claims on Brazil ($95 billion at that time) accounted for 11.2 percent of their total exposure to emerging economies, with 24 percent held by US banks and 18 percent by Spanish banks (IMF, 2002).

But Spanish banks held even larger shares of the debt of other Latin American countries, including Chile, Colombia, Mexico, and Venezuela (IMF, 2002). The concentrations in holdings of emerging economies' debt by individual banks and groups of banks from a given country underscored the vulnerability of lenders and their national banking systems to troubles that arose in these borrowing economies. But they also constituted a problem for developing nations whose funding needs increasingly depended on market conditions in countries that supplied the preponderance of their credit.

Among the effects loosed incongruously on Latin America was concern about war in the Middle East and its potential impact on the US economy. This concern, rather than concerns about their domestic policies or national economic developments that could have been anticipated or avoided, caused both the Brazilian *real* and the Mexican peso to drop sharply after April 2002. But these concerns about policy choices in the US had deep and lasting repercussions not only on debt service requirements but also inflation expectations and growth prospects.

Ironically, the *real* and peso were declining against the greenback at the same time the dollar was falling and *because* the dollar was falling. Recognizing that 89 percent of Mexican exports were sold to the US, investors were concerned that a weaker dollar would lower US imports and erode dollar earnings needed to service Mexican debt. Moreover, a weaker peso would increase Mexico's competitiveness and make it harder for rival Latin American exporters to earn the dollars needed to service their debts. For Brazil—with the majority of its external borrowing and half of its domestic debt linked to the value of the dollar—these same debt-service and trade dynamics acted to push the country harder in the direction of debt restructuring and further unraveled investor confidence (BIS, 2002a).

Hanging over all these déjà vu phenomena was the region's disheartening track record of economic growth. Between 1994 and 2001, developing countries in the Western Hemisphere saw their GDP increase by an annual average of 2.9 percent—barely more than half the growth rate for all emerging economies (5.3 percent) and equal to Latin American growth in 1984–93, a period that included the "lost decade" when debt service payments produced a cumulative $116 billion net capital outflow to industrial-country creditors (IMF, 2003a).

As United Nations economist José Antonio Ocampo pointed out, the region's economies grew only half as rapidly in 1997–2002—the heyday of liberalized economic policy—as they did during the era of state-led industrialization from the mid-1940s through the 1970s. He also observed that output growth for 1997–2002 fell well below the average annual rate (4.1 percent) needed to meet the goal of reducing Latin America's 1990 poverty levels by half. Equally telling, economic activity failed to keep up with population increases. From 1984 through 1993, the region's average annual economic growth registered a paltry 0.9 percent on a per capita basis. Between 1997 and 2000, average annual per capita growth slipped to zero (Ocampo, 2002).

As the effects of the crisis rolled across emerging countries, policy discussions focused on how to deal with the next ones, assuming more would come—as they did. Countries were given advice about how to manage debt structures that amplify external shocks, such as excessive reliance on floating rate instruments, very short maturity structures, or loans indexed to foreign currency movements. While this advice may have been sensible as far as it went, it failed to confront the central problem to which its prescription so clearly alludes: emerging economies possess at best an extremely limited ability to use their own currencies in transactions outside their own borders. Having been encouraged to open those borders and engage in the global economy, they had, as a group, incurred mounting debts denominated in strong currencies. And as developments in Latin America in the early 2000s confirmed, even careful management of external debt could not guaranty sustained adequate growth or insulation from future external crises.

NOTE

1. The agreement acknowledged the right of a party to take prudential measures to protect the domestic customers of foreign financial institutions and to maintain the safety, integrity, and stability of the country's financial system. Moreover, it stated that nothing in the agreement restricts "non-discriminatory measures of general application taken by any public entity in pursuit of monetary and related credit policies or exchange rate policies" (chapter 14, article 1410).

17. Liquidity expansion in the period before the crisis

Flows to and from the US seemed to demonstrate that the rapid expansion in global liquidity created by industrial countries' stimulative monetary policies did not abate with the Federal Reserve's measured increases in policy rates in 2004. In fact, those rate hikes spurred a sharp jump in foreign private investment as rising dollar yields encouraged carry trade strategies based on borrowing in yen (at low rates) for investments in higher-yielding dollar assets. According to the Commerce Department's Bureau of Economic Analysis, US banks' liabilities to foreign investors grew by a record three times the level of the 2003 increase as, over the course of the year, these rising liabilities formed the primary channel for carry trade transactions (US Department of Commerce, 2005).

At the same time, US banks' loans to foreign borrowers jumped $356.1 billion in 2004 (compared to an increase of only $9.6 billion in 2003) and stocks of cross-border and foreign exchange claims surged by $1.23 trillion as banks joined hedge funds and other leveraged players in a rising tide of investment in higher-yielding emerging-market assets. These exports of excess liquidity tended to increase dollar reserves in the recipient emerging economies and thereby triggered return flows to the US in the form of foreign investment. Dollar reserves doubled from 1996 to 2003 and accounted for 70 percent of total international reserves (BIS, 2004). For the year ending in March 2004, official financing flows to the US rose to 2.9 percent of US GDP (US Department of Commerce, 2005).

Many emerging economies accumulated foreign exchange reserves as a result of official attempts to prevent domestic liquidity build-ups by buying dollar inflows rather than permitting their conversion to local currencies. However, by subsequently using the dollars to buy US Treasury securities, these countries re-exported the problem back to the US. Their purchases augmented the highly liquid conditions in US financial markets, drove down interest rates on medium- and long-term securities even as the Fed was raising short-term rates, relieved Americans of some of the burden of financing fiscal deficits, facilitated the growth of US household debt, and fueled another round of capital outflows from the US that would make the same round-robin trip back to the US in a relatively short period of time.

As the BIS and IMF stated in separate reports (BIS, 2003, 2004; IMF, 2004), low interest rates and abundant liquidity in 2004 sparked a worldwide search for yield and encouraged borrowing for leveraged investments. But, as already noted, the flows generated by these transactions became a mechanism for a further expansion of global liquidity and additional downward pressure on interest rates. While these accommodative market conditions supported strong growth in the world economy in 2004, they facilitated an excessive expansion of debt relative to output that contributed to the financial crisis, recession, and stagnation.

Meanwhile, the expanded use of credit derivatives and structured products such as collateralized debt obligations was changing the systemic transmission of liquidity risk. The BIS triennial survey in 2005 revealed that the market for these instruments grew 568 percent in the three years ending June 2004, with "robust" expansion in over-the-counter (OTC) contracts. For example, the notional value of credit default swaps (CDS) rose to $6.4 trillion, of which $2.7 trillion (42 percent) represented contracts between reporting dealers (BIS, 2005c).

As these data illustrate, rising concern about the systemic threat of concentration in financial markets was not misplaced. In the US, a handful of the largest banks dominated OTC derivatives markets and the fact that this limited number of dealers accounted for both sides of 42 percent of all CDS contracts meant that liquidity in derivatives and their underlying markets would drastically shrink if one or more of these institutions were compelled to unwind their positions.

Nevertheless, official as well as private views of derivatives markets at the time heralded the beneficial changes they had introduced. They were said to have expanded the investor base, provided more opportunities for diversification, tightened market integration, and increased the depth of trading (i.e. market liquidity). On the other hand, many acknowledged that it was doubtful that all market participants understood the complexity of these instruments and their hidden risks. Moreover, market participants' penchant for using similar quantitative models to assess value could lead to herding behavior that drains liquidity (BIS, 2005).

But the BIS continued to stress the need to curb excess liquidity and urged central banks to raise interest rates, arguing that:

> tendencies to boom and bust behavior might be aggravated by easy monetary conditions ... Being able to borrow at very low interest rates provides incentives to credit creation, carry trade behavior and leverage, all of which have been increasingly evident in financial markets in recent years. From this

> vantage point, the fact that the prices of all non-monetary, "illiquid" assets (long-term bonds, credit instruments, houses, etc.) have risen rapidly over the last few years, and that measures of implied volatility are down sharply ... could reflect a generalized effort to "buy liquidity" or "sell liquidity" given a surfeit of the latter ... Thus, one important task for policymakers in this new environment is to assess what policies might best help limit the costs of something going wrong. (BIS, 2005, pp. 9–10)

In prescribing interest rate hikes to curb leverage and speculation in this period, the BIS and IMF appear to have remained committed to the deregulated system even as they acknowledged that problems had been fueled on the supply side. Such an admonition—to raise policy rates to curb speculation—seems a woeful acknowledgment of the extent to which lack of financial regulation can undermine the tools needed to support and stabilize economic growth.

Meanwhile, the build-up in international liquidity continued in 2005 for the fourth consecutive year, with claims in the external banking market rising 18.2 percent to $20.7 trillion (BIS, 2005b). The US current account deficit also rose and was largely financed by private carry trade investments in US assets using borrowings in low-interest rate yen to exchange for dollars. Low interest rates on dollar assets narrowed the profitability of traditional carry trades and induced investors into value trades that used credit derivatives such as collateralized debt obligations to boost returns. In the fall of 2005 and the spring of 2006, the IMF and BIS warned that borrowing for speculative purposes had come to dominate cross-border transactions (IMF, 2005, September; BIS, 2006a).

Another critical development in 2005 was the increased use of low-risk government debt as collateral for private financial transactions—this amounted to about 20 percent of the stock of US and Japanese government debt and over half the stock of euro-area government debt. Of the total public debt used as collateral for carry trades, repos, and other transactions, 30 percent ($1.7 trillion) of the combined claims were held by banks not chartered in the countries that issued the debt (BIS, 2006).

This development laid the foundation for the problems that governments of Mediterranean members of the euro area would face after the crisis emerged. The banks using these government debt obligations as collateral assumed that all euro-denominated government debt was equally marketable and would remain so. Moreover, they assumed there was no special risk in buying euro-denominated government debt paying higher interest rates. Given the scarcity of debt issues of the larger countries, they poured funding into government debt in smaller economies and encouraged its expansion—especially in Greece. It seems no one thought this might create problems down the road and, when it did, the blame was placed squarely on the shoulders of the borrowers, not the lenders. Having accepted the belief that regulation by market forces was superior to that of government agencies, the regulators of the financial institutions engaged in such an exceptional level of speculation in this period took no responsibility for either the causes or consequences of the outcome.

PART V

Debt and the collapse of monetary control

18. The failure to halt the emergence and growth of the debt bubble

Monetary policy played a major role in creating the conditions that culminated in the financial crisis of 2008. Understanding that role and why the Federal Reserve was unable to end the credit freeze afterwards are critical components of the analysis needed to implement effective reform. The link between the excess liquidity created by foreign capital inflows, the build-up in debt, and the asset bubbles inflated by unbalanced and excessive lending are outcomes of monetary as well as regulatory policy failures. The first section of Part V deals with the Fed's seeming obliviousness to these causes. The second section focuses on the Fed's failure to fully recognize and correct the substantial weakening of its ability to implement countercyclical initiatives.

One underlying cause of the Fed's failure was its adherence to ideology. Belief in the efficient markets hypothesis and the adoption of capital requirements for banks as the macroprudential tool most compatible with market forces replaced the Fed's earlier commitment to using the link between open market operations and changes in reserve requirements as its primary lever to curb and stimulate credit. The Fed's complicity in accepting the inevitable severing of that lever by deregulation and structural change led it to rely on open market operations to achieve only one objective: to influence the demand for credit by changing the short-term policy rate. The other, critical component of the countercyclical tool-kit, the central bank's ability to influence the credit *supply*—the truly monumental contribution to macroeconomic policy that the Fed itself had initiated in the first half of the twentieth century—had been lost (D'Arista, 1994).

Rather than restore a direct influence over credit expansion and contraction, the Fed adhered to outdated tools and policies in ways that became increasingly counterproductive. Too often its actions exacerbated cyclical behavior in financial markets, even when the intent was to exert a countercyclical influence. Looking back at developments in the first decade of the new millennium, it seems reasonable to ask if the central bank itself had contributed to instability and, if so, what must be done to reconstitute a constructive path for monetary policy.

A no less important subject for analysis is the ineffectiveness of the Fed's role as a lender of last resort (LOLR) during the crisis. The bailout of Bear Stearns in March 2008 demonstrated that the Fed was unprepared to face a systemic crisis. Throughout 2008, it struggled to act systemically, joining with the Treasury in a series of inconsistent and sometimes frantic improvisations that relied on merging large, weak institutions into often incompatible entities. The result was the creation of ever larger "too big to fail" conglomerates, starved for capital but too bloated to function.

To be fair, the Fed itself was not unaware of the weaknesses in its ability to confront the problems it faced. In the fourth quarter of its century-long existence, the Federal Reserve System (FRS) was guided by two chairmen, Alan Greenspan and Ben S. Bernanke, both of whom assured Congress and the public that the central bank had the tools to successfully execute its mandate to promote economic and job growth. Nevertheless, they offered this assurance with some qualification. Chairman Greenspan admitted that:

> the fairly direct effect that open market operations once had on the credit flows provided for businesses and home construction is largely dissipated ... [While the Fed] can still affect short-term interest rates, and thus have an impact on the cost of borrowing from banks, from other intermediaries and directly in the capital markets ... this effect may be more indirect, take longer, and require larger movements in rates for a given effect on output. (Greenspan, 1993)

Chairman Bernanke's view, offered in August 2010 after two years of financial turmoil, anemic output, and growth in unemployment, was:

> The issue at this stage is not whether we have the tools to help support economic activity and guard against disinflation. We do ... the issue is whether, at any given juncture, the benefits of each tool, in terms of additional stimulus, outweigh the associated costs or risks of using the tool. (Bernanke, 2010)

During the tenure of these two chairmen, the Fed's ability to support economic activity and guard against inflation and disinflation had, in fact, been undermined by the risks and costs of using the tools it chose to implement policy. It failed to prevent the huge expansion in the debt of the household, business, and financial sectors in the 1990s and 2000s, and failed to acknowledge and curb an unprecedented inflation in asset prices. Moreover, it had ignored the extent to which capital inflows had augmented the credit supply as it flooded markets in its own efforts to maintain low interest rates.

The story of these failures begins with the emergence of the debt bubble in the 1980s and its heady growth throughout the years before the crisis. The outstanding debt of all United States (US) sectors had increased throughout the post-Second World War period as the US economy expanded and debt rose further during the dislocations caused by inflation in the 1970s. From 1982 to 1990, however, the debt of all US borrowers—federal, state, and local governments; corporate and non-corporate businesses and farms; households, non-profit organizations, and the financial and foreign sectors—doubled from $5 trillion (the total accumulated debt since the beginning of the republic) to $10 trillion and kept mounting through the decade and a half that followed.[1] Spurred by capital inflows in the 1980s and 1990s, growth in the debt-to-gross domestic product (GDP) ratio was unusually robust at the end of the 1990s, capping a decade in which total outstanding debt doubled from $12.8 trillion to $25.6 trillion, despite a decline in outstanding federal government debt.

Debt accelerated when the Fed flooded the market with excess liquidity in the aftermath of the collapse of tech stocks in 2000—a strategy cited by many as a key factor in the development of the housing bubble. Excess liquidity also contributed to the increase in funding for leveraged speculation that spurred an escalation in carry trade transactions, proprietary trading, and off-balance sheet or "shadow" banking (BIS, 2003, June; D'Arista, 2009). As a prelude to crisis, total outstanding US debt reached 352.6 percent of GDP at year-end 2007, up from 255.3 percent in 1997. Over the same decade, household debt rose from 66.1 percent to 99.9 percent of GDP. Even more dramatically, the debt of the financial sector soared from 63.8 to 113.8 percent of GDP. In some periods, financial institutions borrowed more than the aggregate amount borrowed by their non-financial customers as the larger institutions expanded transactions for their own accounts at the expense of their role in intermediation.

In short, the central bank helped create monetary conditions that resulted in a debt bubble. One manifestation of that bubble was rising asset prices, a situation which the Fed failed to see was no less damaging to the economy than increases in prices of goods and services. But the Fed's greatest failure was not attempting a rigorous analysis of the cumulative effect of debt on the real economy.

The debt-to-GDP ratio provides a useful tool for assessing credit growth in terms of the level of economic activity needed to service debt. When economic activity slows, debt becomes more difficult to service. The higher the level of debt, the more borrowers must forgo other expenditures to service debt and that, in turn, jeopardizes growth.

Moreover, the cautionary lesson is that debt levels cannot readily be reversed during a downturn. Indeed, they tend to prolong recessions as borrowers with stagnant or declining incomes struggle to meet debt payments. Servicing debt—both domestic and foreign—had already claimed a much larger share of national income at the end of the 1990s than in the past and constrained the use of financial resources for other purposes.

The rate and uses of credit expansion are surely variables for which a nation's monetary authority bears responsibility. But if the Federal Reserve had concerns about a potential or actual debt bubble, it did not voice those concerns nor address them with effective action. In its February 1999 Humphrey-Hawkins report to Congress, the central bank acknowledged that household debt-service burdens had risen to historic levels (FRB, 1999). Yet it also asserted that the growth in non-financial sector debt had moderated in relation to nominal GDP growth during the 1990s. This claim misleadingly used the decline in public sector debt to mask a decade-long increase in non-financial private sector debt that outpaced GDP growth. Moreover, the Fed's report ignored the degree to which rising dependence on foreign investment had supported credit expansion. On the subject of sky-rocketing financial sector debt and commensurate financial sector vulnerability to market reversals, the Fed's report was simply silent.

Despite its public inscrutability on the subject, during the period before its 1999 Humphrey-Hawkins report to Congress, the Fed very likely was targeting excessive credit with its campaign to raise interest rates. But that strategy clearly had not dampened overall credit demand. Those rate hikes had, in fact, augmented the supply of credit by attracting inflows of foreign capital seeking higher yields on debt securities.

Ultimately, these unintended outcomes can be traced to the growth of external financial markets during the 1970s and 1980s that, as discussed in Chapter 2, had undermined financial structure and regulation. The precipitous expansion of these so-called Eurocurrency markets in the 1990s created difficulties for all central banks in their efforts to influence the supply of credit at home and abroad. But despite the limits of traditional rate-adjustment remedies, neither the Fed nor other monetary authorities were inherently powerless to address explosive credit growth. By judiciously imposing quantitative constraints such as reserve and liquidity requirements on all financial firms operating in the US (and on US institutions operating offshore), the Fed could have gradually reined in the supply of credit without triggering an interest rate spike that would possibly have quashed demand.

Instead, under the thrall of the regulatory passivity embodied in free market ideology and its own unyielding commitment to a strong dollar policy, the Fed accommodated an historic run-up in debt by households, businesses, and financial institutions. By the end of the 1990s, the magnitude of these sectors' vulnerability had already reached a level that would present unusual challenges for monetary and fiscal authorities seeking effective policies to counter a slowdown or a recession.

NOTE

1. These and other data on debt, sectoral borrowing, and net worth in Part V are drawn from various issues of the Federal Reserve's *Flow of Funds of the United States*.

19. Rising imbalances in credit flows

Within the overall trend of rising debt, various sectors of the economy exhibited marked differences in borrowing patterns. State and local government borrowing declined sharply in the 1990s after ballooning in earlier decades. Federal government borrowing continued to rise at double-digit rates through 1992, then diminished every year thereafter, until pay-downs of outstanding debt began in 1998. During the last two years of the decade, federal debt held by the public shrank by about 2 percent annually.[1] As a result, both private and official foreign investors turned to government-sponsored enterprise (GSE) securities as substitutes for Treasuries, accelerating the shift in the burden of debt from the federal government to the private sector.

Borrowing by households and businesses—strong throughout the 1990s—slowed somewhat in the second half of 2000. But even as the US economy fell decisively into recession in the third quarter of 2000, total borrowing by domestic non-financial sectors continued to rise, fueled by falling interest rates at home and abroad and a continued high level of foreign investment in US credit market instruments. Credit expansion remained remarkably vigorous for an economy experiencing a period of decelerating output and this undoubtedly softened some of the effects of declining economic activity. But the failure of substantial increases in new borrowing to produce a comparable spurt in real growth suggests that borrowers used some of the additional debt to consolidate and service outstanding obligations. In the household sector, for example, declining stock prices precipitated a pay-down in security credit in the fourth quarter of the year, after a surge in borrowing to buy stocks in the first three quarters when the Fed declined to exercise its authority to raise margin requirements.

As the US entered recession in 2000, the imbalances in credit flows had become glaringly apparent. As noted, the most dramatic increases in debt in the decade before the crisis occurred in the household, business, and financial sectors. In addition to the structural and regulatory changes discussed in Parts I and II, the investment choices of the foreign sector also played a significant role in the allocation of credit to US borrowers. The overall impact of credit allocation in the 1990s and during the aftermath of the tech stock crisis, and its impact on individual sectors, is discussed in the following subsections.

HOUSEHOLDS

Mortgage borrowing expanded at a fairly rapid rate in the 1990s and rose 10.4 percent in 1999, the highest annual growth in the decade. Increased use of home equity loans sharply slowed the rate of growth of consumer credit after 1996, but the combined increases in consumer and mortgage borrowing in 1999 pushed up overall household debt at an annual rate (9.5 percent) well above the 5.6 percent increase in disposable personal income.

By 2000, the Fed reported that the share of total income that households used to service debt had reached 14.08 percent of disposable income—a level not seen since 1986–87 in the aftermath of the historically high interest rates in that decade. Meanwhile, mortgage payments as a ratio of disposable income topped the peak recorded during the recession in the early 1990s and homeowners' equity-to-debt ratio fell to 54 percent in the third quarter, down from 70 percent in 1982.

In addition to these signs of vulnerability, the gap between the amount of households' borrowing and the value of their financial assets widened to a total of –$274.5 billion for the year. The shrinkage of that cushion (needed to service debt in the event of job losses) was reflected in the first annual decline in families' net worth in over 50 years, triggered by the decline in stock prices.[2] Households continued to borrow but did so under deteriorating circumstances as disposable income fell almost 2 percent and saving as a percentage of personal income plummeted to 0.4 percent. By the end of 2000, some of households' responses to the crisis could have been predicted.

BUSINESSES

Business borrowing also surged in 1998 and 1999, at rates of 10.9 and 10.6 percent, respectively. While small business and farm debt rose substantially in those years, the corporate sector increased its borrowing at a much faster pace and stepped up the pace of stock buy-backs. From 1994 through 1999, the net shrinkage in non-financial and financial corporate equities totaled –$780 billion. Although the stock holdings of wealthier households dropped by –$2.08 trillion, avid stock buying by pension funds and the foreign sector augmented the impact of retirements in bidding up the market value of equities to historic levels. To replace the funds used for stock buy-backs, corporations increased their outstanding issues of bonds from $1.25 to $2.02 trillion over the same period. This wholesale replacement of equity with debt was reminiscent of the "decapitalizing" trend associated with mergers, takeovers, and bidding wars in the 1980s.

Analytic measures based on market values revealed that the debt binge of the late 1990s resulted in a significantly weaker position for the non-financial corporate sector. Debt as a percentage of net worth rose from 51.5 percent at the end of 1998 to 56.3 percent in 2000. As a share of outstanding corporate equities, debt jumped from 33 percent to 38.4 percent over this same short period. No less worrisome, debt as a share of tangible assets continued to climb, rising from 40 percent in 1990 to 45.8 percent in 2000. Although huge in absolute terms, the 88.4 percent increase in outstanding corporate debt over those years produced a smaller expansion in domestic productive capacity than did past borrowing sprees.

For small businesses, residential mortgages constituted more than three quarters of their new debt as bank loans shrank to about 15 percent. This pattern, firmly in place in 2000 as banks expanded their securitization strategies, changed the channel for credit to small business, offering equity loans against owners' residences in place of direct bank lending. It was a strategy that made small businesses dependent on rising home prices for continued access to credit and made the owners of these businesses doubly vulnerable to a bust in the rising housing boom.

THE FINANCIAL SECTOR

The most dramatic rise in indebtedness was recorded by the US financial sector. Over the years from 1990 to 2000, the total debt of all financial institutions rose by $5.8 trillion or 222.3 percent, far outstripping debt accumulation by households, businesses, and all other sectors. Using another measure of its increased absorption of credit market resources, financial debt soared from 31.3 percent of non-federal, non-financial debt in 1990 to 56.4 percent at year-end 2000. These extraordinary increases provide vivid evidence of the shifts in the financial sector's structure, products, and practices during the 1990s and of one of the major imbalances in credit flows affecting US financial markets and the US economy.

Rising levels of mortgage lending and buying by GSEs[3] had become the primary force driving up financial sector leverage. From 1990 to

2000, their outstanding debt tripled to a level of $2.9 trillion—more than the $2.3 trillion increase in outstanding home mortgage debt over the same period.

Asset-based securities (ABS) issuers also became dominant borrowers among private financial institutions. In addition to private issuers of mortgage-backed securities, these firms include automobile companies and retailers that issue securities against pools of car loans and consumer receivables. ABS issuers accounted for 51.1 percent of net borrowing by financial sectors in 2000 and their outstanding debt had sky-rocketed 542 percent to more than $1.5 trillion during the years of unprecedented securitization activity in the 1990s.

Another major channel that fueled the escalation of financial sector debt was the $824.2 billion (221.4 percent) growth in outstanding security repurchase agreements (repos) from 1990 through 2000. Like broker dealers, depository institutions had become increasingly reliant on repos for funding and their dependence grew over the following years in the run-up to the crisis.

While the scale of leverage within the financial sector at year-end 2000 was unprecedented, both the mounting debt and its possible repercussion in the event of a cyclical downswing were ignored. Given the unsupportable debt levels carried by lenders and their customers, the potential for a recession to cause unusually large losses for financial institutions had escalated. The avoidance—or, as it turned out, the postponement—of a financial crisis depended on sources of funding that would continue to support high levels of borrowing.

THE ALLOCATIVE ROLE OF FOREIGN INVESTMENT

While non-US residents continued to borrow dollars in offshore markets, the foreign sector became and remained a large net supplier of credit to American borrowers in the domestic market in the 1990s and in the new millennium. As noted, their investments mitigated the impact of the recession in 2000 on US financial markets and the American economy. For example, foreign residents bought $153.3 billion (30.6 percent) of net issues of GSE securities in 2000 and $181 billion (45.6 percent) of net new issues of corporate bonds. Private foreign investors also favored corporate stocks in 2000. Their net purchases of $172 billion offset net sales by US pension funds and personal trust accounts held by banks and sustained the bull market in equities for the year. Private non-resident investors were net sellers of Treasury securities in the fourth quarter, but net purchases by foreign official institutions in the first quarter of 2000 had raised the foreign sector's total share of outstanding Treasuries above 36 percent—nearly double their 18.3 percent share in 1990.

The influence of foreign investment on US markets was not new. As discussed, foreign inflows accounted for more than 10 percent of net new funds supplied in domestic credit markets during most years in the 1990s and topped 20 percent of the total between 1995 and 1997. Given the scale of its investments, the foreign sector inevitably played a substantial role in directing credit flows to various sectors in US markets. The breadth of that allocative role raises important policy concerns about the effect of foreign investment on credit access and costs for various domestic borrowers in these and subsequent years.

The foreign sector's overall impact on US markets also raises concerns about the effectiveness of macroeconomic policy. When it raised interest rates in 2000, the Federal Reserve attracted additional foreign investment that augmented the domestic supply of credit. While its interest rate hikes dampened demand for residential mortgages, the foreign-fueled growth in the credit supply allowed corporate and consumer borrowing to boom unabated.

NOTES

1. From 1998 through the first two quarters of 2001, federal debt declined by $570 billion, a drop of about 15 percent. Federal borrowing turned negative again in the fourth quarter of 2001, even as state and local government borrowing rose sharply.
2. The drop in households' net worth from $42.3 trillion to $41.4 trillion amounted to 2 percent.
3. GSEs include Fannie Mae, Freddie Mac, Ginnie Mae, and federally related mortgage pools.

20. Mounting risks of the continuing debt bubble in the new millennium

The flip side of US dependence on foreign savings was the requirement that Americans buy the imports that generated the dollars non-residents funneled into US financial assets. But the foreign sector was required, in turn, to invest their trade surpluses in US assets to provide the credit US consumers needed to buy those imports. The burgeoning current account deficit produced by this dynamic and the massive GSE-facilitated movement of domestic credit into housing markets had become the leading indicators of an unbalanced and highly vulnerable US economy. By the end of 2001, debt burdens that could hobble US spending had become a threat that would begin to unravel the growth dynamic of the 1990s.

The changes in credit markets associated with the rapid growth in borrowing and lending by GSEs and federally related mortgage pools after 1995 were also clear indications of the roles played by financial structure and regulation in determining channels for credit flows and shaping macroeconomic outcomes. The fact that such influences were—and still are—largely ignored in decisions about structure and regulation created the potential then—and now—for unforeseen damaging consequences. At the beginning of 2000, a fall in housing prices would have undermined the support that home equity borrowing and refinancing provided to meet consumer and small business demand for credit. And by lowering the value of both tangible and financial assets when the economy fell into recession in the fourth quarter of that year, falling housing prices would have exerted a further negative effect on demand by precipitating a drop in households' net worth. A financial crisis less catastrophic than the one that broke out in 2008 could have occurred then, but was kept at bay by the ongoing expansion of credit provided by the foreign sector.

One of the problems already evident at the beginning of the 2000s was the fact that real-estate values had begun to lag the growth in household mortgage debt. Moreover, the extraordinary rise in the value of housing—up $4.63 trillion or 52.7 percent from 1997 to the middle of 2002—had not produced substantial increases in owners' equity. In fact, the opposite had occurred. When housing prices dipped during the recession in the early 1990s, equity declined as a percentage of household real-estate value, from 65 percent in 1989 to 59 percent in 1993. Over the rest of the decade, the equity ratio continued to inch down until, in 2002, increases in home equity borrowing and cash-out refinancing pushed owners' equity down to 56.4 percent. The continuation of this trend ensured that an ever larger number of households would see their equity disappear altogether when housing prices fell.

Despite their rising debt-to-income ratio, the Fed expressed little concern about stress on households in its *Monetary Policy Report to Congress* in 2002 (FRB, 2002). It asserted that extremely low interest rates had helped families and individuals carry more debt overall while keeping their debt-service burdens at manageable levels. But the Fed's *Survey of Consumer Finance* (*SCF*) for 1999–2001 reported that the benefits of income growth, lower mortgage rates, and rising home prices had not extended to all households. Over those three years, families with above-median incomes enjoyed the fastest growth in income and net worth. As the value of their stockholdings and homes increased, these same households experienced declines in debt-to-asset ratios as well as declines in the share of income devoted to debt repayment. By contrast, families with low levels of wealth and income saw their ability to service debt deteriorate. And the frequency of late debt payments by this group rose accordingly (FRS, 1999–2001).

As household debt continued to rise over the five years before the crisis, the level of inequality already noted in this early period intensified. The benefits for high-income families were ongoing while the ability of families with less wealth and rising debt-service payments deteriorated further, increasing their vulnerability to unstable and volatile market developments. As the *SCF* reported, half of all American families owned stock, whether directly or indirectly through pension or mutual funds. As was widely noted, the broadened ownership of equities helped many households realize spectacular gains in wealth during the latter half of the 1990s. But the so-called "democratization" of stockholding had intensified the impact of collapsing equity prices by including less wealthy families whose primary financial savings were no longer held in insured bank deposits but as indirect holdings of stocks and other marketable securities in pooled funds.

Between 1999 and year-end 2000, for example, the combination of a burst stock bubble and rising household debt levels drained households' net worth by $3.1 trillion or 7.4 percent. Despite sizable gains in the value of real estate and consumer durables, the largest annual drop in this three-year period occurred in 2002 ($1.7 trillion or 4.3 percent). As a result of these losses, the ratio of household net worth to disposable income sank below 1995 levels. In no period since the 1930s had so many American families lost so large a share of their wealth in such a short period of time.

Equally troubling for households and other investors was the potential effect on financial markets if domestic and foreign investors were to question the then widespread assumption that GSE securities are government obligations. In the market for securities issued by housing finance agencies, the GSEs played a commanding role. At mid-year 2003, the market for agency debt ($5.5 trillion) was much larger than the market for Treasury securities ($3.88 trillion) and provided a structure that facilitated the participation of virtually all financial sectors (as well as non-financial and foreign investors) in housing finance. Given the broad distribution of holdings of GSE securities among financial institutions, losses in the value of these securities would lower earnings of intermediaries and cause a drop in credit availability.

As noted, the creation of the market for GSE securities in the early 1970s was strikingly successful in terms of its efficiency in meeting allocative objectives. In creating a secondary market for home mortgages where none existed, the federal government inaugurated a dedicated institutional framework for housing finance that led to broad gains in homeownership. By the beginning of the 2000s, however, that framework had become a problem in terms of balancing credit flows as it absorbed other channels for lending (to consumers and small businesses) and tilted too heavily in the direction of residential real estate to the detriment of other borrowing sectors.

While corporations had been well favored in the debt binge of the 1990s, their channels for borrowing narrowed during the recession in 2001. Profits fell and net worth declined as outstanding corporate debt jumped relative to other indicators. Questions about creditworthiness were reflected in downgrades in ratings. Downgrades by Moody's credit rating agency outnumbered upgrades 14 times over, while delinquency rates on banks' business loans and default rates on outstanding bonds both rose.

With less access to bank credit and the commercial paper market, many companies found themselves unable to secure working capital and were forced to draw down liquid assets. The more creditworthy corporations relied on ongoing foreign interest in purchasing their bonds to lengthen the maturity of debt and alleviate strains on cash flows. The main concern, however, was that business investment had contracted and its revival was seen by the Fed and other analysts as essential to a sustained pick-up in growth. A robust equity market in which to raise funds to pay down debt would have helped, but the collapse in tech stocks had weakened the market and blocked that possibility.

Small businesses outperformed their corporate brethren in terms of net income and net worth gains during and after the 2001 recession. Small business borrowing grew nearly three times faster than corporate borrowing in 2002. Mortgage borrowing remained their primary source of credit as bank loans continued to contract. In the fourth quarter of 2002, this sector's outstanding mortgages climbed to $1.59 trillion, an increase of 36.5 percent from the level in 1998. The vast majority of that debt was not backed by commercial real estate but by residential real estate which, at that time, had risen to 68.2 percent of small firms' tangible assets.

These data show how effectively family-owned businesses tapped into the burgeoning mortgage market in those years and how their continued access to credit contributed to recovery from the recession in 2001 and to the growth that followed. But they also underscore the sector's vulnerability to a decline in housing prices—a development that would imperil small firms' ability to raise future funding against residential real-estate collateral. In other words, small businesses became part of the mortgage machine that provided the main engine for growth in the years before the 2008 crisis but, in its aftermath, their position as borrowers with underwater collateral and no credit became a significant and tragic drag on recovery.

The multifaceted risks embedded in the housing boom in the years before the 2008 crisis became a relevant part of the emerging debate over the role of central banks in targeting asset prices. Chairman Alan Greenspan defended the Federal Reserve against charges that it failed to prick the tech stock bubble in time, arguing that bubbles are inherently difficult to discern, that raising interest rates to deflate stock prices would also have flattened the economy, and that regulatory interventions such as adjustments to margin requirements would have proven ineffectual (FRB, 2002).

More importantly, Greenspan and his Fed colleagues—like the majority of central bankers around the world—declined to take responsibility for the conditions that cause market bubbles. As evidence over the past two centuries suggests, bubbles typically arise out of excessive and unbalanced credit flows. And Greenspan's assertions notwithstanding, large increases in debt relative to economic growth[1] provide a fairly reliable signal that a bubble is evolving. Moreover, common sense evaluations should have suggested that home equity borrowing is a poor substitute for increases in employment and disposable income as a source for financing consumption. Consumption spending financed by rising debt helped drive what many economists termed a "job loss" recovery in 2002. It was not a path to sustainable growth.

Indeed, the massive expansion in borrowing in the second quarter of 2003 both helped and imperiled the US recovery by giving yet another large boost to housing. Monetary authorities gave no indication they were aware that the source of funding for that borrowing was foreign inflows and that potential problems might emerge due to growing US dependence on foreign investment. They also seemed unaware that differences in interest rates among the major developed markets still exercised a strong influence on foreign investment and that credit availability could change abruptly if the Fed did not maintain an interest rate differential that favored the dollar. As a consequence, when US interest rates remained low and the dollar continued to fall in the third quarter of 2003, the usual channels for capital outflows reopened: foreign banks in the US repatriated funds, US banks increased lending to their foreign branches, and US businesses moved more operations offshore.

Not openly discussed at that time was the possibility that a shrinkage in foreign investment could endanger the ability of US borrowers to service debt and set off a process of debt deflation. As discussed below, analysts at international institutions such as the Bank for International Settlements (BIS) and the International Monetary Fund did warn that the excessive debt of US households could deepen another slowdown and make economic activity more difficult to revive. But US policymakers continued to adhere to the view that adjustments should be left to markets. Given their ideological commitment, Fed and Treasury officials ignored the vulnerability of US markets and their participants, and thus ensured no effort would be made to address the problem.

Outside the mainstream, some argued that the Fed need not have stood by passively and let another sector follow the *fin de siècle* trajectory of NASDAQ, leaving sizable losses in output, jobs, and asset values in its wake. As will be discussed more fully, the central bank could have made judicious use of new and existing regulatory and quantitative tools to moderate and balance credit flows.

NOTE

1. The ten-percentage point jump in mortgage borrowing as a share of GDP from 1997 to 2002 is an example of the debt/growth imbalance that characterizes a bubble.

21. How eroding monetary tools facilitated debt creation

The erosion of effective monetary policy implementation is closely linked to the advance of deregulation and was often a response to problems caused by deregulation. After the Carter administration and the Federal Reserve revived and implemented the Credit Control Act in March 1980 to curb inflation, and Congress passed the Monetary Control Act ending interest rate ceilings, the central bank began a substantial shift away from the use of traditional monetary and regulatory tools and gave market forces a greater role in determining the supply and demand for credit.

One major change was, as noted, the virtual abandonment of reserve requirements and the introduction in 1983 of explicit capital requirements for banks as the primary means to moderate changes in bank credit. The Fed also began to ignore and let lapse such macroprudential tools as loan-to-value ratios which had been long-standing components of prudential banking practice and a focus for supervision by regulatory authorities. However, as discussed in Part I, banks' role in credit markets was shrinking as financial intermediation moved to the capital markets, making any policy tool focused solely on depository institutions less effective in influencing the credit supply.

As it slipped into a passive role, the Fed, which had made no attempt to sterilize the huge inflows of foreign capital that inflated the credit supply,[1] operated as though its own ongoing—and by the year 2000, exorbitant—additions to liquidity were the sole source of monetary stimulus. In February 2005, Chairman Greenspan told the Senate Banking Committee that he was surprised that long-term interest rates had fallen lower than they had been when the Fed started raising its short-term policy rate in 2004. He noted that there had been similar declines in long-term rates in Europe and other countries and concluded that, "For the moment, the broadly unanticipated behavior of world bond markets remains a conundrum" (Greenspan, 2005).

For some analysts, these developments were not surprising. They saw falling long-term rates as an inevitable outcome of monetary policy decisions beginning in 2000 that had flooded US and global markets with excess liquidity. In the aftermath of the collapse of major stock indices, the Fed had been concerned about the economy's sluggish response to stimulus and the potential for deflation. To address these concerns, it maintained a nominal federal funds rate of 1 percent from June 2003 through the year 2004 by generating a continuous stream of liquidity that pushed the real rate of interest into negative territory over the period. As investors' so-called "search for yield" intensified in the low interest rate environment, the unprecedented increase in the availability of funding spurred escalating amounts of leveraged speculation using carry trade transactions. Borrowing short term at low rates to invest in higher yielding, longer-term assets drove down rates on the longer-term assets in which the funds were invested.

Dissenting from the Fed's view and its policy choices, the managing director and staff of the BIS argued in their June 2004 *Annual Report* that there was a link between accommodative monetary policies in the G3 countries (the US, the euro area, and Japan) and mounting liquidity in global financial markets. The report pointed to quantitative measures such as the monetary base, broad money, and credit to the private sector—all of which had expanded rapidly in a large group of countries after 1999—as clear evidence of exceptional liquidity growth.

In 2003, the BIS had, in fact, specifically criticized the Fed for creating a situation in which a potential US downturn could become more severe due to the domestic debt build-up encouraged by monetary ease. It had also warned about increasing speculation, pointing to a rising volume of leverage in domestic and international financial systems in 2002 that was fueling the credit expansion (BIS, 2003). It addition, it published research establishing a link between asset bubbles and excessive credit growth (Borio and Lowe, 2002).

Less than a month after Greenspan's confession of puzzlement, a major sell-off in bond markets introduced a stress test for a widening circle of leveraged investors. However, continuing to ignore the BIS's warnings, the Fed and other leading central banks made no effort to address the troubling link between excess liquidity and debt-financed speculation. Indeed, that link and the even more problematic connection between liquidity and credit growth had seemingly slipped below their radar screens. Oblivious to the final link in that chain—the asset bubbles inflated by debt—and lulled by stable wholesale and consumer price indices, central banks took no action to deal with inflated asset prices.

As discussed above, sizable, pro-cyclical capital flows played an important role in augmenting global liquidity and undermining the impact of changes in the policy rate on developments in domestic financial markets and the real economy. Raising the short-term policy rate not only failed to halt the decline in long-term rates in 2004 but also failed to prevent a surge in new borrowing in 2005 and 2006. But the Fed's efforts to implement countercyclical strategies had already failed in earlier periods.

During the recession in the early 1990s, for example, relatively little of the Fed's substantial infusion of liquidity was transmitted to the real economy. The Fed had successfully lowered interest rates but the search for higher yields by domestic and foreign holders of US assets prompted capital outflows—mostly to Mexico—that prolonged the recession. Credit growth resumed when the Fed raised interest rates in March 1994 and US and foreign investors returned to US assets, leaving Mexico in crisis.

By the middle of the 1990s, the rise in cross-border carry trade strategies had further undermined the ability of the Fed and other central banks to expand or curtail liquidity in their national economies. Low interest rates in one national market provided an incentive for carry trade strategies that used borrowing in that currency to fund investments in higher-yielding assets denominated in other currencies. Triggered by interest rate differentials in different currencies, these strategies propelled leveraged speculation to increasingly higher levels and fueled yet another set of asset bubbles to add to the string that began in Japan in the 1980s, moved through the emerging markets in the 1990s, and started to afflict the US and other advanced economies at the turn of the millennium. The pattern that developed in those decades suggests that relying on changes in interest rates as the primary tool of monetary policy can set off pro-cyclical capital flows that reverse the intended outcome of the action taken. As a result, monetary policy can no longer perform its countercyclical function—its *raison d'être*—and its attempts to do so may even exacerbate instability.

NOTE

1. It would, of course, have been impossible for the Fed to sterilize capital inflows at that point, given the stock of foreign investment in US assets. The best opportunity to use this tool occurred in the 1970s when the Fed reached agreement with other central banks to invest dollar reserves in US Treasury securities. In those years, the Fed could have sold Treasuries from its own portfolio and replaced them by investing in foreign government securities. That form of sterilization would have moderated the expansionary impact of the build-up in dollar reserves on US financial markets and would have created a portfolio of foreign exchange reserves for the US while effectively diversifying the aggregate portfolio of international reserves and expanding the use of other currencies in the global economy.

22. Monetary tools: what they are and how they function

From the period after the Second World War to the middle of the 1960s, the US monetary authority was effective in doing what Fed chairman William McChesney Martin famously claimed it could do: remove the punch bowl when the party got rowdy and bring it back when spirits were flagging. In that period, as noted in the opening of Part V, countercyclical policy depended on two tools: the policy interest rate to influence the demand for money and credit, and quantitative restraints to influence the supply of money and credit. While central banks in other countries imposed limits on increases in lending to curb credit expansion in the years before they bowed to deregulatory pressure, the US depended on reserve requirements to influence lending. The shift in financial structure from a bank-based to a market-based system has obscured the fact that, in the US before the 1980s, bank reserves created by—and held with—the Fed served as a *systemic* control on money and credit as well as a publicly created liquidity cushion for the financial sector as a whole.

RESERVE REQUIREMENTS

Long before they were reinvented as a macroeconomic tool for policy implementation, reserve requirements were a widely accepted soundness requirement and had been mandated by state banking regulators in three states after the panic of 1837. As early as 1858, it was argued that excessive credit growth led to boom and bust cycles and that reserve requirements were useful in restraining credit growth (Carlson, 2013). Concerns about what assets should be included in reserve holdings and where they should be held drove discussions throughout the nineteenth century and were part of the decision-making process in shaping the Federal Reserve Act of 1913.

One of the major reforms of the Federal Reserve Act was to require banks to hold a given percentage of their reserves with their regional Federal Reserve banks, rather than as deposits with larger private banks in so-called "reserve cities," whose losses tended to amplify the reach of frequent crises. The balance sheet configurations for the FRS reflect the roles assigned to the regional reserve banks and their member banks: for member banks, reserves were assets available to be cashed in when they lost liabilities to customers; for Reserve banks, they were liabilities backed by the assets they acquired through discounts and, later, through open market purchases.

As the FRS evolved in the 1920s and 1930s, the Fed no longer needed (or required) member banks to pay in reserves; using gold holdings as backing, the Fed created and extinguished bank reserves by buying and selling assets in open market operations on its own initiative. Raising and lowering reserves became the primary tool to achieve the objective that had evolved within the Fed itself in its formative years: a commitment to implement countercyclical monetary policy using bank reserves and open market operations that transformed the Fed from a passive to an active institution and introduced a strong monetary role in the development of macroeconomic policy (D'Arista, 1994).

The Fed can exercise its influence on interest rates and on the credit supply by buying and selling securities in the open market. It buys (or sells) securities from (or to) dealers in the financial sector and pays for them (or receives payment from them) by crediting (or debiting) their reserve accounts or the reserve accounts of other banks acting on behalf of themselves or their customers. Gains in reserve holdings allow these banks to increase their lending and/or sell their excess reserves to other banks in what is called the federal funds market. The additional credit available in the system lowers interest rates. To tighten policy, the Fed sells securities and debits the reserve accounts of banks that buy the securities or act as buyers for customers. Fed sales extinguish reserves, reducing banks' ability to lend and raising interest rates.

The effectiveness of this monetary tool—creating reserves as central bank liabilities by adding assets to the Fed's balance sheet through open market purchases—began to erode in the late 1960s when the largest banks moved operations to unregulated offshore markets to avoid interest rate ceilings and eliminate the cost of holding reserves. The ability of these large banks to lend into the US markets from offshore offices at higher rates of interest undercut the competitiveness of smaller banks and savings associations without offshore operations. This set off changes in financial structure driven by pressure for a "level playing field" to rectify the disadvantages on one sector or another.

Eventually, banks' domestic offices shook off reserve costs by sweeping deposits into overnight money market accounts where, with acquiescence from the Fed, they were not classed as deposits subject to reserve requirements. The Fed acquiesced further by removing reserve requirements on savings accounts to even out domestic and offshore funding costs. Domestic offices began to emulate their offshore branches by increasing the use of non-deposit liabilities such as securities repurchase agreements and commercial paper to fund an expanding volume of non-bank and off-balance sheet activities. In addition, as ATMs proliferated, they began to increase the amount of cash held and counted as reserves. In time and given growing foreign demand for US cash, currency in circulation displaced bank reserves as a major share of the Fed's liabilities.

These developments left the Fed without a tool to control the supply of credit and, at that point, credit ceased to be a topic of discussion. As the outstanding debt of financial and non-financial sectors soared, the Fed argued that its primary role was to curb inflation and pointed to the absence of inflationary pressure as validating its policy tools and goals. Rising imports of cheap manufactured goods, and lower wages for American workers as those imports eroded jobs in US manufacturing, were never acknowledged as contributing to keeping down traditional measures of inflation during this period. The increasingly apparent link between credit expansion and asset inflation and between the explosion of borrowing in the financial sector and the speculative orgies it funded were also ignored (BIS, 2005).

DISCOUNT WINDOW OPERATIONS

A consensus view during the debate on the 1913 Federal Reserve Act was that the new central bank should issue an "elastic" currency that could increase and decrease in quantity to meet the needs of trade. The discount window served as the channel for issuing the new currency—Federal Reserve notes—in the FRS's early years and provided the liquidity needed to smooth seasonal strains.

Given the frequency and severity of panics throughout the nineteenth century, discussions following the panic of 1907 also centered on the need to create a central bank that could act as a LOLR during financial crises. Those who supported that role for the Fed argued that only central bank notes or reserves would remain liquid during a crisis and were the only assets that could be expanded to meet the need for liquidity (Carlson, 2013).

Debates on the legislation and discussions within the FRS itself in the early years indicate that some favored developing countercyclical responses from the beginning. Nevertheless, with the discount window as the primary monetary tool, the Fed's role was essentially passive. It had to wait for banks to take the initiative to change the money supply, credit availability, and interest rates by repaying debt, rolling over borrowings, or borrowing more. The Fed could only respond to pro-cyclical market forces and had no means to influence the supply or demand for money and credit. Impatient with these limitations, Governor Benjamin Strong, Jr. of the Federal Reserve Bank of New York began to purchase securities in the open market, issuing currency and creating reserves backed by the mounting supply of gold that had flowed into the US during and after the First World War, rather than using discounted trade bills as backing (D'Arista, 1994).

The successful use of open market operations during the 1920s led the FRS to ignore the ongoing flaw in the legal framework for the monetary system: the continued omission of a role for the expanded amount of government debt that had been issued to finance the war. In the early 1930s, banks saw Treasury debt as the safest investment for deposits, but the fact that it could not be discounted by the Fed led to a sharp contraction in the money supply. The financial system was effectively frozen when gold outflows shrank the gold backing the Fed had used to issue currency by buying government securities in the open market.

The Fed's inability to expand liquidity to respond as LOLR set the stage for new legislation, beginning with the Emergency Relief and Construction Act of 1932 that authorized the Fed to discount Treasury securities. It was followed by the Glass-Steagall Act of 1933 that, among other important reforms, clarified the responsibility of the Federal Reserve Board in Washington relative to the regional banks in authorizing open market operations. Meanwhile, the 1932 act had reinstated the discount window as the primary channel for emergency liquidity.

OPEN MARKET OPERATIONS

By 1938, "The Fed began to use open market operations to adjust available reserves in the banking system as a primary monetary policy tool" (Carlson, 2013, p. 23) and began to use its ability to change its balance sheet to conduct countercyclical operations in the post-Second World War period. In 1951, when banks held 65 percent of financial sector assets and liabilities, and their reserve balances with the Fed accounted for 11.3 percent of bank deposits, changes in bank reserves could and did have a powerful effect on the credit supply. Fifty years later, reserve balances accounted for only 0.2 percent of bank deposits and the Fed's open market operations were used to influence the level of interest rates rather than to adjust reserve balances (FRS, *Flow of Funds*).

Since 1994, the federal funds rate—the interest rate banks charge one another for overnight or short-term loans—has been used as the benchmark or target rate for policy implementation. In most periods since the mid-1990s, the Fed has been able to use open market operations to maintain the policy rate at the desired level. As noted, Chairman Greenspan and other Fed officials asserted their belief that the central bank's ability to influence the demand for credit through control over the Fed funds rate was sufficient, that market forces would respond by supplying the appropriate amount of credit demanded (Greenspan, 1993).

But relying on open market operations to influence interest rates as the primary policy tool, rather than relying on the raising or lowering of reserve balances, failed to curb demand sufficiently to prevent the unprecedented run-up in debt that occurred over the last 40 years. And the Fed's quantitative easing (QE) strategy to stimulate recovery produced an outcome that failed the test of countercyclical policy. Despite its maintenance of a virtually zero-level target rate, the Fed's asset purchases failed to stimulate an increase in borrowing by non-financial sectors proportionate to the amount of assets it bought.

Questions about the cost of using open market operations to control the target rate must also be addressed in a broader context. A major problem for the Fed or any central bank in globally integrated financial markets is the way foreign capital flows respond to changes in interest rates in national economies. Sizable pro-cyclical capital flows weaken the impact of changes in policy rates on the availability of credit in both emerging and advanced economies.

Throughout 2004 and 2005, for example, borrowing reached truly massive proportions both in the US and abroad. The Fed's measured increases in the policy rate had no cooling effect on rising debt levels. In fact, they spurred private foreign inflows into dollar assets at home and abroad by encouraging carry trade strategies that borrowed low interest rate yen to purchase higher-yielding dollar assets. Escalating speculation was reflected in record-breaking growth in borrowing in external banking markets, the great majority of which was channeled to financial institutions and used for position taking by commercial and investment banks and hedge funds (BIS, 2005, 2006).

In 2005, capital inflows into the US had risen to twice the amount needed to finance the current account deficit, and the US financial market had, in effect, assumed an *entrepôt* or "pass through" function for global markets. Excess flows into dollar assets triggered borrowing to finance sizable outflows for investment in higher-yielding emerging market assets

(US Department of Commerce, 2006). As an excess of dollars from foreign investment on top of current account surpluses flooded their markets, central banks in those countries responded by buying dollars to prevent their conversion into local currencies. Their sterilized intervention strategies helped moderate a build-up in liquidity in their markets and an appreciation of their currencies.

But, as discussed, needing to invest the dollars they had acquired, emerging market countries bought US Treasury securities and other dollar assets and re-exported the problem back to the US. The accumulation of dollar reserves by these countries augmented the highly liquid conditions in US financial markets, exerting downward pressure on medium- and long-term interest rates and fueling another round of capital outflows from the US back to emerging markets, as well as additional binge borrowing by US residents.

The downward pressure on long-term interest rates in advanced economies and the easing of domestic monetary conditions in emerging economies constituted an unprecedented global response to the build-up of excessive liquidity in this period (White, 2013). While, as noted, net foreign lending in US credit markets averaged about 15 percent of the annual supply of funds from the mid-1990s through 2007, the advent of monetary ease after 2001 introduced a new dynamic: the generation of liquidity through the spillover effects of leveraged cross-border investment flows. The round-robin nature of those flows constituted a sorcerer's apprentice scenario that was bound to lead to crisis when uncertainty—from whatever source—threatened the highly leveraged financial sector's ongoing need for funding. As excessive liquidity and rising debt set the stage for the crisis, a major contributing factor was the Fed's failure to recognize and respond to the volume and impact of capital inflows and their relation to changes in US interest rates.

MACROPRUDENTIAL POLICY

Macroprudential policy has been described as a "system-wide, top-down approach to regulation and financial stability that seeks to 'curb the credit cycle' through countercyclical regulatory interventions by directing and sometimes directly constraining the commercial activities of private institutions" (Baker, 2013, p. 2). The tools used to implement macroprudential strategies include capital requirements, loan loss provisions, liquidity requirements, caps on aggregate lending, reserve requirements, limits on leverage, interest rate ceilings, underwriting and margin requirements, loan-to-value ratios, transactions taxes, constraints on currency mismatches, and capital controls (Baker, 2013. p. 2).

A critical legislative tool in this arsenal is limits on loans to individual borrowers as a percentage of capital—a constraint enacted in the US in the National Bank Act of 1865 that did not, however, include constraints on loans to individual financial institutions. A continuation of this relaxation from the rule amplified interconnectedness in the financial system and, as discussed in Part II, was one of the primary causes of what became a systemic implosion in US and global financial markets in 2008.

Except for capital requirements—introduced in the US in 1983—many of these macroprudential constraints had long-standing histories as tools of soundness regulation, but most were removed, allowed to lapse, or ignored in the surge toward deregulation in the 1980s. Based on growing acceptance of the efficient markets hypothesis, the deregulator juggernaut that rolled through financial markets in the 1980s and 1990s instated market forces as the preferred regulatory paradigm, with risk management enhanced by Value-at-Risk (VaR) models. The constraint most compatible with this new paradigm was capital requirements and it became and has remained the dominant tool for soundness regulation in US and global financial markets.

As early as 2000, however, a series of papers and the *Annual Reports* published by the BIS criticized the ascendency of free market ideology and warned of the consequences of an expansion of credit that increased systemic risk and the potential for a financial crisis. Hyman Minsky's work on financial fragility also began to be recognized as presciently descriptive of developments already underway (Minsky, 1986). As the financial crisis unfolded in 2008, over-reliance on VaR models came to be seen as one of the causes of the crisis and the efficient markets hypothesis was supplanted in policy discussions by a renewed interest in macroprudential policy tools (Baker, 2013). Indeed, in December 2007, the Fed's belated proposals for regulating all mortgage lenders suggested that it was engaged in the proverbial closing of the barn door after the horses were out. That it hadn't considered such restrictions necessary at an earlier point seemed to confirm the Fed's ideological commitment to deregulation rather than its pragmatic assessment of developments that could potentially cause market disruption and systemic fragility.

Recent analyses of macroprudential policy include reserve requirements among the tools under discussion. Ignoring the link between open market operations and reserve creation, a working paper published by the Office of Financial Research (OFR) describes it as a tool that allows credit to be controlled independently of monetary policy (Elliott et al., 2013). This, in fact, more accurately describes capital requirements rather than reserve requirements. And, by contrast, the authors' research supports a strong monetary role for reserve requirements, noting that they were the most significant tool used in 1980 when the Fed implemented the Credit Control Act to curb excessive inflation in the wake of the substantial drop in the value of the dollar.

The OFR paper also describes the expanded use of reserve requirements to cover net borrowing under securities repurchase agreements (repos) in 1969, imposed on new borrowing by banks from overseas branches, on large certificates of deposit, and, in August 1970, on commercial paper issued by banks and their affiliates. In addition, the activation of the Credit Control Act in 1980 imposed reserve requirements on any type of company, financial or non-financial, by requiring all lenders to hold special deposits on certain types of consumer credit and a special deposit of 15 percent (later reduced to 7.5 percent) against increases in total assets of money market funds.

The OFR working paper also discusses proposals offered by then Federal Reserve Bank governor Andrew Brimmer in the 1970s and subsequently by others to use reserve requirements based on loans (asset-based reserve requirements) to channel credit toward or away from particular sectors. The authors see this as foreshadowing risk-weighted capital requirements which, like asset-based reserve requirements, also have an allocative function, if not always the one intended. Another difference between reserve requirements and capital requirements is the fact that the monetary authority can directly change reserve requirements and make them effective quickly and flexibly to counter the effect of market forces on credit, while changes in capital requirements must await the response of market forces. In view of the re-emergence of reserves on the Fed's and banks' balance sheets after inauguration of the QE programs, assessments of both the monetary and soundness roles of reserve requirements should take precedence in any discussion of the Fed's ability to meet its objectives.

23. The inability of capital requirements to prevent or moderate financial crises

The Dodd-Frank Act (2010) reaffirms the role of capital requirements as the primary tool to influence the supply of credit and maintain soundness in the post-crisis regulatory framework. The capital requirements of that act and the rules proposed to implement them build on the most recent evolutionary stage of the Basel Agreement that, since 1988, has functioned both as a regulatory tool to moderate leverage and, theoretically, as the sole cushion against insolvency for individual institutions and the global financial system as a whole. The adoption and continuation of reliance on capital requirements reflects the view that market forces, not regulators, can and should constrain unsound bank behavior by providing or withholding capital from individual banks. The assumption that undergirds this framework is that markets can maintain equilibrium without government intervention; this led proponents to favor dismantling the earlier regulatory framework based on quantitative restrictions, believing that it undermined innovation and impeded market efficiency.

The focus on capital requirements in the two decades before the crisis led regulators to adopt an atomistic approach, focusing on the individual institution in isolation, ignoring the ever tighter linkages between institutions and sectors and the systemic interactions they created. Changes in the quantity and quality of lending went unchallenged as did increasing concentration in the size of institutions and the types of assets they held. Because profits were high, financial institutions were able to attract capital and the apparent adequacy of capital ratios—at least as measured against on-balance sheet assets—supported the belief that relying on market forces had, as promised, promoted a sound and efficient financial system.

But in the aftermath of the crisis, it is clear that capital requirements are a tool that failed. While the Dodd-Frank Act and Basel III added some important revisions and additions to the capital adequacy paradigm, its reinstatement once again as the primary regulatory tool suggests the need for a more skeptical analysis of how capital functions to prevent or moderate the effects of financial dislocations. During the 2008 crisis, capital evaporated. What was originally seen as a liquidity crisis rapidly morphed into a threat to systemic solvency that required governments, not markets, to provide the capital cushion needed to prevent total collapse. Moreover, the ongoing pressure on capital in the aftermath of the crisis impeded efforts to revive credit flows and restart economic activity. Legislators and regulators promised taxpayers that they would never again be called on to shore up the system, but it is unlikely that the reforms in place can buttress the regulatory foundation they perpetuate to sufficiently withstand future strains.

Meanwhile, the crisis demonstrated just how strongly capital requirements pushed institutions and the system as a whole in a pro-cyclical direction. Not only will markets supply capital in a boom and withhold it in a downturn, but the impact on capital of changes in the value of assets also has the same pro-cyclical effects. The downward spiral set in motion by falling prices and charges against capital in the fall of 2008 argues for a view of capital as a *threat* to solvency, not a cushion. There is simply not enough capital available in a downturn to safeguard individual institutions, let alone an entire financial system.

Moreover, the suggestion that financial institutions in good times raise and store large amounts of capital that can be run down, if needed, also raises concerns. It seems reasonable to ask how much of the available capital generated by savings in an economy should be allocated to finance, as opposed to non-financial sectors, to ensure balanced growth in economic activity. As economist Jan Toporowski noted, "A regulatory requirement to increase bank capital reduces the amount of capital available to nonfinancial firms" (Toporowski, 2009, p. 2). Indeed, the run-up in capital that supported the growth of the largest institutions in the decade before the crisis necessarily contributed to the rise in financial corporations' profits relative to non-financial corporate business. Meanwhile, given that the larger institutions have an advantage in attracting capital from institutional investors, requiring more capital may tend to increase levels of concentration within the financial sector. An additional concern is that requiring ever higher levels of capital to address heightened risk taking may have the opposite effect. The amount of growth and profitability needed to attract higher levels of capital tends to increase, not decrease, incentives to take risk.

While it is true that debate on reform included discussion of ways to make capital, as well as provisioning requirements, countercyclical, the outcome was to endorse the idea and call for efforts to find ways to make it happen. Meanwhile, in some emerging economies, central banks that had used reserve requirements to moderate the impact of capital flows attracted by direct increases in the policy rate had also built up a cushion of reserves before the crisis, and were able to act countercyclically by lowering reserve requirements in 2008 to provide liquidity relief and restore the monetary transmission mechanism (Montero and Moreno, 2011).

It is also true that there is agreement on the need for institutions to pay more attention to macroprudential risks but, in the US, concerns about such risks are articulated as suggestions for undertakings by institutions on a voluntary basis. They reflect, at best, half-hearted efforts to restore elements of the previous regulatory and monetary paradigm—efforts that underscore what was lost in the process of installing capital requirements in place of the reserve system that evolved in the US after the creation of its central bank.

While the major reform of the Federal Reserve Act of 1913 was the creation of a new monetary system for America, a no less important reform was, as discussed, the creation of a systemic cushion for banks by requiring them to hold a given percentage of their reserves with their regional Federal Reserve banks. The role of reserves as a cushion for the system was weakened in the late 1920s but re-established under the Banking Act of 1935 that clarified and facilitated the ability of the Fed's open market committee to create and extinguish reserves by buying and selling Treasury securities. As noted, reserve balances with the Fed accounted for 11.3 percent of bank deposits in 1951 and constituted a remarkably comfortable cushion for a segregated system in which banks, the dominant sector, loaned to other financial sectors with which they were not in competition. Fifty years later, however, the shift in credit flows away from banks and their use of borrowed funds, and other strategies to reduce holdings of deposits subject to reserve requirements, had virtually wiped out that cushion.

During the 2008 financial crisis, the absence of a monetary cushion provided by reserves weakened individual financial institutions and made them more vulnerable to stops in external funding. As institutions' confidence in the solvency of their financial counterparties eroded, borrowing and lending among financial institutions through repurchase agreements collapsed as a channel for distributing liquidity. Had there been a large cushion of reserves held by the Federal Reserve banks, transfers of reserve accounts among financial institutions would not have been questioned and the credit crunch and the threat to the payment system could have been avoided. But the missing monetary cushion also impeded the Fed's ability to provide liquidity to the system as a whole. As discussed below, it was forced to use unconventional means to address the collapse of liquidity in funding markets by swapping Treasury securities for riskier debt, extending its emergency borrowing program to non-banks and providing term loans to banks.

A cushion of reserve balances owned by financial institutions but held by the Fed would be a far more effective way to maintain liquidity in the event of future shocks to the system. Because reserve balances retain their face value, an established pool of reserves is a more certain liquidity buffer than capital or the Fed's lending facilities, because the reserve holdings of financial institutions are not subject to charges against their value as the value of institutions' assets decline. The reserve pool would, as it did in the past, help moderate pressure for asset sales, stem the decline in their prices, and thus protect institutional capital.

While capital is and will remain a useful tool of soundness regulation as a constraint on leverage, a numerator for ensuring the diversification of credit exposures and asset concentrations, and a measure of solvency for individual institutions, capital alone cannot protect the financial sector in the event of a systemic crisis. The Fed's struggle to ensure systemic reach for its efforts to provide liquidity suggests that it and other central banks should attempt to build a source of systemic funding within the monetary system that, like reserves, is renewable and immediately available to all financial sectors in a downturn.

24. How crisis reshaped the monetary toolkit

The depth of the financial collapse in 2008 and the duration of the recession that followed confronted central banks with a series of recurrent, real-time stress tests. The Fed responded by adopting new strategies and extending the range of assets it acquired in executing these strategies. It was also willing to interact with other central banks and other segments of the global financial system in the early stages of the crisis. In a broad sense, the tools it used were traditional—lending, conducting open market operations, and creating bank reserves—but they were used in ways that changed the toolkit.

The following sections focus on the major programs the Fed used to deal with the crisis and address the recession. The outcome of these efforts suggests that revisions in the toolkit are a work in progress; that a revaluation of both old and new strategies is needed to deal with financial crises and moderate credit cycles that disrupt economic activity.

FED LENDING DURING THE CRISIS

In 1984, the Fed made heavy use of the discount window to contain a potential crisis involving Continental Illinois Bank and its holding company. Fortunately, the problem at that time centered on only one bank, but it foreshadowed some of the problems the Fed would face in 2007 and 2008: loss of confidence in a major institution by other institutions it relied on for funding; the threat to the bank from its non-banking activities, and an outflow of a critical source of funding—commercial paper—outside the traditional asset base for Fed discounts and open market purchases. The Fed's struggle to ensure a soft landing for Continental Illinois and prevent contagion was one that was watched very carefully by other banks. The transparency of the Fed's balance sheet revealed the amount of lending required daily and discouraged other banks from using the discount window for fear that they, too, would be seen as weak—a concern that persisted after 1984 and shaped the way the Fed responded as the crisis unfolded in December 2007.

For example, the first of the more than 12 lending programs or facilities the Fed created, the Term Auction Facility (TAF), reflected awareness of what was called the "stigma problem": the unwillingness of banks to reveal their identity as borrowers or the amount of their borrowings as individual institutions. Thus, the program was structured to allow banks to borrow in groups and negotiate the rate as an auction. The largest of the facilities in terms of the number of banks participating and the longest in duration, the TAF nevertheless accounted for only 22 percent of the total lending. Even so, it was indicative of the overall character of Fed lending in this period: the largest banks were the dominant borrowers, many of these were foreign banks, and the interest rate averaged slightly above or below 1 percent (Matthews, 2013).

While the TAF was open to many banks, the bulk of Fed lending (62 percent of the total lending of $1.7 trillion) was to only 20 so-called "primary dealers" through the Term Securities Lending Facility (TSLF) and the Primary Dealer Credit Facility (PDCF) at a mean interest rate of 0.48 percent. The TSLF provided high-quality collateral to investment banks to back repo borrowing, while the PDCF (51 percent of the Fed's total lending) loaned cash for collateral. Other important facilities included the Asset-Backed Commercial Paper Money Market Mutual Fund Liquidity Facility (AMLF), that acted primarily to support money market mutual funds and the asset-backed commercial paper market by making loans to intermediary financial institutions for on-lending to the AMLF.

Nicola Matthews' 2013 analysis of these lending facilities makes the point that the duration of the programs and the fact that the interest rate was not a penalty rate indicate that the Fed was dealing with insolvency rather than a liquidity crisis. Moreover, she argues that maintaining low rates on the loans and allowing banks to negotiate their rates of borrowing from the Fed through auctions were an effort to improve bank profitability. In conclusion, she questions the Fed's use of its LOLR powers to deal with insolvency on the grounds that it validated unstable banking instruments and practices and may have set the stage for an even greater crisis (Matthews, 2013).

QUANTITATIVE EASING

The Fed began the first round of QE in November 2008, the second in November 2010, and the third in September 2012. In December 2012, it announced that its purchases of securities under QE3 would continue until the unemployment rate had fallen to 6.5 percent or the outlook for medium-term inflation had risen to 2.5 percent. By May 2013, the Fed had bought almost $3 trillion of US Treasury and mortgage-backed securities. As a share of the US economy, the Fed's purchases were slightly less than the amount of UK government bonds ($569 billion) as a share of the UK economy bought by the Bank of England in the aftermath of the crisis. Meanwhile, the Bank of Japan also adopted QE as a strategy by announcing that it would double the nation's money supply. In addition, the Japanese government, unlike its US and United Kingdom (UK) counterparts, announced a new stimulus package to be financed by the central bank's purchases of government bonds, in contravention of the long-held prohibition against monetizing government spending (Appelbaum et al., 2013).

It is generally assumed that the QE strategy was prompted by Chairman Bernanke's view that an insufficiently easy monetary policy had increased the severity of the Depression in the 1930s. His view had the support of a majority of the Fed's Open Market Committee, one of whose members, James Bullard of the St. Louis Reserve Bank, urged the European Central Bank to consider large bond purchases to drive down interest rates (Ewing, 2013). Economists who supported the Fed's action dismissed the argument that the build-up of reserves that resulted from the Fed's large-scale purchases could lead to inflation if banks began to use excess reserves to back new lending. They argued that the problem was disinflation; that lost jobs and wage growth had suppressed demand and would keep inflation and interest rates low until monetary stimulus helped bring recovery.

But QE also had other critics. Some thought the problem with QE was not prospective; that it was already evident that the Fed, once again, was focusing on consumer prices and ignoring bulges in asset prices. In their view, the Fed's use of QE to maintain a zero-bound target rate had prompted a "search for yield" that fueled record highs in stock markets in the US, UK, and Japan—a form of asset inflation that contributed to further increases in inequality (Eisinger, 2013). Other critics noted that low short-term rates encourage financial instability (White, 2013; Zumbrun, 2013) and credit-driven speculation in the financial sector, and that, for many, low returns discourage saving and thus discourage capital formation over time while, for others, their effect is to dampen current consumption by requiring more saving to provide adequate retirement income (White, 2013).

But the larger cause for concern about QE was that, by mid-year 2013, it had not worked; the Fed was not getting what it wanted: jobs and recovery. Donald L. Kohn, a former Fed vice-chairman, said he was "not sure why we're not getting more response … why we have negative real interest rates everywhere in the industrial world and so little growth," and Mervyn King, former governor of the Bank of England, took the view that there was a limit to what monetary policy could do to spur recovery (Appelbaum et al., 2013). William R. White, a former BIS official who was one of the principal supporters of macroprudential policy, saw "significant grounds for believing that the various channels through which monetary policy might normally operate are at least partially blocked" (White, 2013, p. 29).

THE BUILD-UP IN EXCESS RESERVES

The Fed's assets more than doubled as it created new lending facilities and expanded the menu of securities it bought. On the liability side of its ledger, the reserves created in the process of paying for these new assets grew from $2.1 billion in the fall of 2008 to $900 billion in January 2009 and $1.5 trillion at year-end 2012 (FRS, *Flow of Funds*). To encourage banks to hold reserves in excess of what was legally required, in September 2008 Congress granted the Fed's request for authority to pay interest on reserves. As economist Robert Pollin noted, interest on reserves (0.25 percent) gave banks a generous spread over the federal funds rate (0.07 percent in 2011) on a safe, par-valued asset—one uniquely not subject to price adjustment (marking to market). While this strategy certainly helped preserve capital by supporting bank earnings, paying interest on reserves further weakened banks' incentive to lend. Their failure to resume lending while maintaining high levels of reserves suggests the strategy was the latest version of the 1930s liquidity trap and a new wrinkle on the Fed's usual post-trauma policy of saving the banks at the expense of the economy (Pollin, 2012).

Control over the federal funds rate had weakened after the collapse of Lehman Brothers and, in the fall of 2010, the Fed tried to justify paying interest on reserves as a way to regain influence over interest rates. Chairman Bernanke argued that banks would not lend in the money market at an interest rate lower than the rate they could earn risk-free from the Fed and that increasing the interest rate on reserves would put significant upward pressure on all short-term interest rates (Lanman, 2010). While other central banks used interest on reserve deposits as a policy tool in bank-based systems, the institutional shift in the US toward a market-based system had already limited the systemic effect of this strategy, since the primary influence would be on bank lending. Meanwhile, critics of the policy proposed abolishing interest payments to encourage lending and/or taxing excess reserves (Palley, 2011; Pollin, 2012).

Other than using payments on reserves as a new target rate, the Fed seemed reluctant to reinstate a role for reserve requirements in curbing credit. Others, however, had renewed the call for asset-based reserve requirements. Economist Thomas Palley, for example, proposed their use as "targeted discretionary counter-cyclical balance sheet controls on the financial sector," including shadow banks and hedge funds. He argued that, unlike reserve requirements, interest rates are not selective and are not efficient in curbing sectoral imbalances. Moreover, even without sectoral targeting, reserve requirements can be used as both a curb on excessive leverage, and as assets that meet liquidity requirements (Palley, 2011, p. 19).

THE NEED TO REBUILD THE FED'S TOOLKIT

Recognition that the anemic outcome of four years of implementing its QE strategy and discussions of proposals to strengthen control of the policy rate suggest that the Fed needed to reassess its countercyclical policy tools. A first step in such an assessment would be to ensure that any current and proposed tool can be effectively implemented in the context of a radically changed US financial system in which traditional relationship banking has been replaced by a "collateralized market system with the repo market at its heart" (White, 2013, p. 41). Unless monetary initiatives can impact all financial intermediaries and credit markets, the Fed will be unable to counter the pro-cyclical boom and bust effects of market forces. Asking Congress to extend reserve requirements to all financial institutions would be one way for the Fed to regain influence over the credit supply and would enable it to target imbalances by raising and lowering requirements without creating competitive disadvantages for individual sectors and institutions.

Reserve requirements as a principal monetary tool, operating in tandem with open market operations, would also improve the Fed's ability to act as a LOLR. As the events of 2008 and 2009 demonstrated, capital is a necessary support for institutions but offers no protection against insolvency in a systemic crisis, either for the individual institution or the system itself.

A new *systemic* cushion is needed: one that, unlike capital, can be created and extinguished countercyclically by a public body. Part VI offers a proposal for extending the systemic reach of monetary policy within the framework of the current structure of the US financial system. The author hopes it will spur others to join in creating proposals to address the failure of monetary policy to channel the balanced flow of credit needed to restore sustainable economic activity. In the aftermath of its failure to prevent the most costly financial crisis and economic recession since the Great Depression, the Fed must be charged to use its immense intellectual capital to offer the American people a realistic appraisal of the strategic changes that must be made.

PART VI

An agenda for monetary reform

25. Introducing a systemic approach

As noted in Part V, beginning in the 1970s various proposals for using asset-based reserve requirements to improve the channeling of credit through allocative strategies opened discussions of the need for monetary reform. More recently, analysts have shown interest in constructing a framework for macroprudential stabilization. For example, in its June 2005 *Annual Report*, the Bank for International Settlements (BIS) proposed a framework that strongly endorsed the use of countercyclical techniques by central banks to implement both regulatory and monetary policies. The BIS framework would reintroduce quantitative measures, such as liquidity requirements, loan-to-value ratios, collateral requirements, margin requirements, and tighter repayment periods. It would also set prudential norms relating to the growth in credit and asset prices and, as former BIS economist William R. White argued, "use monetary and credit data as a basis for resisting financial excesses in general, rather than inflationary pressure in particular" (White, 2007, p. 81).

This is an ambitious and admirable agenda that represents a 180-degree turn away from the deregulatory and inflation-targeting practices put in place over the two decades following the rise of free market ideology. But, as a proposal to reinstate effective countercyclical strategies, it falls short of what is needed. The quantitative measures it recommends would apply only to banks and not to other financial sectors. Moreover, these mechanisms deal mainly with credit standards governing loans to non-financial borrowers, not their financial counterparts. They therefore ignore the distinctive systemic issues and threats that have emerged as a result of changes in financial structure: the rapid growth and enhanced role of sectors other than banking in channeling savings and credit; the extensive linkages among all financial sectors that result from changes in funding strategies; increased leverage and the use of derivatives to hedge positions; and the proliferation of non-public, opaque markets that operate without up-to-the-minute information about the price of transactions and the volume of trading.

Part VI proposes a new system of reserve management that assesses reserves against assets rather than deposits, and applies reserve requirements to all segments of the financial sector. It is an approach that would increase the Fed's ability to respond to credit contractions or expansions because it would be implemented by supplying (or withdrawing) interest-free liabilities in exchange for purchases (or sales) of assets on the balance sheets of the financial sector.

In a downturn, for example, purchases of assets by the central bank in exchange for *free* liabilities held by Federal Reserve banks would more effectively accomplish what the Fed tried to do during the crisis of 2007–2008 to halt asset sales that drive down prices and erode the capital of financial institutions. Removing assets and providing interest-free liabilities would encourage financial institutions to rebalance their books by lending or expanding their holdings. In dealing with an expansion, however, the Fed would extinguish reserves by selling assets back to financial institutions. The addition of those assets and the loss of free reserve liabilities would force institutions to remove assets from their balance sheets, thus contracting credit and raising its price.

In addition, the expansion of reserve requirements to all financial sectors would permit all institutions to draw on reserve accounts held with the Fed to make payments to one another. Restoring a publicly guaranteed channel for intrasystemic transactions would alleviate concerns about counterparty risk and maintain confidence in financial markets. Moreover, a supply of new no-cost liabilities emanating from the central bank would make it possible for individual institutions to write off or restructure the terms of loans or securities and replace them with more credit-worthy assets—a new and powerful use of a monetary tool that would moderate the destructive force of future financial disruptions for borrowers as well as lenders.

The chapters in Part VI lay out the framework and rationale for such a system. This proposal is offered in the hope that it will stimulate discussion and, in time, result in additional proposals to restructure what is called the transmission belt for monetary policy. The flaws in the current system contributed to the financial crisis in 2007–2008, as well as the length of the Great Recession that followed. The need to identify and correct those flaws is as great now as it was in the 1930s, when a series of emergency measures were taken that culminated in the Banking Act of 1935. The revisions of the structure and powers of the monetary authority in that Act revived a countercyclical role for the Federal Reserve in dealing with the Depression, financing the Second World War, and contributing to growth in the post-war years. But while the 1935 act successfully addressed the problems of those years, the profound changes in the financial system that have occurred since the 1970s have made it ineffective in providing the monetary conditions necessary to promote stability and growth.

For example, no plausible scenario suggests the likelihood that banks and other depository institutions will regain their once hegemonic role in credit creation. And no likely series of events promises to diminish the substantial influence of institutional investment pools and global capital flows on credit expansion. As a result, any practical effort to rebuild effective countercyclical financial and monetary strategies must establish new channels for exercising monetary and regulatory influence over *all* financial institutions. Simply put, banks alone can no longer shoulder the transmission-belt function that ensures the stability of the link between the financial and real sectors of the economy, nor can non-bank financial firms participate meaningfully in transmitting policy initiatives unless those firms also come under the direct influence of the central bank.

How might such a system be inaugurated? The Fed's sweeping inclusion of all mortgage lenders, state or federally regulated, under the proposed regulations it issued in December 2007 (Andrews, 2007), is an important precedent for introducing system-wide requirements and one that acknowledges that omitting any institutional segment would vitiate the intent of the action. A systemic approach could use the 1999 Gramm-Leach-Bliley Act's definition of activities deemed financial in nature and apply the same regulatory and monetary strategies to all entities engaged in a given function to moderate the rise and fall in credit growth.[1] The first step would be to extend the influence of the central bank to the entire financial system by imposing reserve requirements on all sectors and institutions.

The next step in bringing non-depository institutions under the Fed's monetary control would mean creating a reserve system that targets changes in assets, not liabilities. Such a system would demand significant adjustments to a reserve structure tailored to fit banks' unique role in the financial system.

Despite their growing dominance in channeling credit, non-bank financial intermediaries are not designed to engage in money creation. Unlike banks, they do not create new liabilities for customers when they add assets by making loans or investments. Moreover, the liabilities of institutional investors such as pension funds and insurance companies are in longer-term contracts, rendering reserve requirements on changes in liabilities impractical. In short, the current liability-based system doesn't permit central banks to create and extinguish reserves for non-bank financial firms.

While the proposal outlined here differs from earlier strategies that target assets, the concept of holding reserves against assets is not new (Thurow, 1972; Pollin, 1993; D'Arista and Schlesinger, 1993; Palley, 2000). Thomas Palley provides a full exploration of the advantages of asset-based reserve requirements as a tool of stabilization policy and points out that the concept actually embodies a range of real-world experiences, including the current model for United States (US) insurance regulation.[2] Similarly, the liquidity requirements proposed by the BIS and suggestions that margin requirements be extended to assets other than equities are also examples of quantitative monetary tools that target assets.

The experience of European countries during the Bretton Woods era provides additional examples of asset-based reserve systems—some designed to control overall credit expansion, others to shield key sectors from cyclical excesses and drought,[3] and still others to increase credit flows to privileged sectors. Another example includes the Federal Reserve's imposition of reserve requirements on loans by US banks' foreign branches to their home offices in 1979 to restrain the run-up in domestic credit fueled by this source of funding.

When applied to non-bank financial institutions, these earlier asset-based reserve systems were used to implement allocative strategies. They required non-banks to hold reserves on the asset side of their balance sheets as banks do now. Non-interest-bearing reserves could be turned into interest-earning assets by non-banks only if they were loans to, or investments in, privileged sectors such as housing, exports, or tourism, or loans to other financial institutions that made credit available to such sectors. If they did not lend to privileged sectors, non-banks had to hold the reserves as non-interest-bearing loans to the central bank.

Asset-based reserve strategies intended to expand or restrain credit growth were usually applied to banks. In the case of US banks' borrowings from their foreign branches, the reserve requirements were not effective in restraining credit growth since they could not cover loans from the home offices of foreign banks to their US branches. Nevertheless, these strategies were generally effective within national economies in earlier periods and might even have been effective in the US in cases where bank credit fueled a bubble. For example, imposing asset-based reserve requirements on banks' commercial real-estate loans in the late 1980s, when such loans were rising by over 20 percent a year in New England banks, might have prevented or moderated the collapse in values that followed.

However, since banks do not hold equities on their balance sheets, asset-based reserve requirements could not be used to defuse the bubble in high-tech stocks without imposing reserves on non-banks. Moreover, this strategy could not have defused the subsequent bubble in housing if it had not been applied to all financial institutions. By that time, securitization had distributed mortgage lending across the entire financial system. Raising reserve requirements on banks' holdings of mortgages, mortgage-backed securities (MBS), or mortgage-related derivatives would have shifted holdings of these assets to other investors without moderating their expansion.

In any event, industry resistance and pressures for deregulation had already doomed these earlier asset-based approaches, and the many changes that have occurred in financial markets since the 1970s make it unlikely that those models would fit the current institutional framework. Nevertheless, no other models offer more promising paths for modernizing the Fed's policy tools today. Only by targeting financial firms' assets can a reserve system hope to effectively influence most of the total credit extended to non-financial and financial borrowers and ensure greater balance in the distribution of credit across all sectors over the business cycle.

Creating a reserve system that extends the Fed's influence over the financial system as a whole requires that reserves be issued to and held by financial institutions as liabilities to the central bank. Shifting reserves to the liability side of financial institutions' balance sheets would permit the monetary authority to create and extinguish reserves for both bank and non-bank financial firms. By contrast, attempting to extend reserve requirements to non-bank institutions under the old framework—with reserves held on the asset side of the balance sheet—would, in fact, have pro-cyclical effects.

For example, if the Fed's objective were to augment the supply of reserves, adding reserves on the asset side of a mutual fund's balance sheet would require it to balance its position by adding liabilities. Because, unlike a bank, it can't *create* liabilities, the mutual fund would have to sell additional shares to customers. If unable to attract additional shareholders, it would have to sell a commensurate amount of assets or sell its reserves to another institution—responses that could either defeat or reduce the expansionary intent of the action. Similarly, if the Fed were attempting to restrain an expansion by extinguishing reserves, the effect on the mutual fund would be to reduce its overall holdings of assets, providing an incentive to buy other assets to balance an unchanged liability position—again, defeating the Fed's objective.

In short, using the reserve requirement framework developed in the era when bank-based systems were the norm would work only as an allocative strategy. It could be introduced as a special intervention to stimulate credit flows to a sector under stress or to moderate expansion in a particular financial sector. It might also be used to reduce excessive leverage within the financial system. But these interventions would tend to be cumbersome and could disadvantage some financial sectors more than others. As a tool to maintain financial stability on an ongoing basis or to implement countercyclical policies, requiring non-bank financial institutions to hold reserves on the asset side of their balance sheets would undercut the effort to strengthen the monetary authority's systemic influence because it would not make reserve requirements a permanent tool applicable to all.

NOTES

1. Requirements needed to implement those strategies would be imposed only on those portions of a company engaged in financial activities, but not those portions conducting non-financial operations. Drawing this distinction would strengthen the crucial separation between banking and commerce and prevent commercial entities from making emergency liquidity claims on the lender of last resort.
2. Although reserves are imposed on insurance companies for soundness purposes (as opposed to conducting monetary policy) and are held by the firms themselves (rather than a public agency), they nonetheless illustrate the feasibility of systematically reserving and classifying institutional investors' assets.
3. For example, Sweden required all financial sectors to hold a given percentage of their total portfolio in housing-related assets. Institutions that did not make real-estate loans could meet the requirement by purchasing the liabilities of institutions that did. As noted, financial firms that failed to meet the required percentage had to enter the shortfall on their balance sheet as reserves, thereby making an interest-free loan to the government rather than an interest-earning loan for housing. Similar strategies for other purposes were used by the Netherlands, the Bank of England, Italy, Switzerland, and France (US House of Representatives, 1972, 1976).

26. Creating a system-wide asset-based reserve system

To create the asset-based reserve system proposed here would require changes in the way the Federal Reserve conducts monetary policy and in the structure of its balance sheet. The first of these changes would entail making securities repurchase agreements (repos) the Fed's primary operating tool. Used by the Fed in transactions with primary dealers since the 1920s, repos allow both the central bank and private financial institutions to buy an asset, with an agreement to resell it in a given amount of time. As an old and proven tool of monetary policy, they are ideally structured to allow the Fed to interact with all financial firms on the asset side of their balance sheets in assessing reserve requirements against a broad range of financial assets. Under the proposed system-wide reserve regime, for example, the Fed could use repos to buy loans, mortgages, MBS, government or agency securities, commercial paper, corporate bonds, or any other sound asset from any of the many financial institutions that hold these assets, including banks, investment banks, mutual funds, pension funds, insurance and finance companies, or government-sponsored enterprises (GSEs).

While the Fed has already expanded the range of assets it buys or lends against in implementing its recent crisis-management strategies, authorizing it to accept a wide variety of sound assets as backing for repurchase agreements[1] would bring the US central bank closer to the successful practices of other central banks and enable it to exercise monetary control over an assortment of assets much larger than the shrinking universe of reservable deposits that now constitute its lever for direct influence over credit growth. Equally important, authority to conduct repos in any sound asset would strengthen the Fed's ability to halt runs, moderate crises, and curb excessive investment across the entire financial system. It would, in short, restore the Fed's ability to function as a *systemic* lender of last resort.

Implementing an asset-based reserve system would require balance-sheet adjustments for financial firms and the Federal Reserve as well as changes in the conduct of policy. Tables 26.1 through 26.4 and the accompanying text summarize balance sheet categories and open market operations under the current reserve system (in which reserves are assessed against bank deposits) and explain how the proposed system (in which reserves are assessed against the assets of all financial institutions) would make policy implementation more effective.

Tables 26.1 and 26.2 show how reserves are booked on the balance sheets of banks and other depository institutions and on the Fed's balance sheet under the current bank-based reserve system. As discussed, they are carried as assets of depository institutions and liabilities of the Fed.

Table 26.1 Current balance sheet structure for depository institutions

Assets	Liabilities
Reserves	Deposits
Loans	Capital
Securities	Borrowings
Other	Other

Table 26.2 Current balance sheet structure for the Federal Reserve System

Assets	Liabilities
Government securities	Currency in circulation
Repurchase agreements	Bank reserves
Discounts	Government deposits
Foreign exchange reserves	Other

Under the proposed system of universally applied reserve requirements shown in Table 26.3, financial institutions would book reserves on the liability side of their balance sheets rather than on the asset side. Shifting reserves from one side of their balance sheet structure to the other would have important consequences for banks. And booking reserves as liabilities would have implications for the broader financial industry as well.

First, defining reserves as liabilities to the Fed would clarify and make explicit the fact that reserves represent the financial sector's obligation to serve as a transmission belt for policy initiatives intended to affect economic activity.[2] Second, recognizing reserves as liabilities would make moot the contentious issue of paying interest on reserves while eliminating the expense for taxpayers that was approved in 2008.[3]

Table 26.3 Balance sheet structure for financial institutions using asset-based reserve requirements

Assets	Liabilities
Loans	Deposits
Securities (government and private)	Open market paper
Shares	Loans
Mortgages	Bonds
Open market paper	Shares
Other assets, advances, and contracts	Mortgages
Repos and fed funds	Repos and fed funds
Cash	Other liabilities, advances, and contracts
	Capital
	Reserves

Finally, defining reserves as financial sector liabilities would remove the motivation for using sweep accounts to reduce reserve requirements on demand deposits and the use of vault cash by banks as a substitute for reserve accounts with the Fed. Cash holdings are assets, not liabilities. As such they represent one component of the financial sector's total portfolio of assets against which reserves would be held.

The shift in booking reserves for financial institutions in Table 26.3 would require a symmetrical shift in the Fed's balance sheet. As shown in Table 26.4, bank reserves—now held as Fed liabilities—would be recorded on the asset side together with the reserves of all other financial institutions. Meanwhile, repurchase agreements and discounts would move from the asset to the liability side of the Fed's balance sheet to reflect the central bank's liability for the private sector assets it acquires when it creates reserves. Foreign exchange holdings (international reserves) would remain on the asset side since they, too, would be acquired through repurchase agreements which would be liabilities of the Fed. Outstanding currency would remain a liability, manifesting the delegation to the Fed of Congress' constitutional authority to create money and manage its value.

Table 26.4 Federal Reserve balance sheet structure using asset-based reserve requirements

Assets	Liabilities
Financial sector reserves	Currency in circulation
International reserves	Government deposits
	Repurchase agreements
	Financial sector discounts

As a result of this rearrangement, financial sector reserves would constitute the Fed's principal assets under the proposed system. The central bank would no longer hold a huge portfolio of government securities as backing for Federal Reserve notes, bank reserves. and government deposits, ending the fiction that one government obligation is needed as backing for another. This would mean, however, that the Fed would no longer earn interest on assets other than its foreign exchange holdings and, with non-interest-earning reserves backing its repurchase agreements and discounts, the central bank would no longer have income to pay interest on its purchases. However, the fact that financial institutions would receive invaluable interest-free liabilities when they sell their assets to the central bank under repurchase agreements supports the argument for compensating the central bank for its role in creating liquidity by allowing it to receive earnings on the collateral backing those repos, as private financial borrowers do now.[4]

NOTES

1. A proposal to broaden the portfolio of assets eligible for purchase by the Fed was offered by former Fed chairman Marriner S. Eccles during hearings on the Banking Act of 1935. He argued that the Fed should be free to buy "any sound asset" (Eccles, 1935, p. 194). Then as now, broadening the Fed's portfolio would eliminate the central bank's need to own a vast amount of Treasury securities. A large stockpile of Treasuries held as backing for reserves and outstanding currency, and the even larger aggregate holdings of foreign central banks, tend to restrict the availability of this risk-free, highly liquid asset for use in private transactions where it is needed as collateral to support market stability. In the reserve management system proposed here, the Fed could still acquire Treasuries, support Treasury auctions and the market for government securities while releasing a substantial portion of its current holdings for purchase by investors and financial institutions seeking the ultimate safe-haven asset.
2. Defining reserves as financial institutions' liabilities to the Fed would finally, if belatedly, achieve a fuller measure of consistency between the central bank's balance sheet and its actual operations. During the drafting of the Federal Reserve Act, lawmakers forged a political compromise with the banking industry that made the new monetary authority

appear to be nothing more than a bankers' bank—a repository for the reserves that banks would pay into the system as a safeguard in the event of future financial panics. In that conceptual framework, reserves could legitimately be viewed as a passive type of central bank liability.

Soon after the Fed's establishment, however, the invention of open market operations gave the system the ability to create reserves and exercise a level of influence on financial markets and economic activity not envisioned when the legislation was enacted. Later, the Banking Acts of 1933 and 1935, the Employment Act of 1946, and the Humphrey-Hawkins Full Employment and Balanced Growth Act of 1978 fully recognized and ratified this influence. Nevertheless, the Fed has maintained a set of bookkeeping arrangements that continue to treat its assets and liabilities like those of a mere bankers' bank. Defining financial sector reserves as assets of the central bank would modernize these outdated arrangements by confirming that the Fed's major function is to create and extinguish liquidity and that it enjoys the unique ability to create the reserves that accomplish this function.

3. Under an asset-based reserve system, it might be argued that financial institutions should pay interest on reserves to the Fed. But it is likely that policy objectives would be achieved more efficiently if financial firms simply hold reserves as non-interest-bearing liabilities to the Fed.
4. If the Fed kept the earnings on financial assets held under repurchase agreements, that income—along with fees for clearing and other services—should prove sufficient for it to continue operating at or near current levels of expenditure. It is highly unlikely that income from this source would be insufficient but, if it were, the Fed, like all other government agencies, would receive supplementary funding through the appropriations process. While this might be seen as an assault on the post-Second World War assumption that central banks must be free of political influence, that assumption should be revisited in light of the Fed's failure to maintain financial stability before and after the 2008 crisis and its unique role as an agency to which Congress has delegated its constitutional responsibilities.

27. Implementing policy under the current and proposed systems

Table 27.1 shows the balance sheet changes that result from *current* monetary policy initiatives. As discussed, the Fed's acquisition of assets (government securities, repos, discounts, or loans) causes a symmetrical increase in bank reserves on the liability side of its balance sheet and adds reserves to the asset side of depository institutions' balance sheets. This allows depository institutions to create new liabilities (deposits) by making loans. Similarly, the Fed's sales of assets reduce reserves, and the loss of reserves on the asset side of depository institutions' balance sheets theoretically forces them to reduce deposits by selling assets.

Table 27.1 Current open market operations

Depository institutions		Federal Reserve System	
Assets	Liabilities	Assets	Liabilities
		Expansion	
		1) + government securities	1) + bank reserves
2) + reserves			
3) + loans	3) + deposits		
		Contraction	
		1) – government securities	1) – bank reserves
2) – reserves			

Currently, however, depository institutions need not and do not reduce their overall liabilities or sell assets when they lose reserves. They can substitute borrowings for deposits under repurchase agreements with other financial institutions and add, rather than subtract, assets—especially if policy rate increases attract foreign inflows that increase the availability of credit. This weakening of the effect of changes in outstanding reserves may also result in little change in banks' balance sheets when the Fed attempts to expand credit by adding reserves. In 2008, for example, banks allowed reserves to pile up as sterile assets—especially after the Fed began to pay interest on them—rather than make loans that would create deposits. With capital erosion caused by falling prices on their holdings of securities and on the collateral they had posted to back repos, derivatives, and other off-balance sheet commitments and borrowings, banks had lost confidence not only in their counterparties but in their ability to manage their own balance sheets to preserve capital. Moreover, given the need to raise $1 of new capital to back every $12 of new loans, the fact that reserves were not subject to the weightings of capital requirements and that they (unlike other assets) retained their face value increased the likelihood that banks would begin to hoard reserves.

To implement an expansionary policy under the proposed system-wide reserve management system, the Fed would add to reserves by engaging in repurchase agreements with financial institutions. The expansion of reserves would occur in two steps, as shown in Table 27.2.

Table 27.2 Expansionary open market operations using asset-based reserve requirements

Financial institutions			Federal Reserve System	
	Assets	Liabilities	Assets	Liabilities
Step 0: Before expansion				
	$1000	$900 to customers, investors, lenders; $100 reserves	$100 reserves	$100 cash, deposits, repos, discounts
	$1000	$1000	$100	$100
Step 1:	–$10 assets		+ $10 reserves	+ $10 repos
	+$10 repo	+$10 reserves		
	$1000	$1010	$110	$110
Step 2:	+$10 assets			
	$1010	$1010	$110	$110

In Table 27.2, Step 1, the central bank buys assets from a financial institution—Met Life, JPMorgan Chase, or Fannie Mae, for example—and agrees to resell the assets in a designated period of time. The Fed pays for the asset by crediting the seller's reserve account with its local

Federal Reserve Bank. In the step shown here, the Fed has added $10 of liabilities to its balance sheet (repos) and created $10 of assets (financial sector reserves).

On the asset side of the financial institution's balance sheet, the transaction is a wash; the addition of a $10 repurchase agreement offsets the sale of $10 of assets to the Fed. However, the repo with the Fed (unlike the asset acquired by the Fed) does not bear interest. Meanwhile, on the liability side of its balance sheet, the financial institution has gained $10 of interest-free reserves. At this point, the financial institution has more liabilities than assets and needs to adjust its balance sheet.

In Table 27.2, Step 2, the financial institution would use its newly acquired, interest-free reserves to buy additional assets to replace the earnings it lost when it sold assets to the Fed under a non-interest-bearing repo agreement. If there were a fractional reserve requirement under the proposed system, the financial institution could acquire a larger amount of assets than the reserves it has received from the Fed, if it could acquire additional liabilities from customers, investors, or lenders.

As is the case under current operating procedures involving only banks, reserves would be distributed throughout the financial system by means of purchases and sales of reserves among private institutions in the federal funds market. The system might not maximize the expansionary potential of the reserve increase due to the voluntary nature of this process. But the addition of a given amount of interest-free liabilities would provide a powerful incentive—nothing to lose and more earnings to gain—for financial institutions to acquire income-producing assets and lead to a fairly predictable increase in credit.

By providing this incentive, the proposed reserve management system would, as discussed, remedy a major flaw in the existing model. Under the current system, the Fed can create excess reserves that aren't used (push on a string) in the kind of credit crunch that developed during the 1990–91 recession and returned with even deeper and longer-lasting consequences in 2008. Under the proposed system, a string turns into a stimulus to meet the countercyclical objective.

In a deflationary environment, this change could prove the difference between recovery and prolonged recession. With the tools available in the proposed system, the Fed could create reserves to encourage cancellations of non-performing debts and debt securities, allowing the financial sector to replace them with earning assets. This would channel liquidity directly to households and businesses, helping to avoid the stagnation that develops when financial institutions resist issuing new credit and cannot cancel debt for troubled borrowers without jeopardizing their own survival. By thus strengthening private sector balance sheets, monetary policy could powerfully reinforce fiscal initiatives designed to revive demand and investment.

As Step 2 of Table 27.3 shows, the Fed would initiate a contractionary policy by allowing repurchase agreements to mature without renewal or engaging in reverse repurchase agreements, causing a reduction in outstanding reserves. The Fed extinguishes its liability to the seller of the repo by returning the collateral and debiting the financial institution's reserve account. In this way, the central bank reduces its balance sheet by $10 of liabilities (repos) and $10 of assets (reserves). In the process, the financial institution has exchanged $10 of non-interest-bearing assets (the repo with the Fed) for $10 of interest-bearing assets (the collateral backing the repo with the Fed). The amount of its assets has not changed but it has lost $10 of non-interest-bearing liabilities (the reserve deposit with the Fed). With insufficient liabilities to back its assets, it must adjust its balance sheet.

Table 27.3 Contractionary open market operations using asset-based reserve requirements

Financial institutions			Federal Reserve System	
	Assets	Liabilities	Assets	Liabilities
Step 0: Before contraction				
	$1000	$900 to customers, investors, lenders; $100 reserves	$100 reserves	$100 cash, deposits, repos, discounts
	$1000	$1000	$100	$100
Step 1:	–$10 repos + $10 assets	–$10 reserves	–$10 reserves	–$10 repos
	$1000	$990	$90	$90
Step 2:	–$10 assets			
	$990	$990	$90	$90

In Table 27.3, Step 3, since the financial institution no longer has enough required reserves to back total assets, it adjusts its balance sheet by selling $10 of assets. Again, a change in the supply of reserves triggers adjustments that ripple throughout the financial system via the federal funds market. At the end of the contractionary process, both the total supply of credit and the value of total credit market assets will be lower.

28. Implications of the proposed system for the conduct of policy

Under the proposed reserve management system, the Fed's method of implementing expansionary and contractionary monetary policies would closely parallel its current implementation process in three significant ways: the central bank would continue to buy and sell financial assets in transactions with private financial institutions; the Fed's actions would still have the effect of simultaneously changing the amounts of its own assets and liabilities as well as those of private financial institutions; and reserves would continue to be distributed throughout the financial system by means of purchases and sales among private institutions in the federal funds market. The Fed would also continue to have the (little-used) power to change reserve requirements, raising or lowering the amount of reserves needed to back one or more or all classes of assets, as part of either an allocative or stabilization strategy.

Another aspect of current operating procedures that would remain unchanged would be the Fed's ability to influence asset prices. Some have argued that the Fed does not and should not directly exert such an influence. But the Fed's open market operations already impact asset prices through changes in interest rates and liquidity, both of which trigger portfolio shifts that disseminate the effects throughout asset markets. Though they do so indirectly and, as has been argued, sometimes with unintended results, the Fed's interest rate changes have exerted and continue to exert profound effects on the value of pension fund assets, mutual fund shares, equities, and housing.

In practice, all efforts to conduct monetary policy must take asset-price movements into consideration—at least at some level of the analytical or decision-making process. And, targeted or not, all efforts to conduct monetary policy must influence those price movements. As long as the Fed's basic objectives—sustainable output, low unemployment, stable prices—remain constant, it makes little philosophical difference whether policy transmits those influences indirectly (as in the current bank-centered reserve system) or directly in a system-wide reserve regime. The point is to ensure that the process is efficient and produces the intended outcomes.

In practical terms, the Fed's influence on asset markets likely would function far more efficiently under a system-wide reserve regime. With all financial institutions holding reserves and participating in the federal funds market, volatility would decline as a wider number of institutions began making portfolio adjustments by purchasing and selling reserves rather than assets. This is particularly important in the event of market disruptions, when forced sales of assets increase downward pressure on prices and financial sector capital and threaten the ability of markets to function. The fact that reserves retain their face value enhances their role as a cushion, ensuring that trades settled by debiting an institution's reserve account with the Fed are accepted with confidence.

But an additional contribution to efficiency under the proposed system would be its ability to deal with the often unintended and counter-productive effects of capital flows. As discussed, foreign capital inflows and outflows change the availability and price of credit in domestic markets and, under current operating procedures, the Fed does not—and cannot—directly offset their effects on the supply or distribution of credit. It could only change the impact of capital flows if foreign investors held the majority of their US investments in bank deposits rather than in Treasury, GSE and MBS securities, corporate bonds, and stocks. Given this handicap, the central bank cannot play an effective restraining role when foreign inflows or outflows cause substantial shifts in the issuance or price level of these and other tradable assets.

In the proposed system-wide reserve regime, using repurchase agreements as the principal operating tool would allow the Fed to respond more effectively to excessive investment or disinvestment of foreign funds in one or more US asset markets. For example, allowing the run-off of repos backed by holdings of the kinds of assets purchased by foreign investors, and replacing them with repos in foreign assets, would effectively mop up an inflow, leaving reserves, interest rate levels, and credit conditions largely unchanged. Alternatively, to counter the contractionary effects of an outflow, the Fed could acquire assets sold by foreign investors, increasing the amount of reserves in the system. But the Fed's ability to conduct repurchase agreements in foreign securities would, as it does now, eliminate the central bank's need to hold international reserves as precautionary investments.

The benefit of introducing such transactions would be to enhance the Fed's capacity to maintain stable conditions in domestic financial markets. But increasing effective US intervention in foreign exchange markets would not necessarily contribute to global stability.

The issue of capital flows is complex and contentious. As argued in Chapter 15 and elsewhere, a rising volume of speculative flows in response to interest rate differentials has contributed to widening global imbalances, with results that have underscored the need for international as well as national monetary reform. Nevertheless, the Fed's inability to moderate the impact of capital flows on US credit expansion has exacerbated the problem of global payments imbalances even as it has facilitated the build-up of historic levels of domestic and external debt in the US economy.

In short, the purpose of creating and implementing monetary policy tools is to enhance overall macroeconomic performance, and the purpose of reinstating quantitative policy tools is to reinstate a system that can do that job more effectively. Because it can constrain or stimulate specific asset types or institutional sectors and thus deal more effectively with asset bubbles or credit crunches, a reserve management system that creates and extinguishes financial sector liabilities to influence holdings of credit-creating assets is a more efficient channel for monetary control.

In the case of credit crunches, for example, if financial institutions were required to back assets by holding reserve liabilities that retain their face value, a fall in the price of any asset would increase the value of reserves relative to assets and allow intermediaries to buy more of either the affected instruments or other assets. Similarly, an increase in the value of assets without an offsetting increase in the reserve liabilities that back them would limit the rate of increase in prices of one or more classes of assets and thus moderate the development of bubbles. This automatic countercyclical aspect of the proposed system would do more to stabilize movements in asset prices than changes in interest rates, or margin or capital requirements.

Last but certainly not least, a system-wide reserve management regime would give all financial institutions direct access to the lender of last resort. For example, if mutual funds faced runs by shareholders, they could avoid selling assets (and thus prevent downward pressure on prices) by transferring assets to the Fed under repurchase agreements and acquiring the reserves needed to offset customers' withdrawals. Of course, the Fed would, as now, act in that capacity at its own discretion. But it would not need to pressure banks to lend to others the funds that it traditionally loaned primarily through depository institutions to address systemic disruptions.

If bundled with complementary reforms in prudential supervision and regulation and a much needed overhaul of financial sector guarantees, the comprehensive lender of last resort facilities achievable under the proposed system-wide reserve regime would make the Fed's crisis interventions more coherent, less costly, and probably less necessary. Like the other benefits of the system proposed here, this improvement in crisis management would begin to forge a policy framework that, by promoting greater stability, could promote a higher level of sustainable economic activity.

PART VII

Reforming the privatized international monetary system

29. Can special drawing rights replace the dollar and other national currencies as a reserve asset?

The Bretton Woods international monetary system began to unravel when European currencies and the Japanese yen became convertible in the late 1950s and early 1960s. Marshall Plan grants and the growth of their exports to the United States (US) made it possible for these countries to acquire sufficient reserves of gold and dollars to be able to exchange their currencies for those of other countries and begin to expand their contacts with trading partners. The positive effect of this development was a substantial increase in growth in industrial countries in the 1960s, largely due to the expansion of trade. Throughout the decade, however, there was an increase in private speculative sales of dollars for other currencies and some official demand for gold in expectation of dollar devaluation (Dam, 1982).

As discussed in Chapters 2 and 12, the external (Eurodollar) market was seen as a way to absorb excess dollars without changing the US international balance sheet after the first dollar crisis in 1960. But the second run on the dollar in 1967 demonstrated that offshore transactions would affect the exchange rate for the dollar; change the demand for dollars as effectively as transactions involving capital flows into and out of the national market; and expand foreign holdings of dollars if other currencies were not used in cross-border transactions with countries other than the US. The continued "dollar glut" resulted from an ongoing preference for using dollars in international payments, but a waning preference for using the dollar as a store of value. Demands on the US to convert dollars for gold contributed to the unraveling of the dollar/gold exchange standard and forced President Nixon to end the dollar's convertibility into gold in August 1971, and end the monetary system established under the Bretton Woods Agreement (D'Arista, 2009a).

As the unsustainability of the dollar/gold exchange standard became increasingly obvious in the 1960s, the noted international economist Robert Triffin led the way in calling attention to the need for a post-Bretton Woods system. His proposals were an integral part of the discussions that led to the Rio Agreement in 1967 that authorized the International Monetary Fund (IMF) to create and issue special drawing rights (SDRs) to be used as reserve assets. Since then, other crises—in the 1980s, in 1997, and in 2008—prompted a re-emergence of interest in international monetary reform. Most of the discussion has continued to focus on expanding the role of SDRs; the amended IMF Articles of Agreement state the intention of making the SDR the principal reserve asset in the international system. But a total of only 21.4 SDRs ($33 billion) were issued after their creation in 1969 and the IMF's approval of a new issuing of $250 billion in 2009 reveals how minor the SDRs' role remains, compared with trillions of dollars of outstanding dollar-denominated reserves (D'Arista, 2009a).

Nevertheless, SDRs have played an important role in providing reserves to developing countries. In the absence of the ability or willingness of any country or group of countries to fund grants on a scale comparable to the US Marshall Plan, the SDR is the only debt-free source of liquidity at the international level for economies in crisis. Loans from the IMF are not a desirable solution for crisis countries. Since they are no different than debt owed to the private sector and, since debt to the IMF has priority status and must be serviced before other obligations, these loans tend to compound the pressure on countries to export their way out of additional IMF loans. On the other hand, new SDR allocations provide a uniquely benign alternative to bailout loans that compound the underlying inequities in the system. Given these benefits and the fact that the SDR is an established component of the current international monetary system, we begin this section by examining the potential benefits and limitations of relying on SDRs as a vehicle for monetary reform.

Robert Triffin believed that the central achievement of the 1967 Rio Agreement—the creation of new reserve assets to strengthen the balance of payments adjustment mechanism—was a first step in the right direction. But he warned that it would not constitute a viable reform effort if it failed to take a more comprehensive approach in assigning roles to all three components of reserves—gold, foreign exchange, and collectively created assets—especially since he predicted that gold would be demonetized internationally as it had been nationally since the 1930s (Triffin, 1968).

Triffin's created reserve assets were similar to the reserve asset that Keynes called "bancor" in his 1940s proposal for an international clearing union to hold international reserves. Unlike Keynes, however, Triffin proposed that the distribution of reserves created by the IMF be linked to development finance. But the major industrial countries with the majority of votes in the IMF linked the distribution of SDRs to the size of existing quotas. Triffin complained that their decision to link issuance to quotas was "as indefensible economically as it [was] morally," especially since two of the richest countries in the world (the US and the United Kingdom (UK)) were assigned about one-third of the total (Triffin, 1968, p. 194).

One outcome of the decision to allocate so large a share of SDRs to the US was that it effectively destroyed the ability of the SDR to assume an important role in the system, since it made the US, the holder of the largest share of SDRs, reluctant to exchange dollars for SDRs offered by other countries. As a result, it undermined the potential to forge the needed link between the reserve asset and the medium of exchange. Moreover, continuation of the system of allocating SDRs in proportion to quotas has perpetuated the inequity in the system. The new issuing of $250 billion approved in 2009 allocated less than $100 billion to developing countries and only about $20 billion to low-income countries (United Nations, 2009).

Under the system created in 1969, SDRs are valued in relation to a basket of currencies and serve as the unit of account in which all IMF transactions are denominated. Member countries' obligations to and claims on the fund are also denominated in SDRs. SDRs may be used as reserve assets by a member country in exchange for another country's currency in cases where the former needs to finance a balance of payments deficit and the latter has a strong balance of payments position. Such transactions can take place at the direction of the IMF or through the mutual consent of the two countries, but only if both countries agree. In addition, SDRs can be used in loans, swap arrangements, and the settlement of other financial obligations among member countries, and between a member country and the IMF (IMF, 1987).

Like past proposals for new issues of SDRs, the objective of the 2009 allocation was to move beyond the key currency system by creating an international reserve unit under multilateral governance. While new issues of SDRs have been used as a mechanism for expanding reserves, they have the potential to contribute to global stability by removing the credit-generating attribute of foreign exchange reserves that, as discussed in Chapter 13, introduced a pro-cyclical aspect to reserve holdings and exacerbated booms and busts. Using the SDR as a reserve currency could accomplish that objective without the loss of national sovereignty because national central banks would continue to issue national currencies. But while the SDR could be used in transactions among central banks and with the IMF—and like the European Currency Unit created by the European Monetary System before the adoption of the euro, could serve as a unit of account in private transactions—it could not be used to finance transactions in the private sector. In other words, the SDR as currently structured cannot be used as a means of payment.

In an effort to overcome this problem, economist Joseph Stiglitz proposed creating a "global greenbacks" system in which new reserves could be created every year and would not be given largely to the wealthiest countries. His proposed system would include a trust fund of conventional hard currencies to enable countries in crisis to exchange their global greenbacks for currencies that can be used to pay private creditors and for imports. A more ambitious version of the system, he noted, "would allow global greenbacks to be held by individuals, in which case there would be a market price for them and they would be treated like any other hard currency" (Stiglitz, 2006, p. 263).

Unlike other proponents of SDR issuings, Stiglitz acknowledges the need to forge a link between a reserve asset not based on national currencies and the currencies used in private international transactions. His proposal improves on the current system for exchanging SDRs for hard currencies in that the pool of hard currencies that would be created would be used at the direction of the IMF rather than the national central banks that issue those currencies. Nevertheless, the trust fund would necessarily rely on contributions from those countries; he does not suggest how the IMF would ensure that their contributions would be sufficient to create a pool large enough to be effective in managing crises.

As for the more ambitious proposal to allow the global greenback to evolve into a transaction currency, Stiglitz is vague on the institutional arrangements that would be required. One assumes that global greenbacks would not be issued directly to individuals or private institutions, but might leak into the system through sales to private institutions by central banks. Or, again, like the European Currency Unit, they could be used to denominate private transactions without being exchanged at settlement.

After the 2008 crisis, the Commission of Experts of the President of the United Nations General Assembly on Reforms of the International Monetary and Financial System published a report calling for a global reserve currency issued by a public international institution to replace the dollar. The report offered several alternative arrangements for this core proposal, including the following:

> One institutional way of establishing a new global reserve system is simply a broadening of existing SDR arrangements, making their issuance automatic and regular. Doing so could be viewed simply as completing the process begun in the 1960s when SDRs were created. The simplest version, as noted,

> is an annual issuance equivalent to the estimated additional demand for foreign exchange reserves due to the growth of the world economy. But they could be issued in a countercyclical fashion, thereby concentrating issuances during crisis periods. One advantage of using SDRs in such a countercyclical fashion is that it would provide a mechanism for the IMF to play a more active role during crises. (United Nations, 2009, p. 117)

Forging institutional means to use a more plentiful supply of SDRs in trade and debt-servicing transactions might constitute an effective incremental path toward substituting an international unit of account for national currencies as both the primary reserve asset and as a means of payment in the international system. As noted, the SDR is already part of the international monetary system; additional creative proposals on how it could be used in managing crises appear to be the most fruitful path toward reform. As these proposals are developed, however, they must place restraints on the role of the private financial sector in pricing or distributing SDRs or similar reserve assets. Failure to do so would likely expose the reserve asset once again to the perils of speculation. Given the damage done by the process of privatizing the international monetary system since the 1970s, the debate on reform must include discussions of the appropriate criteria for determining changes in exchange rates and how those determinations should be made.

30. Restructuring flows of private international investment into emerging and developing economies

While a larger role for the SDR might deal with some of the problems faced by developing and emerging economies, it would not address either problems associated with private foreign capital inflows or the issue of how channels for capital inflows affect these countries' stability and growth. As portfolio investment became the dominant channel for private foreign inflows in the 1990s, the damage they caused became a critical part of the ongoing crisis scenarios that have plagued these countries in recent decades. As a result, establishing a channel for private foreign investment that can promote stable and sustainable growth is another important issue that must be addressed in reforming the international financial and monetary system.

Developing and emerging economies need to attract capital to augment the more limited resources available in their own markets. Recognizing that need, the Bretton Woods system created a specific institution to fund development—the International Bank for Reconstruction and Development, more commonly known as the World Bank—that was authorized to issue its own liabilities to private investors, backed by contributions and guarantees from its member countries. But, like bilateral aid given by individual countries, private capital flows had dwarfed amounts loaned by either the World Bank or other public sources by the middle of the 1970s. At that point, as discussed in Chapter 2, the large international banks located in developed countries undertook the role of recycling the surpluses of Organization of Petroleum Exporting Countries and became the pre-eminent intermediaries for private capital flows.

Beginning in the 1980s, however, three interrelated developments gradually established the supremacy of private foreign portfolio investment in funding development. First, patterns of saving and investment underwent a major shift in the larger industrialized countries. Increasingly, individuals put their savings in pension plans and other institutional pools that invest those funds directly in securities rather than placing them in the hands of intermediaries such as depository institutions. How this development reshaped the US financial system is discussed in Chapter 4; as it progressed in other developed countries, it transformed their traditional bank-based systems into market-based systems, as it had in the US. In Canadian, German, Japanese, and UK financial markets, assets of institutional investors more than doubled as a percentage of gross domestic product (GDP) from 1980 through 1995. In the US, the percentage of assets held by institutional investors rose from 59 to 151 percent of GDP over the same period. The rapid increase in institutional holdings of bonds and equities among the G7 countries rose from 35 percent of their combined GDP in 1985 to 140 percent in 1995 (IMF, 1995, 1999).[1]

The explosion in cross-border securities transactions was aided and abetted by a second key event: the dismantling of controls on capital movements by rich, poor, and middle-income countries alike. The US took the lead in 1974, removing controls that had been imposed in the 1960s to halt capital outflows: the interest equalization tax on issues of foreign securities in US markets, restrictions on transfers of funds by US multinational corporations to their foreign affiliates, and limits on new foreign lending by US banks (D'Arista, 2000, 2006).

In 1979, the UK eliminated controls on capital outflows. During the following decade, other European countries repealed limits on both outflows and inflows (such as reserve requirements and taxes on foreign borrowing) to comply with the timetable set for unification and the implementation of the European Monetary System. Ending capital controls also became a prerequisite for membership in the Organisation for Economic Co-operation and Development, which prompted their removal by Mexico and South Korea when they became members in the 1990s. Under pressure from the US government and foreign investors, other emerging market countries also lifted restrictions on inflows in the 1990s.

In many countries, the wholesale removal of capital controls took place against the backdrop of a vast privatization of state enterprises. The wave of privatization extended from the Thatcher government in England to the restructuring of centrally planned economies, and generated more securities issues in a wider range of national markets than in any previous period. This third critical development ensured the rise of portfolio investment worldwide. As cross-border securities transactions mushroomed in volume and scale, national capital markets expanded accordingly, markets grew more integrated worldwide, and capital mobility accelerated.

For most of the 1980s—a period of easy fiscal and tight monetary policy that drove up real interest rates and the value of the dollar—the

US reigned as the primary recipient of foreign portfolio investment. As the Third World Debt Crisis (triggered in part by those same policies) stretched across the decade, debt service payments provided a large, continuing source of inflows to the US. But the end of the decade recession that sapped demand and depressed asset prices in America and other industrialized countries caused investors to redirect funds into developing economies. Between 1989 and 1993, private investment flows into emerging markets multiplied more than 12 times over as a percentage of total foreign securities investment by industrial countries.

This pattern superficially resembles other ebbs and flows in post-Bretton Woods economic and financial activity in the era immediately after the collapse of the Bretton Woods gold/dollar exchange standard. During the 1970s, for example, rapid oil price increases produced recession and falling interest rates in industrialized countries, which set the stage for a wave of private bank lending to developing countries.

But international investment in the early 1990s differed from preceding periods in at least two important ways. First, developing countries absorbed a much larger volume of funds than ever before. As unrestrained foreign portfolio investment poured into national markets, it bid up the prices of financial assets at unprecedented rates. Aggregate capital inflows to Mexico from 1990 to 1993 totaled $91 billion—an amount equal to one fifth of all net inflows to developing countries in those years—and most of it was channeled into the stock market, which rose 436 percent between 1990 and 1993.

Second, the opening of financial markets to massive flows of foreign portfolio capital exposed countries to short investment horizons and hair-trigger investor judgments. Rather than residing as long-term assets on the books of banks, developing nation investments became overnight guests on the constantly changing balance sheets of pension funds, mutual funds, and hedge funds. Freed from restrictions on entry or exit, institutional investors could now shuffle their investments in bonds and equities from market to market in response to cyclical developments that raised and lowered returns—a privilege that subtly but inexorably weakened the impact of countercyclical monetary policies.

As the notion of "hot money" entered the popular lexicon, central bankers discovered that the increasingly potent interest- and exchange-rate effects of capital flows were undermining their ability to control credit expansion and contraction. As discussed in Chapter 17, lowering interest rates in an effort to revive economic activity was instead likely to precipitate or intensify capital outflows and reduce credit availability in their national economies. By raising interest rates to cool economic activity, central banks tended to attract foreign inflows seeking higher returns. If large enough, the inflow might stimulate rather than suppress borrowing and lending. In other cases, of course, hiking interest rates to attract foreign funds to finance a current account deficit or halt a drain on reserves might fail if investors are not convinced the rate is high enough or will be maintained for long enough to sustain the inflow and prevent a fall in the exchange rate.

The danger of these pro-cyclical pressures manifested itself with a vengeance in the mid-1990s as industrialized countries pulled out of recession and increased their demand for credit. After skyrocketing from $29 billion to $142 billion between 1990 and 1993, the annual net value of foreign portfolio investment by US residents fell to $50 billion in 1994. The Federal Reserve played a decisive role in this reversal by initiating in March 1994 what became a seven-step monetary tightening that narrowed the spreads between US and emerging market debt issues.

As these spreads narrowed, equity prices fell in Mexico and other emerging markets, eroding their value as collateral for bank loans. Meanwhile, an appreciating peso had lowered the cost of imported consumer goods and hammered Mexico's export sector, pushing the country's current account deficit to a whopping 8 percent of GDP by the final quarter of 1994. As new foreign investment in private securities diminished, the Zedillo government attempted to finance the deficit by issuing dollar-indexed, short-term debt—the so-called *tesobonos* that promised to protect their holders against the possibility of currency devaluation.

Although temporarily effective, this response only increased Mexico's exposure to a loss of confidence by foreign investors. Amid a series of political shocks and mounting concern over the country's dwindling international reserves, domestic and foreign investors began to take flight, forcing Mexico to devalue the peso in December 1994. Ultimately, the *tesobono* overhang contributed to what was called a $50 billion bailout of Mexico by the Clinton administration. In reality, it was a bailout of foreign investors by international public sector lenders that was repaid by Mexican taxpayers over time.

In the wake of the peso crisis, many emerging market countries took measures to counter the heavy investment inflows that inflated exchange rates (thereby eroding the competitiveness of export sectors) and increased the volatility of capital markets (thereby heightening the vulnerability of their financial systems). According to the IMF (1995), these remedial measures included increases in bank reserve requirements, increased exchange rate flexibility, and the imposition of exchange controls. The Bank for International Settlements (BIS, 1995) reported widespread agreement that short-term financial transactions should not be free from controls until developing nations could assure the soundness of their financial systems.

This agreement, however, ran up against what became known as the far more powerful Washington Consensus. Leading American financial firms, the Democratic administration, the Republican Congress, the Federal Reserve, the IMF, and elite opinion makers all continued to press for unimpeded financial liberalization, insisting that greater freedom for capital movements was the solution, not the problem. Portraying capital inflows as wholly beneficial, these influential advocates claimed that mass outflows were an inevitable response to bad policies and an acceptable tool of market discipline (D'Arista, 2008).

As the Mexican crisis subsequently replayed itself in different forms throughout the world, the shortsightedness of the Washington Consensus became clear. When capital raced out of East Asia, Russia, Brazil, and other emerging economies in the late 1990s in successive waves of panic, the ripple effects on exchange rates, asset values, commodity prices, employment, incomes, and financial systems brought a downturn in the global economy that was felt in industrialized as well as emerging markets. After these experiences, views on capital controls began to shift and countries began to look back to earlier models, such as Chile's requirement that foreign investors hold securities for a year or more, and that Chilean companies maintain reserve requirements on direct borrowing abroad—requirements that had proved successful in the 1990s (D'Arista, 2008).

But these controls don't always succeed in deterring the destructive fluctuations in asset prices and exchange rates that are associated with pro-cyclical surges in capital flows. Moreover, they can undermine the effort to attract long-term private capital into emerging markets in amounts that are both sizable and stable and not directed solely to companies in the export sector that can earn foreign exchange. Institutional investors necessarily have narrow interests and limited time horizons, despite the potential for such investors to use long-term savings to promote growth and stability in emerging economies. Therefore, a public purpose market innovation will be needed to accomplish that task and will require that governments take the lead in laying the institutional groundwork.

A PROPOSAL TO TAME INVESTMENT FLOWS TO EMERGING ECONOMIES

One innovation that might be equal to this task is a closed-end investment fund for securities that would fund private enterprises and public sector agencies in developing and emerging economies. Such a fund could issue its own liabilities to private investors and buy stocks and bonds, or make loans to borrowers in a wide spectrum of developing countries, including those that do not have markets large enough to absorb direct inflows of foreign portfolio investment or the credit standing to attract them. Both the number of countries and the size of the investment pool would need to be large enough to ensure diversification. The fund's investment objectives would focus on the long-run economic performance of enterprises and countries rather than short-term financial returns. Selecting securities in consultation with the host government would help the fund meet those objectives.

Unlike open-end mutual funds which must buy back an unlimited number of shares whenever investors demand it, closed-end investment pools issue a limited number of shares that trade on a stock exchange or in over-the-counter markets. This key structural difference makes the holdings of closed-end portfolios much less vulnerable to the waves of buying and redemptions that sometimes characterize open-end funds. A closed-end fund would therefore provide emerging markets with a measure of protection by allowing the prices of shares in the fund to fluctuate without triggering destabilizing purchases and sales of the underlying investments.

To further balance the goals of market stability and economic dynamism, the closed-end fund should possess a solid capital cushion. Between 10 and 20 percent of the value of shares sold to investors should be used to purchase and hold government securities of major industrial countries in amounts roughly proportional to the value of the closed-end fund shares owned by residents of those countries. These holdings would provide investors a partial guaranteed return, denominated in their own currencies. And the government securities would explicitly guarantee the value of the fund's capital—a double guarantee that would moderate investors' concerns about potential risk.

Creating one or more closed-end funds on this model would reduce the need for capital controls, especially in countries that choose to accept foreign portfolio investment solely through this channel. And these funds would have several additional benefits. They would help pension plans in developing and developed countries diversify their portfolios while minimizing country risk and transactions costs. And it would help institutional investors in developing countries share the cost of information and collectively combat the lack of disclosure by domestic issuers in those markets.

The institutional structure of the proposed closed-end fund does not reinvent the wheel. Just as the mechanisms and potential assets of a closed-end fund based on emerging economies already exist in the marketplace, the capacity for managing such a fund falls well within the reach of an existing public institution. Indeed, this management function is wholly consistent with the World Bank's mandate to facilitate private investment in developing countries. Moreover, the Bank's experience in issuing its own liabilities in global capital markets would expedite the start-up of a closed-end fund.

In addition, creating a closed-end fund under the World Bank umbrella could make another important contribution to global financial and monetary reform. If emerging and developing countries were to use their current account surpluses to purchase the liabilities of the fund, those liabilities would become a new form of international reserve asset—a safe and productive channel for the investment of their international reserves.

As discussed in Chapter 17, the spillover effects of the investments of their current account surpluses in the US and other major national and international markets assures not only that these poorer countries are financing the rich, but that some portion of those funds are recycled back to those same creditor economies in the form of foreign acquisition and ownership of their financial assets and productive facilities. The current channel for the reflow of the savings of these countries does not always reflect investment strategies that are concerned with development. In fact, portfolio and direct investment by foreigners necessarily entails the need for returns to reward individuals and institutions that have acquired ownership of these assets. Moreover, as discussed, it tends to encourage and facilitate export strategies that increase the accumulation of external currencies.

In view of this aspect of the reserve accumulation process, one of the more pressing issues in dealing with global imbalances is to find ways to recycle the savings of these countries back into their own economies in support of development strategies that increase demand and income more equitably and reduce dependence on export-led growth. Investing the reserves of developing countries in one or more closed-end funds would redirect external savings back into the economies of the countries that own them rather than into the financial markets of strong currency countries. Like proposals for additional issues of SDRs, these investment funds could inaugurate a meaningful shift into a non-national reserve asset and help phase out a system in which the choice of financial assets as reserve holdings centers on a few countries whose wealth supports the strength of their currencies. One incentive for emerging and developing countries to hold the securities of the proposed closed-end funds as reserves is that they would provide a multilateral (rather than a unilateral) guarantee from industrial countries and, in time, from wealthier emerging economies as well.

NOTE

1. Cross-border transactions data for the G7 countries excluded the UK because of the uniquely international nature of its financial markets.

31. Reforming the international payments system

The proposal to use public multilateral credit liabilities as reserve assets is incremental in nature and, while it addresses a critical flaw in the current international financial and monetary system, an equally critical one—the means of payment—must also be addressed. As discussed above, permitting a strong currency regime for cross-border transactions to continue would perpetuate the export-led growth paradigm that requires the majority of countries to shape their economies to ensure that they can earn—or borrow—key currencies in order to engage in external trade and investment. It also requires the key or strong currency country to import more than it exports to meet demand for its currency and to accept the resulting current account deficits and build-up in debt described by Nicholas Kaldor in Chapter 12. The global economy can only regain balance if every country is able to use its own currency, backed by the wealth created within its own borders, to participate in the global economy. To achieve that goal, a new system must enable national governments and central banks to reclaim from financial markets their sovereign capacities to conduct appropriate national economic policies, including the ability to implement effective countercyclical policies at a national level.

One way to create such a system would be to revive John Maynard Keynes' Bretton Woods proposal for an international clearing union as the underlying structure for a new institutional framework.[1] While Keynes' overall proposal was designed for a very different world, the basic structure in his concept could be revised to serve as the institutional platform for a new global payments system that would foster egalitarian interactions and more balanced outcomes. Such a platform—an international clearing agency (ICA)—would function as a clearing house and repository for international reserves. As a public sector entity, its creation would demand significant collaboration among nations, but it would not be a supranational central bank. It would not issue a single global currency. Indeed, it would not issue currency at all. That would remain the prerogative of national central banks, as would making monetary policy decisions for their own national economies. But, by providing a multinational structure for clearing payments, the ICA would both enable and require countries to make cross-border payments in their own currencies.

The balance sheet of the proposed ICA defines its operational framework. It would hold debt securities of its member nations as assets and their clearing accounts as liabilities. These assets and liabilities would allow the agency to clear transactions denominated in members' own currencies by crediting and debiting their clearing accounts in transactions with their national central banks. These clearing accounts would, in fact, constitute the international reserves of the system, held for the member countries by the ICA and valued using a trade-weighted basket of all members' currencies. At the time of initiation of the ICA, the decision about the size of an individual country's reserve account would be based on the size of its GDP, with additional reserves allocated to developing countries whose GDPs are small relative to population.

The clearing process would change the ownership of reserves and permit exchange rates to increase or decrease within a given range and set a period of time in response to changes in reserve levels. Thus, the clearing mechanism would preserve the valid role of market forces in shaping currency values through trade and investment flows while ensuring that speculators would no longer dominate the process.

The ICA could also reintroduce Harry D. White's Bretton Woods proposal to authorize open market operations at the international level as central banks do at the national level.[2] It would do so by permitting the new clearing agency to acquire government securities from its member countries to back additions to their reserve holdings or sell securities to reduce the backing for those holdings—actions that would directly influence the effects of changes in reserves on national market conditions.

In addition, when approved by a supermajority of its members, the ICA could also act as an international lender of last resort—a role the IMF cannot play given its dependence on taxpayer contributions. In this capacity, the ICA could assist a national central bank in supplying liquidity by buying government securities from residents in the national market and augmenting the country's international reserves.

Given these powers, it would be important to create a governmental and institutional structure for the proposed ICA that would reflect democratic and egalitarian standards. To begin, membership in the ICA would be open to national central banks of participating countries, and branches of the clearing agency would operate in every major financial center across the globe. Its egalitarian framework could be constructed by ensuring that population as well as economic activity would determine governing power within the agency. For example, the executive committee in charge of the ICA's operations and policies should be appointed on a rotating basis, with the requirement that its members at all times represent countries that, in the aggregate, constitute over half the world's population and over half its total output. To bring diverse inputs into policy deliberations, the ICA's staff and advisory bodies should represent a variety of regions, occupations, and sectors and include constituencies that are frequently overlooked in the formulation of national central bank policies.

Like national central banks, the ICA should be equipped with a highly skilled transactional, policy, and legal staff attuned to market dynamics and alert to the needs of commercial banks and other financial institutions. But the ICA's mandate must focus on the interests of the citizens of member nations and their institutions of self-government. It must not view private financial institutions as its primary constituency nor include them on its advisory committees.

The Agency's independent directors should be the co-equals of national central bank officials, but their obligations and perspective must be mega-economic. In seeking to influence the course of national economic policy, the ICA must operate primarily through persuasion and negotiation rather than resorting to unilateral exercise of its financial leverage through open market operations. It would have the power to redirect national policy but could do so only by establishing a consensus agreement among its members and acting in the long-term interest of all.

This aspect of the ICA's operations may seem radical, even with an unprecedented degree of transparency and accountability built in. It is, however, far less radical and far more respectful of national sovereignty than financial markets' existing capacity to override national policy goals and undermine democratic institutions. Moreover, numerous precedents exist for international efforts to reshape economic policy in one country in the interests of global stability through existing institutions such as the IMF, the World Bank, the G7, and G20.

BENEFITS OF THE PROPOSED CLEARING SYSTEM

Restoring the public sector to its role as facilitator and guardian of the international payments system would have deep and lasting benefits. A stable regime of currency relations is key to reversing current global economic system incentives for lower wages and the export of goods and capital on ruinous terms. In effect, the proposed ICA would eliminate over-the-counter foreign exchange activities of large multinational banks, ending the wasteful reign of the enormous daily volume of foreign exchange transactions and curbing the volatile movements in currency values that undermine real economic activity. It would bar speculators from raiding the world's currency reserves by requiring that those reserves be held by the ICA and by periodically using changes in reserve levels to determine adjustments in exchange rates.

In such a system, individuals or firms could not accumulate sufficient foreign exchange balances to influence the values of currencies. And allowing only authorized participants access to an international payments system would radically diminish the ability of individuals, firms, or unregulated havens to initiate or encourage off-market transactions. Most importantly, by requiring each country to pay for cross-border transactions in its own currency, an ICA-based system would allow national governments and central banks to focus on the needs of the domestic economy.

During the last several decades, the debt-service imperative of the current key currency system has relentlessly focused economic competition on labor costs rather than on broader measures of comparative advantage. In addition, the deregulated international financial environment dominated by portfolio investment has fostered powerful, built-in incentives for austere monetary and fiscal policies in almost all nations. Now the deflationary consequences of these trends have produced huge global imbalances in productive capacity and effective demand. Volatile movements in the huge, privatized foreign exchange market compound the deflationary effect and reinforce the deflationary bias of countries that issue currencies, such as the euro or the pound sterling, that are used in cross-border payments but are subordinate on a global scale to the ubiquitous dollar.

An international clearing system could have helped moderate the build-up of the huge global imbalances in place when the financial crisis erupted in 2007–2008. And by pre-emptively absorbing some of the excess liquidity flooding into both advanced and emerging market countries in the years since the 1970s, the ICA could have reduced the damages of both booms and busts. Lowering the need to build up foreign exchange reserves for countries that required and still require foreign capital to develop would have helped these countries control capital inflows and outflows, as discussed in Chapter 17. Equally importantly, they would have been able to develop more diversified economies with broader, more diversified domestic markets for goods and services.

Moreover, in its capacity as an absorber and provider of liquidity, the ICA could also undercut the pressure for austerity by giving nations greater freedom to instate prudent expansionary policies based on their domestic needs. However, since exchange rates would be determined by a clearly articulated set of ICA rules, as well as by underlying trade and investment flows, the agency would not provide a blank check or unconditional safety net for wrongheaded policies. Nevertheless, awareness of the ICA's ability to help mop up excess liquidity or provide new liquidity would obviate the need for capital controls which have proven in past instances to be of only limited and temporary effectiveness.

THE RULES OF THE GAME FOR AN INTERNATIONAL CLEARING AGENCY

The term "rules of the game" refers to the practices and conditions that nations accept as the framework for participating in an international payments system. At the national level, such practices may be informally adapted to international transactions or may formally conform to multinational agreements. Examples of informal agreements include the gold and gold/exchange standards in effect at various times before the Second World War or the current fiat currency standard. Bretton Woods is an example of a formal multinational agreement, ratified by member countries. But any international monetary system that involves public sector institutions requires adherence to certain conventions. Those that would apply to the proposed system—that is, the rules of the game for the ICA—include the following:

1. All cross-border payments would be made in the payer's domestic currency.
2. Commercial banks in member countries would be required to accept checks denominated in any other member country's currency. ("Commercial banks" means any financial institutions that are part of a country's payments system.)
3. Commercial banks in member countries would be required to present foreign currency-denominated checks to their national central banks for payment. Payment would be made by crediting individual banks' reserve accounts with the central bank to provide support for the creation of a domestic currency deposit of equal value. In this way, commercial banks would not be permitted to hold foreign currency deposits or make foreign currency payments.
4. National central banks in member countries would be required to present all foreign currency-denominated payments received by their national commercial banks to the ICA for payment. Foreign currency payments received by the ICA would be processed

through credits and debits to member countries' international reserve accounts. Consequently, all international reserves would be held by the ICA.

5. International reserves would constitute bookkeeping entries on the asset side of the balance sheet of national central banks and on the liability side of the balance sheet of the ICA. The value of these reserves would reflect the aggregate value of all member countries' currencies—a comprehensive basket—with a trade-weighted basis used to set the initial value of individual reserve accounts. Thereafter, changes in the value of individual reserve accounts would reflect gains and losses in their share of the comprehensive basket.
6. National central banks would be required to accept all checks denominated in their currencies and finalize payment by debiting the domestic reserve accounts of the originating commercial banks.

In summary, international payments would take place through the simultaneous debiting and crediting of a) reserve accounts held by commercial banks with their national central banks; and b) the reserve accounts of national central banks held with the ICA. No payments would be made directly between national central banks. Nor would national central banks provide foreign currency to private sector financial and non-financial institutions. All international reserves would be held by the ICA and denominated in a weighted basket of all members' currencies.

This structure would not prevent non-residents from holding domestic currency assets or deposits in another country's national market. Nor would it prevent foreign financial institutions from acting as authorized intermediaries for making loans and investments in the domestic currency within the national market of another country. The rules would, however, restrict the use of a nation's currency in transactions outside its national market since only financial institutions holding reserves with national central banks could accept payments in foreign currency or make payments to non-residents in the domestic currency. In other words, this framework would effectively disband and prevent the re-creation of external financial markets like the so-called Eurocurrency markets which have become a main impediment to effective implementation of monetary policy and financial regulation by national authorities.

THE TRANSACTIONAL FRAMEWORK FOR AN INTERNATIONAL CLEARING SYSTEM

The following description of the transactional framework for the ICA international monetary system is likely to be of limited interest to most readers, even those with a general knowledge of how monetary systems work. But it is important to work through these balance sheet transactions to ensure that the overall concept is valid. Therefore, I ask the indulgence of the reader as I proceed with this task, hoping most will attempt to follow the explanations of transactions, but accepting the probability that many readers will skip this part of the chapter.

The transactional work of the ICA begins when a check is written in country B to pay for goods, services, or investments purchased in country A. The buyer pays in his own currency. The seller deposits the foreign currency check in her own bank account. Her bank deposits the foreign currency check in its national central bank and receives a credit to its reserve account, which enables it to create a domestic currency deposit for the seller equivalent to the foreign currency she received.

Country A's central bank then submits the foreign currency check to the ICA and receives a credit in that amount to its international reserve account. The ICA, in turn, submits the check to country B's central bank and accepts payment for it by debiting country B's international reserve account. The final step in the process comes when country B's central bank submits the check to the buyer's bank and debits that institution's reserve account the way the Fed and other central banks currently clear checks on a domestic basis. The check is then canceled and returned to the buyer.

This kind of transaction would be repeated millions of times during the course of a day and involve many buyers and sellers in a number of countries. At the end of the day, however, countries A and B might end up in the same place as in the solitary transaction described in Table 31.1. Both the international reserves and domestic bank reserves of country A have increased while the international and domestic bank reserves of country B have declined. In the event of such symmetrical transactions, the ICA's balance sheet would reflect a shift in reserves. But neither the ICA's total assets and liabilities—or, therefore, global liquidity—would change as indicated by the balance of payments effects shown in the series of pluses, minuses, and zeros shown below the line in the table.

Table 31.1 ICA clearing function

Country A				ICA		Country B			
Commercial bank		Central bank				Central bank		Commercial bank	
Assets	Liabilities	Assets	Liabilities	Assets	Liabilities	Assets	Liabilities	Assets	Liabilities
1.	+ Country B deposit								–Country B deposit
2. + reserves	B deposit	+ B deposit	+ domestic reserves						
	+ A deposit								
3.		– B deposit + inter-national reserves		+ B deposit	+ A international reserves				
4.				– B deposit	– B international reserves	+/– B deposit international reserves	– domestic reserves	– reserves	

Within the ICA, all member countries' international reserves will fluctuate as a result of payments for international trade in goods and services and investment transactions, just as they do today. However, the job of the ICA will be to manage these fluctuations through a system of appropriate exchange rates determined at the inauguration of the system. Changes in international reserves that exceed an agreed-upon amount in either direction (for example, plus or minus 5 percent) and persist for a given amount of time (for example, more than 30 days) would signal the need for adjustments. Table 31.2 shows how the ICA would perform these adjustments.

Table 31.2 Exchange rate adjustment under ICA proposal

	International clearing agency	
	Assets	Liabilities
Stocks	Country A	Country A
	government securities	international reserves
before transactions in Table 31.1	100%	100%
	Country B	Country B
	government securities	international reserves
	100%	100%
Stocks	Country A	Country A
	government securities	international reserves
after transactions in Table 31.1	100%	105%
	Country B	Country B
	government securities	international reserves
	100%	95%
Stocks	Country A	Country A
	government securities	international reserves
after changes in reserve levels and exchange rates	105%	105%
	Country B	Country B
	government securities	international reserves
	95%	95%

The first and second rows of Table 31.2 show the stock of assets and liabilities of the ICA before and after the transactions in Table 31.1. Assuming that changes in the international reserves of countries A and B are large enough and have persisted long enough to trigger an adjustment in the exchange rates, the third row shows the ICA's response. It will increase or reduce its holdings of these two countries' government securities to bring their values in line with the values of each of their international reserves at the new exchange rate.

Again, these adjustments would produce no change in global liquidity. However, if the ICA had to buy additional government securities from residents of country A or sell government securities to residents of country B in the process of making its adjustments, the agency's actions would reinforce the economic impacts of changes in reserve levels and exchange rates on their domestic financial markets.

In most cases, the central banks of countries A and B would be able to deal with the expansionary or contractionary effects of changes in international reserves and exchange rates in ways that promote their national policy objectives. In the absence of capital controls, however, the interest-rate and asset-price effects that follow an exchange rate adjustment could reinforce the pro-cyclical response of capital flows. If flows were to become excessive and shocks occurred, the ICA could prevent or moderate further exchange rate realignments by adjusting the international reserve holdings of one or more countries, as shown in Table 31.3.

Again, the first row shows the effects of the transactions in Table 31.1 on the stocks of assets and liabilities of the ICA and the central banks of countries A and B. The international reserves of country B have fallen by 5 percent while those of country A have risen by 5 percent. The resulting decline/increase in domestic bank reserves puts contractionary/expansionary pressure on the domestic economies of the two countries.

To cushion the impact of these pressures, the ICA reduces country A's reserves by selling some of its holdings of country A's government securities to its central bank and accepting payment for them by debiting its international reserve account (see the second row). At the same time, the ICA buys country B's government securities from its central bank and pays for them by crediting its international reserve account (also shown in the second row). These reserve adjustments have altered the composition of assets and liabilities at the two central banks and the ICA but, as the third row shows, they do not change the aggregate level of assets and liabilities or alter international liquidity.

Table 31.3 Adjustment in reserve holdings

	Central bank Country A		International clearing agency		Central bank Country B	
	Assets	Liabilities	Assets	Liabilities	Assets	Liabilities
Stocks after clearing transactions	Domestic government debt	Domestic reserves, cash, etc.	Country A Government debt 100%	Country A International reserves 105%	Domestic government debt	Domestic reserves, cash, etc.
	International reserves				International reserves	
			Country B Government debt 100%	Country B International reserves 95%		
Flows (reserve adjustment process)	Domestic government debt +5% International reserves –5%		Country A Government debt –5%	Country A International reserves –5%	Domestic government debt –5% International reserves +5%	
			Country B Government debt +5%	Country B International reserves 5%		
Stocks (after reserve adjustment process)	Domestic government debt International reserves	Domestic reserves, cash, etc.	Country A Government debt 95%	Country A International reserves 100%	Domestic government debt International reserves	Domestic reserves, cash, etc.
			Country B Government debt 105%	Country B International reserves 100%		
	100%	100%	200%	200%	100%	100%

These adjustments give the two central banks additional capacity to wrestle with the effects of international transactions on their domestic economies and financial sectors. The additional capacity does not guarantee a successful result. But it does enable national monetary authorities to use open market operations and other policy tools to cope more effectively with falling employment, rising prices, or other domestic trends.

As Table 31.3 suggests, the ICA's transactional framework enables the agency itself to conduct open market operations at the international level to reinforce national policy objectives, to stabilize global markets in ordinary circumstances, or to act as a lender of last resort in crisis situations. Tables 31.4 and 31.5 outline the transactions involved in the conduct of international open market operations by the ICA.

The ICA would conduct international open market operations much as a central bank does in its own national market by buying or selling government securities directly from or to residents of that country (Tables 31.4 and 31.5, first row). When the ICA buys government securities from residents of a given country, it writes checks payable to the sellers denominated in the currency of that country. The sellers of the securities deposit the ICA checks in their commercial banks and the banks submit the checks to their national central bank and receive credit to their reserve accounts with the central bank (Table 31.4, first and third rows). The potential expansionary effects are shown as increases in the assets and liabilities of both the central bank and the commercial banks.

The real expansion takes place after the central bank submits the check to the ICA and is paid with an increase in its international reserve account (Table 31.4, fourth row). At this point, the commercial banks have excess reserves to make new loans that will expand economic activity in the member country (Table 31.4, first row). But it is the growth in total international reserves that produces an increase in global liquidity.

If the policy objective were to contract global liquidity, the ICA would sell a member country's government securities to its residents and receive checks drawn on commercial banks in that country denominated in its domestic currency (Table 31.5, fifth row). As shown in the second row, the ICA would present these checks to the member country's central bank and accept payment by debiting the central bank's international reserve account. In the third row, the central bank returns the commercial bank checks to the banks they were written on and accepts payment by reducing their reserve accounts with the central bank. In the process, the commercial banks lose reserves and the deposits on which the checks

Table 31.4 International open market operations (expansionary)

International clearing agency		National central bank		National commercial bank		National investors	
Assets	Liabilities	Assets	Liabilities	Assets	Liabilities	Assets	Liabilities
National government debt +	ICA check +					National government debt −	
						ICA check +	
				ICA check +		ICA check −	
				ICA check −			
		ICA check +	Domestic reserves +	Domestic reserves +	Domestic deposit +	Domestic deposit +	
	ICA check −	ICA check −					
	International reserves +	International reserves +					
				Excess reserves −			
				New loan +	New deposit +	New deposit +	New loan +

were written. In a fractional reserve system, the banks must call in loans to balance the asset and liability sides of their balance sheets, with a resulting drop in deposits used by the resident investors of that country to repay loans (Table 31.5, fourth row). In this way, international open market operations initiated by the ICA through sales of a country's government securities result in a contraction in credit in that country. In addition, these sales at the international level also reduce the total amount of international reserves held by the ICA and thus lower the level of global liquidity.

Table 31.5 International open market operations (contractionary)

International clearing agency		National central bank		National commercial bank		National investors	
Assets	Liabilities	Assets	Liabilities	Assets	Liabilities	Assets	Liabilities
National government debt –						Domestic deposit –	
National commercial bank check +						National government debt +	
National commercial bank check –	International reserves –	National commercial bank check +					
		International reserves –					
		National commercial bank check –	Domestic reserves –	Domestic reserves –	Domestic deposit –		
				Domestic loan –		Domestic deposit –	Domestic loan –

The ICA proposal addresses several of the underlying problems discussed in this book. It would help create a multipolar world in which no single national currency would dominate financial markets, forcing damaging constraints on countries that must earn or borrow that currency to participate in the global economy, and on the country that issues that currency. By creating a public sector institution to implement the international payments system, it could provide the meaningful institutional structure needed to curb the rule of speculative capital flows in determining the growth of international reserves and changes in exchange rates. It would strengthen the ability of all countries to implement policies that meet the needs of their economies while meeting the need for a rule-based lender of last resort at the international level. And in the process of solving these problems, it would dismantle the system now in place that generated the level of worldwide debt that caused the previous financial crisis.

CONCLUDING REMARKS

The erosion and collapse of the Bretton Woods Agreement in the 1960s and 1970s caused chaos in the global economy.[3] The particular problem in that period was a "dollar glut" caused by the preference of market participants to use dollars in international payments, but not as a store of value. Since then, the use of the dollar as a store of value has resulted in an immense volume of international reserves denominated in dollars that, in the event of a fall in the dollar's value, would result in losses in the value of international reserves on the balance sheets of national central banks, causing a substantial contraction in the money supply in many national economies that could initiate a global depression.

To prevent such an outcome, it would be possible for member countries of the IMF to authorize it to create and issue the amount of SDRs necessary to offset the loss in value of dollar reserves. But doing so might lead to a series of questions:

1. Would that constrain the use of the dollar in making international payments?
2. If so, could it constrain the volume of international transactions and threaten recession or depression from a slowdown in trade and investment?
3. To counter or moderate that problem, would it be possible to set up a system like the one that used the European Currency Unit before the euro was introduced—a system that would denominate private transactions in SDRs in ongoing accounts with trading or investment partners, without actually exchanging SDRs at settlement?

It is appropriate to ask these questions because a potential loss in the value of the dollar at least as great as the loss at the beginning and end of the 1970s is possible and, at this time, the SDR is the only instrument available to moderate the damage caused by such a loss. But such a solution is clearly not an adequate foundation on which to build a new international monetary system.

While the proposed ICA architecture is by no means the only way to solve current and prospective problems in the international reserve and payments system, a discussion of how it would deal with those problems has, the author hopes, helped to outline the elements required for building a new system and may contribute to renewed discussion of the need for reform. Just as the failures at the international monetary and financial level in the 1930s created the urgency to re-establish the rule of law that led to the Bretton Woods Agreement, the strong possibility that a new financial crisis will ravage a much weaker global economy still recovering from the 2008 crisis and the failure of policies in the aftermath to re-establish sustainable economic activity, in addition to indications of a collapse of the current system, has once again created an urgent need for reform. The case for urgency in addressing the threats to our global and national monetary and financial systems is the subject of Chapter 32.

NOTES

1. For a description of Keynes' proposal, see Skidelsky, 2000.
2. For a full description of White's Bretton Woods proposals, see Boughton, 2006.
3. See Part III and the opening paragraphs of Chapter 29.

PART VIII

Conclusion

32. Building toward crisis in the global economy—again

In its 2016 *Annual Report*, the Bank for International Settlements (BIS) once again warned the international financial community about hugely damaging financial booms and busts and the debt-fueled growth model that spawns them. It argued that: "Debt has been acting as a political and social substitute for income growth for far too long" (BIS, 2016, p. 8); that "the world has been haunted by an inability to restrain financial booms that, once gone wrong, cause lasting damage" (p. 14); and that the "relentless increase in the debt-to-gross domestic product (GDP) ratios, both private and public" (p. 17) suggests the need for a fundamental realignment.

As the BIS critique confirms, high debt-to-GDP ratios were the clear signals that heralded the impending crisis in 2007–2008; today these ratios remain high and still indicate a threat to the global economy. Focusing on the build-up in debt of the highly leveraged United States (US) financial sector, from 22 percent of GDP in 1981 to 117 percent in late 2008, it is useful to remember why economist James Crotty argued that the level of the ratio had become unsupportable:

> It is not possible for the value of financial assets to remain so large relative to the real economy because the real economy cannot consistently generate the cash flows required to sustain such inflated financial claims. It is not economically efficient to have such large proportions of income and human and material resources captured by the financial sector. Financial markets must be forced to shrink substantially relative to non-financial sectors, a process already initiated by the crisis, and the nontransparent, illiquid complex securities that helped cause the crisis must be marginalized or banned. (Crotty, 2009)

While the illiquid complex securities Crotty mentions were among the triggers for the crisis, the rise in private financial and non-financial debt as a share of GDP led to an ongoing series of crises across the global economy from the 1980s through 2008, each of which was followed by a damaging period of deleveraging that hobbled growth. As anticipated, the debt of the US domestic financial sector did shrink by about $2.4 trillion in the wake of the financial crisis, from 2008 to year-end 2016, and fell to 84.3 percent of GDP, but that shrinkage was in effect a transfer of toxic assets from the balance sheets of private institutions to that of the Fed. Few if any of those assets were written off and, while the Fed's quantitative easing (QE) strategy clearly benefited financial institutions, it provided little or no relief for households, businesses, or state and local governments.

Meanwhile, the total debt of all US domestic non-financial sectors rose by $12.3 trillion to $47.3 trillion from 2008 to 2016, but fell from 290 to 254.3 percent of GDP. Outstanding US government debt stood at $19 trillion at year-end 2016, having risen to about 100 percent of GDP in the wake of the adverse effects of the recession on tax revenues. Indeed, as a recent Levy Economics Institute analysis points out, this cycle is the only one in the post-war era in which real government expenditure has decreased—a development that, in their view, is one of the main reasons for the slow recovery (Nikiforos and Zezza, 2017). Nevertheless, policy debates never deviate from an obsessive focus on federal government debt, despite levels of private and financial sector indebtedness that are far more damaging to economic outcomes.

In fact, current levels of US private debt remain historically high and validate concerns about their ongoing drag on actual and potential economic activity, especially in a long period of anemic wage growth. Student debt is worrisome, as is the fact that household debt reached $12.7 trillion in the first quarter of 2017—higher than the level before the collapse in 2008 (Corkery and Cowley, 2017). Moreover, in that same quarter, the International Monetary Fund (IMF) warned that leverage for firms accounting for about half of the economy-wide US corporate sector had reached levels exceeding those prevailing just before the 2008 crisis (IMF, 2017).

Equally importantly, however, but not widely discussed, is the substantial increase in US external debt after the financial crisis. American trade deficits continued to be financed by foreign investment and, while the trade balance remained stationary as a percentage of GDP, by year-end 2016 foreign investment in the US exceeded US investment abroad by $8.1 trillion or 43 percent of GDP—up from $2.9 trillion or 25 percent of GDP in 2002—while total US liabilities to foreigners had risen to $29 trillion or 158 percent of GDP (US Department of Commerce, 2016).

While debt expansion in the US moderated somewhat during the Great Recession, the ongoing inflow of foreign savings into American markets continued to provide a substantial source of financing for the rise in household and corporate debt. Moreover, sparked by low US interest rates and, beginning in 2009, the flood of liquidity the Fed unleashed with its QE strategy, there was a virtual explosion of debt creation in offshore financial markets, with emerging market economies (EMEs) the major recipients of large volumes of capital inflows. Dollar-denominated debt outside the US rose by more than 50 percent from 2009 to 2015; the dollar debt of non-banks in EMEs doubled and the foreign exchange reserves of these countries reached 24 percent of global GDP (IMF, 2017). As these figures suggest, demand for dollars remained strong and the value of the dollar rose about 28 percent from 2011 to 2016 (Appelbaum, 2017). However, from January through July 2017, the dollar fell nearly 8 percent against a basket of currencies, becoming what some have called a medium of expression about the American political environment (Goodman, 2017).[1]

Nevertheless, in the period 2009 to 2015, a sizable share of the additional foreign exchange reserves acquired by EMEs were invested in US financial assets as well as in dollar deposits and securities issued in external markets. Those invested in the US contributed to the ongoing deterioration in the US net international investment position and helped fuel the carry trades that converted borrowings in dollars for investment in higher-yielding EME assets. The resulting round-robin strategies embedded in the global monetary and financial system rebounded quickly after the crisis and continued to finance debt-fueled growth.

As the IMF noted, that build-up in debt in the EMEs made them more vulnerable to developments and policy changes in advanced economies (IMF, 2017). Although the self-insurance they had amassed in the form of international reserves may have seemed adequate in terms of covering payments on foreign currency debts, the substantial growth in foreign investment in their securities markets after the 2008 crisis suggests that reserves might not be adequate to cushion potential outflows (Akyus, 2017). As in the past, outflows from an EME are likely to be precipitated by developments in international financial markets that have nothing to do with confidence in that country's economy, but require the sale of its assets to meet the investor's need to cover losses elsewhere.

The IMF's reminder that, as countries become more integrated into the global economy their financial conditions are more likely to be affected by external shocks, applies to the US as well as to EMEs. The US has become more integrated into the global economy as a result of the substantial rise in its external debt, and any event anywhere in the world that might cause a significant withdrawal of foreign investment in US assets could precipitate destabilizing changes in interest and exchange rates in American financial markets that would spill over to the rest of the world.

The expansion of international reserves backed by the dollar or other national currencies since the crisis is a particular area of vulnerability both for EMEs and for the global economy. A significant drop in the value of the dollar or other widely held reserve currency would reduce the value of reserves that back domestic money and credit, which central banks in emerging markets and developing countries hold as assets on their balance sheets and use to engage in cross-border transactions. The impact of such a drop in value would cause a contraction in those economies that would affect economic activity throughout the rest of the world. It would also affect financial institutions in both developed and developing countries in their roles as creditors and borrowers. And the balance sheets of central banks still bloated from the last crisis—the $3.6 trillion acquired by the Federal Reserve through its QE programs, for example—will make it much harder to respond to a new crisis.

Given their concerns about the problems and dangers identified in their 2016 *Annual Report*, the BIS believes a fundamental realignment in the global financial system is possible if a macroprudential stability framework could be agreed upon.[2] Such a framework is certainly needed to rein in the financial system, even if the current resurgence of free market ideology and deregulation were not a factor. Equally important is the fact that the loss of countercyclical tools by national central banks in the process of deregulation has left the global system without the means to moderate excessive growth in credit. A macroprudential stability framework that would restore the ability of central banks to exercise effective countercyclical policies is a no less critical area for reform to end the potential for booms and busts that continue to inflict permanent loss.

Nevertheless, the financial system is only one problem. The other critical problem is created by the continued reliance on a national currency as the dominant instrument for global trade and investment. It is the key currency-based international monetary system that inexorably reinforces both the export-led and debt-fueled growth models that ultimately drive the US and global economies into crisis.

This author believes that a conference like that held at Bretton Woods at the end of the Second World War must be convened to redesign the monetary and financial structure that governs the global economy. As was the case in organizing the Bretton Woods Conference, all nations must be invited to participate, and the goal must be to structure a multipolar system under public sector guidance that will give all countries equal status in global financial markets. The proposed International Clearing Agency outlined in Chapter 31 would meet those criteria, but other frameworks could be designed that would be no less effective.

In addition, a multinational conference must be convened to discuss ways to reinstate the countercyclical powers of national central banks in a market-based global financial system in which investment and trading are more important functions than traditional bank-based lending and deposit taking. Without a new regulatory paradigm that would restore constraints on the supply of credit, debt-fueled growth will continue to generate booms that then collapse, with highly damaging consequences for both economic activity and the net wealth of households. As the IMF noted, the household sector has become the shock absorber of financial disruption (IMF, 2005, April, p. 5); a shift in the framework for financial protection, like the one proposed in Chapter 11 to cover individuals rather than institutions, is urgently needed to restore financial stability for households and the economy as a whole.

While all proposals that would meet the criteria outlined above appear to have little hope of being adopted in the current political environment, the proposals offered by the United Nations Commission of Experts in 2009,[3] and other proposals concerned with the effects of the debt- and export-led growth models embedded in the international and national monetary and financial systems, must continue to be discussed. The drag of continued high levels of debt in the US and global economies and growing recognition of rising instability suggest that the need to revisit such proposals may soon come in the wake of yet another crisis.

NOTES

1. Over this period, the dollar fell 11 percent against the euro, 7 percent against the pound, 6 percent against the Japanese yen, and 4 percent against China's renminbi.
2. For a discussion of macroprudential tools, see Chapter 22.
3. See Chapter 29 for a discussion of the United Nations Commission of Experts' proposals.

Bibliography

Akyus, Y., 2017. *Playing with Fire: Deepened Financial Integration and Changing Vulnerabilities in the Global South*. Oxford: Oxford University Press.

Albrecht, M., 2009. *Industry Surveys: Financial Services*. Standard & Poor's, November 26.

Andrews, E. L., 2007. "In Reversal, Fed Approves Plan to Curb Risky Lending." *New York Times*, December 19.

Appelbaum, B., 2017. "What the Decline of the Dollar Means." *New York Times*, July 20.

Appelbaum, B., J. Ewing, H. Tabuchi, and L. Thomas, 2013. "Central Banks Act with a New Boldness to Revitalize Economies." *New York Times*, May 28.

Baker, A., 2013. "The Gradual Transformation? The Incremental Dynamics of Macroprudential Regulation." *Regulation and Governance*, vol. 7, no. 4.

Baker, D., 2003. *Mismanaging Money: The Investment Practices of the Pension Fund Industry*. April. Washington, DC: Center for Economic and Policy Research.

Bank of England, 2009. *Financial Stability Report*. June. London: Bank of England. www.bankofengland.co.uk/publications/fsr/2009.

Barth, J. and R. D. Brumbaugh, Jr., 1993. "The Changing World of Banking: Setting the Regulatory Agenda." Unpublished paper prepared for the *Conference on Financial Prosperity in the 21st Century*, Jerome Levy Economics Institute, Bard College, Annandale-on-Hudson, NY, March.

Bernanke, B., 2010. Speech at the Federal Reserve Bank of Kansas City Economic Symposium, Jackson Hole, WY, August 27. Washington, DC: FRB.

BIS, 1995. *Annual Report*. June. Basel: BIS.

BIS, 2000. *International Banking and Financial Market Developments*. February. Basel: BIS.

BIS, 2002. *Annual Report*. June. Basel: BIS.

BIS, 2002a. *International Banking and Financial Market Developments*. September. Basel: BIS.

BIS, 2002b. *International Banking and Financial Market Developments*. December. Basel: BIS.

BIS, 2003. *Annual Report*. June. Basel: BIS.
BIS, 2004. *Annual Report*. June. Basel: BIS.
BIS, 2005. *Annual Report*. June. Basel: BIS.
BIS, 2005a. *Statistical Release*. May. Basel: BIS.
BIS, 2005b. *International Banking and Financial Market Developments*. Basel: BIS.
BIS, 2005c. *Triennial OTC Derivatives Statistics*. Basel, BIS.
BIS, 2006. *Annual Report*. June. Basel: BIS.
BIS, 2006a. *International Banking and Financial Market Developments*. March. Basel: BIS.
BIS, 2008. *Annual Report*. June. Basel: BIS.
BIS, 2016. *Annual Report*. Basel: BIS.
BIS, various issues. *Annual Report*.
Blackburn, R., 2003. "Gray Capital and the Challenge of Pension Finance." New York: New School University.
Blecker, R., 2002. "International Capital Mobility, Macroeconomic Imbalances, and the Risk of Global Contraction." In J. Eatwell and L. Taylor (eds), *International Capital Markets: Systems in Transition*. Oxford: Oxford University Press.
Borio, C. and P. Lowe, 2002. "Asset Prices, Financial and Monetary Stability: Exploring the Nexus." *BIS Working Papers*, no. 114. Basel: BIS.
Boughton, J. M., 2006. "American in the Shadows: Harry Dexter White and the Design of the International Monetary Fund." Working paper no. 06/6. Washington, DC: IMF.
Braudel, F., 1982. *The Wheels of Commerce: Civilization and Capitalism in the 15th–18th Centuries*, Vol. 2. New York: Harper and Row.
Brownstein, R., 1983. "A Wall of Money." *National Journal*, July 30.
Carlson, M. A., 2013. "Lessons from the Historical Use of Reserve Requirements in the United States to Promote Liquidity." Staff working paper no. 201 3-11. Washington, DC: Board of Overseers of the FRS.
Cassidy, J., 2010. *How Markets Fail: The Logic of Economic Calamities*. New York: Farrar, Straus & Giroux.
Cline, W. R., 1983. *International Debt and the Stability of the World Economy*. Washington, DC: Institute for International Economics.
Corkery, M. and S. Cowley, 2017. "Household Debt Makes a Comeback in the US." *New York Times*, May 17.
Cornford, A., 2008. "An Agenda for Financial Reform," SUNS, North-South Development Monitor #6511, July 7.
Crotty, J., 2009. "Structural Causes of the Global Financial Crisis: A Critical Assessment of the 'New Financial Architecture.'" *Cambridge Journal of Economics*, vol. 33, no. 4, July.

Crotty, J. and G. Epstein, 2008. *Proposals for Effectively Regulating the US Financial System to Avoid Another Meltdown*. Working paper no. 181, October. Amherst, MA: Political Economy Research Institute.
Dam, K. W., 1982. *The Rules of the Game*. Chicago, IL: University of Chicago Press.
D'Arista, J., 1976. *International Banking: A Supplement of a Compendium of Papers Prepared for the FINE Study*. Staff report of the Committee on Banking, Currency and Housing, House of Representatives. Washington, DC: US Government Printing Office.
D'Arista, J., 1994. *The Evolution of US Finance, Vol. I: Federal Reserve Monetary Policy: 1915–1935*. Armonk, NY: M. E. Sharpe.
D'Arista, J., 1994a. *The Evolution of US Finance, Vol. II: Restructuring Institutions and Markets*. Armonk, NY: M. E. Sharpe.
D'Arista, J., 2000. "Reforming International Financial Architecture." *Challenge*, vol. 43, no. 3, May–June.
D'Arista, J., 2002. "Financial Regulation in a Liberalized Global Environment." In J. Eatwell and L. Taylor (eds), *International Capital Markets: Systems in Transition*. Oxford: Oxford University Press.
D'Arista, J., 2003. "Balance of Payments Constraints on the Conduct of Independent Monetary Policies in a Globalized World: The NAFTA Experience." *International Journal of Political Economy*, vol. 33, no. 3, 72–89.
D'Arista, J., 2006. "The Implications of Aging for the Structure and Stability of Financial Markets." Background paper for the 2007 *World Economic and Social Survey*, December. New York: United Nations.
D'Arista, J., 2008. "Replacing the Failed Washington Consensus." *Journal of Post Keynesian Economics*, vol. 30, no. 4, 523–39.
D'Arista, J., 2009. "Setting an Agenda for Monetary Reform." Working paper no. 190, Political Economy Research Institute, University of Massachusetts, Amherst, MA.
D'Arista, J., 2009a. "The Evolving International Monetary System." *Cambridge Journal of Economics*, vol. 33, no. 1, July.
D'Arista, J. and G. Epstein, 2011. "Dodd-Frank and the Regulation of Dangerous Financial Interconnection." In M. Konzcal (ed.), *Dodd-Frank: Will It Work? How Will We Know?* New York: Roosevelt Institute.
D'Arista, J. and S. Griffith-Jones, 2001. "The Boom in Portfolio Flows to Emerging Markets and Its Regulatory Implications." In S. Griffith-Jones et al. (eds), *Short Term Capital Movements and Balance of Payments Crises*. Oxford: Oxford University Press.
D'Arista, J. and T. Schlesinger, 1993. "The Parallel Banking System." In G. Dymski, G. Epstein, and R. Pollin (eds), *Transforming the US*

Financial System: Equity and Efficiency for the 21st Century. Armonk, NY: M. E. Sharpe.

Davis, E. P., 2001. *Aging and Financial Stability*. Discussion paper 0111. London: Pensions Institute, University of London.

Eccles, M. S., 1935. "Statement." *Banking Act of 1935: Hearings Before the Committee on Banking and Currency*. Washington, DC: US House of Representatives.

Eisinger, J., 2013. "Why Fund Managers May Be Right about the Fed." *New York Times*, May 15.

Elliott, D. J., G. Feldberg, and A. Lehnert, 2013. "The History of Cyclical Macroprudential Policy in the United States." Working paper no. 0008, Office of Financial Research, US Department of the Treasury. Washington, DC: DOT.

Epstein G. and J. Crotty, 2009. "Controlling Dangerous Financial Products through a Financial Pre-Cautionary Principle." *Ekonomiaz*, no. 72, Quarter 3, 270–91.

European Parliament, 2008. *Draft Report with Recommendations to the Commission on Hedge Funds and Private Equity*. Brussels: European Union, April 18.

Ewing, J., 2013. "In Europe, a Fed President Urges Quantitative Easing." *New York Times*, May 21.

Financial Stability Forum, 2008. *Enhancing Markets and Institutional Resilience*. Basel: BIS, April 11.

FRB, 1999. *Monetary Policy Report to Congress*. Washington, DC: FRB.

FRB, 2002. *Monetary Policy Report to Congress*. Washington, DC: FRB.

FRS, 1998. H.10 Weekly Releases. October–December. Washington, DC: FRS.

FRS, 1999–2001. *Survey of Consumer Finance*. Washington, DC: FRS.

FRS, various issues. *Flow of Funds Accounts of the United States*. Washington, DC: FRS.

FRS, various years. *Federal Reserve Bulletin*. Washington, DC: FRB.

Galbraith, James K., 2009. "Who Are These Economists, Anyway?" *Thought and Action: The NEA Higher Education Journal*, Fall.

Geithner, T., 2008. *Testimony Before the US Senate Committee on Banking, Housing and Urban Affairs*. Washington, DC, April 3.

Gisselquist, D., 1981. *The Political Economics of International Bank Lending*. New York: Praeger Publishers.

Goodman, P. S., 2017. "In the Age of Trump, the Dollar No Longer Seems a Sure Thing." *New York Times*, August 9.

Gorton, G. and A. Metrick, 2009. *Securitized Banking and the Run on the Repo*. Brookings Institution Papers on Economic Activity, 15223.

Greenspan, A., 1993. "Opening Remarks." *Changing Capital Markets: Implications for Monetary Policy*. Conference Proceedings of the Federal Reserve Bank of Kansas City, Jackson Hole, WY.

Greenspan, A., 2003. *Address to the 21st Annual Monetary Conference*. Co-sponsored by *Economist* and the Cato Institute. November. Washington, DC: FRB.

Greenspan, A., 2005. *Testimony on the Federal Reserve Board's Semi-annual Monetary Policy Report to Congress*. Committee on Banking, Housing and Urban Affairs, US Senate, February 16.

Griffith-Jones, S., 2001. "Causes and Lessons of the Mexican Peso Crisis." In S. Griffith-Jones et al. (eds), *Short Term Capital Movements and Balance of Payments Crises*. Oxford: Oxford University Press.

Griffith-Jones, S., P. Calice, and C. Seekatz, 2007. *New Investors in Developing Countries: Opportunities, Risks and Policy Responses, the Case of Hedge Funds*. Paper prepared for BMZ/GTZ.

Group of Thirty, 2009. *Financial Reform: A Framework for Financial Stability*. January. Washington, DC: Group of Thirty.

Hester, D., 1982. *The Effects of Eurodollar and Domestic Money Market Innovations on the Interpretation and Control of Monetary Aggregates*. Working paper. Madison, WI: Social Systems Research Institute.

IMF, 1987. *The Role of the SDR in the International Monetary System*. Staff study. Washington, DC: IMF.

IMF, 1995. *International Capital Markets: Developments, Prospects and Policy Issues*. Washington, DC: IMF.

IMF, 1999. *World Economic Outlook*. September. Washington, DC: IMF.

IMF, 2000. *International Financial Statistics*. April. Washington, DC: IMF.

IMF, 2002. *Global Financial Stability Report*. September. Washington, DC: IMF.

IMF, 2002a. *International Financial Statistics*. September. Washington, DC: IMF.

IMF, 2002b. *World Economic Outlook*. September. Washington, DC: IMF.

IMF, 2003. *Global Financial Stability Report*. September. Washington, DC: IMF.

IMF, 2003a. *World Economic Outlook*. September. Washington, DC: IMF.

IMF, 2004. *Global Financial Stability Report*. April, September. Washington, DC: IMF.

IMF, 2005. *Global Financial Stability Report*. April, September. Washington, DC: IMF.

IMF, 2009. *Global Financial Stability Report*. April. Washington, DC: IMF.

IMF, 2017. *Global Financial Stability Report*. April. Washington, DC: IMF.

Jackson, W., 1985. *Public Rescue of Private Liabilities: The Continental Illinois Case*. Library of Congress, Congressional Research Service Report 85-172E, November 20.

Kaldor, Nicholas, 1971. "The Dollar Crisis." *Times*, September 6, 7, 8 (reprinted in N. Kaldor, 1978. *Further Essays on Applied Economics*. New York, Holmes and Meier, p. 64).

Kaufman, H., 1985. "Dangers in the Rapid Growth of Debt: The Need for a National Policy Response." Address Before the National Press Club. Washington, DC, January 10.

Lanman, S., 2010. "Fed Weighs Interest on Reserves as New Benchmark Rate." *Bloomberg.com*, January 26.

Lewitt, M., 2008. "How to Fix It." *HCM Newsletter*, March.

Little, J. S., 1969. "The Eurodollar Market: Its Nature and Impact." In *New England Economic Review*. May/June. Boston, MA: Federal Reserve Bank of Boston.

Matthews, N., 2013. "How the Fed Reanimated Wall Street: The Low and Extended Lending Rates that Revived the Big Banks." Working paper no. 758, Levy Economics Institute of Bard College, Annandale-on-Hudson, NY.

Maxwell, D. O., 1984. *Testimony, Financial Restructuring: The Road Ahead*. Hearings before the Committee on Energy and Commerce, Subcommittee on Telecommunications, Consumer Protection and Finance, US House of Representatives, April 5.

McCauley, R. and R. Seth, 1992. "Foreign Bank Credit to US Corporations: The Implications of Offshore Loans." *Quarterly Review*, Spring. New York: Federal Reserve Bank of New York.

Mester, L. J., 2007. "Some Thoughts on the Evolution of the Banking System and the Process of Financial Intermediation." *Economic Review*, First and Second Quarters. Federal Reserve Bank of Atlanta.

Minsky, H. P., 1986. *Stabilizing an Unstable Economy*. New Haven, CT: Yale University Press.

Monks, R., 1985. "Will Money Managers Wreck the Economy?" Statement before the US House of Representatives, Committee on Energy and Commerce, Subcommittee on Telecommunications, Consumer Protection and Finance Hearing on *Shareholder Interests and Corporate Takeovers*, May 22.

Montero, C. and R. Moreno, 2011. "The Use of Reserve Requirements as a Policy Instrument in Latin America." *BIS Quarterly Review*, March. Basel: BIS.

Moody's Bank and Finance Manual, Vol. 2, 1990.

Morgenson, G., 2008. "Behind Insurer's Crisis, a Blind Eye to a Web of Risk." *New York Times*, September 28.

Nikiforos, M. and G. Zezza, 2017. "The Trump Effect: Is this Time Different?" *Strategic Analysis*, Levy Economics Institute of Bard College, April. Annandale-on-Hudson, NY.

Ocampo, J. A., 2002. in *WIDER Angle*, no. 2/2002, newsletter of the World Institute for Development Economics Research of the United Nations University, Helsinki.

Office of the Comptroller or the Currency, 2008. *Quarterly Report on Bank Trading and Derivatives Activities*. Second quarter.

Palley, T., 2000. *Stabilizing Finance: The Case for Asset-Based Reserve Requirements*. Howardsville, VA: Financial Markets Center.

Palley, T., 2003. "Asset Price Bubbles and the Case for Asset-Based Reserve Requirements." *Challenge*, vol. 46, no. 3, May/June.

Palley, T., 2011. "Monetary Policy and Central Banking After the Crisis: The Implications of Rethinking Macroeconomic Theory." Working paper no. 8/2011, Hans-Böckler Stiftung, Dusseldorf.

Pollin, R., 1993. "Public Credit Allocation Through the Federal Reserve: Why It Is Needed; How It Should Be Done." In G. A. Dymski, G. Epstein, and R. Pollin (eds), *Transforming the US Financial System: Equity and Efficiency for the 21st Century*. Armonk, NY: M. E. Sharpe.

Pollin, R., 2009. "Tools for a New Economy: Proposals for a Financial Regulatory System." *Boston Review*, January/February.

Pollin, R., 2012. "The Great Liquidity Trap of 2009–2011: Are We Stuck Pushing on Strings?" *Review of Keynesian Economics*, Autumn.

Quint, M., 1991. "Lending When Bankers Won't." *New York Times*, October 7.

Sakoui, A., 2010. "Lehman Unwinding Creates a Blueprint." *Financial Times*, April 21.

Sellon, G., 1992. "Changes in Financial Intermediation: The Role of Pension Funds and Mutual Funds." *Economic Review*. Kansas City: Federal Reserve Bank of Kansas City.

Singh, M. and J. Aitken, 2009. "Counterparty Risk, Impact on Collateral Flows and Role of Central Counterparties." IMF Working Paper 09/173. Washington, DC: IMF.

Skidelsky, R., 2000. *John Maynard Keynes, Volume 3: Fighting for Freedom*. New York: Viking.

Sorkin, A., 2009. *Too Big to Fail*. New York: Penguin Books.

Stiglitz, J. E., 2006. *Making Globalization Work*. New York: W. W. Norton.

Stiglitz, J. E., 2008. "The Financial Crisis of 2007/2008 and Its Macroeconomic Consequences." Paper prepared for a meeting on financial regulation sponsored by the Initiative for Policy Dialogue and Brooks World Poverty Institute, Manchester, July 1–2.

Taub, J., 2010. "A Whiff of Repo 105." *Baseline Scenario*, http://baselinescenario.com/2010/03/16/a-whiff-of-ro-105/.

Thurow, L., 1972. "Proposals for Rechanneling Funds to Meet Social Priorities." In *Policies for a More Competitive Financial System*, conference proceedings of the Federal Reserve Bank of Boston, MA.

Toporowski, J., 2009. *"Enforced Indebtedness" and Capital Adequacy Requirements*. Policy Note 2009/7, p. 2. Annandale-on-Hudson, NY: Levy Economics Institute of Bard College.

Triffin, R., 1968. *Our International Monetary System: Yesterday, Today and Tomorrow*. New York: Random House.

United Nations, 2009. *Report of the Commission of Experts of the President of the United Nations General Assembly on Reforms of the International Monetary and Financial System*. New York: United Nations.

US Department of Commerce, 2003. "US International Transactions." *Survey of Current Business*, Washington, DC: US Department of Commerce, Bureau of Economic Analysis.

US Department of Commerce, 2005. "US International Transactions." *Survey of Current Business*, Washington, DC: US Department of Commerce, Bureau of Economic Analysis.

US Department of Commerce, 2006. "US International Transactions." *Survey of Current Business*, Washington, DC: US Department of Commerce, Bureau of Economic Analysis.

US Department of Commerce, 2016. "The US International Investment Position." *Survey of Current Business*, Bureau of Economic Analysis. Washington, DC: US Department of Commerce.

US Department of Commerce, various issues. "US International Transactions." *Survey of Current Business*, Washington, DC: US Department of Commerce.

US Department of the Treasury, 2008. *Blueprint for Financial Regulatory Reform*. Washington, DC: US Treasury, March.

US House of Representatives, 1972. *Foreign Experience with Monetary Policies to Promote Economic and Social Priority Programs*. Staff report of the Committee on Banking and Currency. Washington, DC: Government Printing Office.

US House of Representatives, 1976. *International Banking: A Supplement to a Compendium of Papers Prepared for the FINE Study*. Staff report of the Committee on Banking, Currency and Housing. Washington, DC: Government Printing Office.

Wade, R., 2009. "Iceland as Icarus." *Challenge*, vol. 52, no. 3, 5–33. Armonk, NY: M. E. Sharpe.

White, W. R., 2007. "The Need for a Longer Policy Horizon: A Less Orthodox Approach." In J. J. Teunissen and A. Akkerman (eds), *Global Imbalances and Developing Countries: Remedies for a Failing International Financial System*, p. 81. The Hague: Forum on Debt and Development.

White, W. R., 2013. "Ultra Easy Monetary Policy and the Law of Unintended Consequences." *Real World Economic Review*, no. 63, 19–56.

Williams, M., 2008. *Governing the Global Financial System.* Paper prepared for a meeting on financial regulation sponsored by the Initiative for Policy Dialogue and Brooks World Poverty Institute, Manchester, July 1–2.

World Trade Organization, 2001. *International Trade Statistics.*

Zuckerman, S., 1991. "As Washington Dithers, Nonbanks Advance." *American Banker*, March 15.

Zumbrun, J., 2013. "Kocherlakota Says Low Fed Rates Create Financial Instability." *Bloomberg Businessweek*, April 18.

Index

Printed and bound by CPI Group (UK) Ltd, Croydon, CR0 4YY

23/04/2025

14660965-0003